A HISTORY

OF

MEDIÆVAL POLITICAL THEORY

A HISTORY

OF

MEDIÆVAL POLITICAL THEORY
IN THE WEST

BY

SIR R. W. CARLYLE, K.C.S.I., C.I.E.

AND

A. J. CARLYLE, M.A., D.LITT.

LECTURER IN POLITICS AND ECONOMICS (LATE FELLOW)
OF UNIVERSITY COLLEGE, AND OF LINCOLN COLLEGE,
OXFORD

VOL. III.

POLITICAL THEORY
FROM THE TENTH CENTURY TO THE THIRTEENTH

BY A. J. CARLYLE, M.A., D.LITT.

THIRD IMPRESSION

WILLIAM BLACKWOOD & SONS LTD.
EDINBURGH AND LONDON
MCML

Agents for the United States
BARNES & NOBLE, INC.
105 5TH AVE., NEW YORK 3, N. Y.

VOL. III.

POLITICAL THEORY

FROM THE

TENTH CENTURY TO THE THIRTEENTH

BY

A. J. CARLYLE, M.A., D.Litt.

PREFACE TO VOLUME III.

In this volume we resume the study of the development of political theory in its immediate relation to the historical events and conditions of the Middle Ages at the point where we left it in the first volume. I venture to hope that historical scholars will agree that it has proved to be of real service to deal with the political ideas inherent in feudalism in close relation to this development.

I should wish to express once again my obligations to the admirable work of Mr R. L. Poole, the most learned of English students of the Middle Ages, who more than thirty years ago, in his 'Illustrations of Mediæval Thought,' pointed out the great significance of the position of Manegold and John of Salisbury in the development of mediæval political theory. The detailed study of the political literature of their times has only served to bring out more clearly the justice and insight of his recognition of their place and importance.

As this work advances I become more and more conscious of the difficulty of handling such large and diverse materials, and I am therefore very grateful to those scholars who have been so kind as to help me with their technical knowledge of particular aspects of the literature ; and I wish therefore to express my most sincere thanks to Miss Pope of Somerville College, who has very kindly examined all the references to Mediæval French writers, to Professor Meynial of Paris, and Mr E. Barker of New College, who have read the proofs of Part I., and to Mr F. Urquhart of Balliol, who has read the proofs of Part II.

The printed texts of Bracton are obviously very defective, and I have used the text of the Bodleian MSS., Digby, 222. Professor Woodbine, in the first volume of his edition of Bracton, has indeed thrown some doubt upon Maitland's judgment of the value of this text, but I have thought it best in the meanwhile, pending the appearance of Professor Woodbine's text, to use it. I am under great obligation to Mr G. C. Winstedt of Magdalen College and the Bodleian Library for furnishing me with its readings throughout.

A. J. CARLYLE.

OXFORD, 1915.

In this edition the text of Bracton is given as in Professor Woodbine's edition, so far as it has been published, and I give the reference to the folios, but I have also retained the reference to Books and chapters, as these may be convenient.

A. J. C.

1928.

CONTENTS OF THE THIRD VOLUME.

INTRODUCTION.

The subject of this volume, 1—the general characteristics of the political ideas inherited by the Middle Ages; the distinction made by the Stoics and Fathers between nature and convention, 3—slavery, property, and government are all conventional, 4—conceptions specifically Christian at least in form; the independence of the spiritual life and the spiritual authority, 6—the divine nature of political authority, 9—Teutonic constitutional principles; supremacy of law over all members of the community, 10—the authority of the law and the ruler derived from the community, 11—mutual agreement to maintain the law, beginnings of conception of social contract, 12—the task of this volume to consider how far these conceptions were modified or developed in the period from the tenth to the twelfth centuries, 13—development of the feudal system in the tenth century, 14.

PART I.

THE INFLUENCE OF FEUDALISM ON POLITICAL THEORY.

CHAPTER I.

PERSONAL LOYALTY.

Difficulty of defining Feudalism, and of determining its effects, 19—the two principles, loyalty and contract, 21—illustrations of the nature of personal loyalty in 'Raoul de Cambrai,' 23—in Fulbert of Chartres, Assizes of Jerusalem, Bracton, and Glanvill, 25—contrast between loyalty to immediate lord, and contempt of overlord, 28.

CHAPTER II.

JUSTICE AND LAW.

Authority determined and limited by law, 30—the function of authority is to
maintain justice, illustrated in ' Couronnement de Louis,' 32—in Assizes
of the Court of Burgesses of Jerusalem, 32—in Bracton, 34—law as the
embodiment of justice illustrated in 'Summa de Legibus,' 37—law as the
foundation of political authority, "There is no king where will rules and
not law," Bracton, 38—the king swears to observe and maintain the
law, 39.

CHAPTER III.

THE SOURCE OF LAW.

Common conception of sovereignty unknown to Middle Ages, 41—primary
mediæval conception of law as the custom of the community, Bracton, 41
—Beaumanoir, 42—Assizes of Jerusalem, 43—beginnings of the conception
of legislative sovereignty, 45—legislation as the act of the king, the great
men, and the people, Glanvill, 46—'Summa de Legibus,' 46—Bracton, 48
—discussion of the conception of Beaumanoir, 48.

CHAPTER IV.

THE MAINTENANCE OF LAW.

The mutual legal obligations of lord and vassal are determined by the feudal
court, 52—composition of the feudal court, 54—the decisions of the court
enforced against the lord by withdrawal of service, Assizes of Jerusalem,
56—the court as judge between lord and vassal, 'Consuetudines Feudorum,' 59—the king liable to judgment of the Count Palatine, 'Sachsenspiegel,' 61—the court as judge between lord and vassal, Pierre de Fontaines,
61—'Etablissements de St Louis,' 62—if king refuses to do justice to his
vassal in the court, vassal can make war against him, 63—court is judge
between lord and vassal, Beaumanoir, 63—relation of king to the law,
Bracton, 66 — question of means of enforcing law against the king,
Bracton, 69.

CHAPTER V.

FEUDALISM AND THE NATION.

Anarchical tendency of principle of loyalty to immediate lord, 75—principle of
fidelity to overlord illustrated, in action of William the Conqueror, 76—
in regulation of Assizes of Jerusalem that all sub-vassals must do "ligece"
to the chief lord, 77—in reservation of fidelity to kin in Glanvill 79—

in 'Jostice et Plet,' 79—in Beaumanoir's statement that obligation to follow lord in war does not extend to summons to war against the king, 80 —discussion of some doubtful phrases in James of Ardizone, 80—judgment of feudal jurists that the king has full jurisdiction over all persons in his kingdom, 'Sachsenspiegel,' 81—'Summa de Legibus,' 82—'Jostice et Plet,' 83—Beaumanoir, 84—Bracton, 84—Summary of influence of feudalism on political theory, 85.

PART II.

GENERAL POLITICAL THEORY IN THE ELEVENTH AND TWELFTH CENTURIES.

CHAPTER I.

NATURAL LAW AND EQUALITY.

Contrast between nature and convention assumed in political literature of the time, 87—this is clear with regard to conception of natural equality and liberty, 88—illustrations of this, Ratherius, 'Sachsenspiegel,' Beaumanoir, and Bracton, 88.

CHAPTER II.

THE DIVINE NATURE OF POLITICAL AUTHORITY.

Continuity of political theory in this period with that of the ninth century, 92— question whether secular authority was divine in nature and origin raised by certain passages in the letters of Gregory VII., 93—consideration of other passages in his letters, 94—conclusions to be derived from a comparison of these with each other, 96—passages in other writers which seem to deny the divine nature or origin of secular authority, 98—the normal view of this period represented by Atto of Vercelli, Wippo, Peter Damian, Gerhoh of Reichersberg, John of Salisbury, Manegold, and Honorius Augustodunensis, 99.

CHAPTER III.

THE MORAL FUNCTION OF POLITICAL AUTHORITY.

The divine nature of political authority finds its rationale in its moral function, 106—the beginnings of organised society, 106—the principle of the just end of political authority illustrated in Abbo of Fleury, 107—Ratherius, 108— Wippo, 109—in imperialist writings, 'De unitate ecclesiæ conservanda,' 109—Hugh of Fleury, 111—in papalist writers, Manegold, 111—Berthold of Constance, 112—and in John of Salisbury, 113.

CHAPTER IV.

THE THEORY OF THE "DIVINE RIGHT."

Divine nature of the state interpreted by some Fathers, especially St Gregory
the Great, as meaning that resistance to the ruler was always unlawful, 115
—illustrations of this in Atto of Vercelli, 117—and in St Bruno of Würzburg,
118—the question raised in acute form by Saxon revolt of 1073, 118—
Henry IV.'s reply to Gregory VII.'s bull of deposition, 119—attitude of
imperialist clergy, 119—Wenrich of Trier, 119—'De unitate ecclesiæ conservanda,' 120—various supporters of Henry IV., 121—Sigebert of Gembloux, 122—most complete statement by Gregory of Catino, 122.

CHAPTER V.

JUSTICE AND LAW.

Patristic tradition that without justice there could be no true authority, 125—
tradition of early Middle Ages, that to govern justly means to govern according to law, 126—the distinction between the king and the tyrant, John of
Salisbury, 126—the true king, Ratherius and Wippo, 127—the political
conflicts of eleventh century compelled men to consider their principles of
political authority, 128—illustrations of this, Lambert of Hersfeld, Bruno,
Berthold of Constance, Herrand, 129—the king and the tyrant, Hugh of
Fleury, 'Tractatus Eboracenses,' Manegold, 134—the political theory of
John of Salisbury, the king and the tyrant, 137—nature and source of law,
140—the tyrant has no rights against his people, but may justly be slain,
142.

CHAPTER VI.

CONSTITUTIONAL THEORY AND CONTRACT.

Political authority in its relation to the community, 147—rulers govern with
advice of great men, &c., Gerbert, Abbo of Fleury, Constitutions of emperors,
148—principle of election or recognition normal in Middle Ages, 150—
elective principle finally established in Germany, 151—legislative action of
ruler limited and conditioned by counsel of great men, 153—assertion of
principle that great men are entitled to take action to secure law and constitutional order against ruler, 155—political theory of Manegold, 160—his
theory of contract in virtue of which the king was appointed, 160—relation
of this conception to the "social contract" of seventeenth and eighteenth
centuries, 168.

CHAPTER VII.

THE CONCEPTION OF A UNIVERSAL EMPIRE.

Conception of the political unity of the world under the empire, 170—Annals of Quedlinburg, 171—life of St Adalbert, 171—Berno of Reichenau, 171—Peter Damian, 172 — Frederick I. (Barbarossa), 173 — Henry II. and Richard I. of England, 175 —contrary conception, Gerbert, 177—Adalbero of Laon, 177—William, Abbot of St Benignus, 177—another work of Peter Damian, 178—the actual trend of European civilisation towards separate and independent states, 179.

CHAPTER VIII.

SUMMARY.

The first principle of the political theory of the Middle Ages is that the function of political authority is to maintain justice, 181—this is the real meaning of the conception that the authority of the king is divine, 182—the second principle is the supremacy of law as the embodiment of justice, 183—the third is that the relation between ruler and people is founded upon the mutual obligation and agreement to maintain justice and law, 185.

TEXTS OF AUTHORS REFERRED TO IN VOLUME III.

Abbo, Abbot of Fleury—Collectio Canonum, Migne Patrologia Latina, vol. 139.
Adalbero, Bishop of Laon—Carmen, Migne Patrologia Latina, vol. 141.
St Adalbert—Vita, Migne Patrologia Latina, vol. 137.
Ardizone, James of—'Summa Feudorum,' in 'Tractatus Universi Juris,' vol. 10, Part 1.
Assizes of Jerusalem—
    Assizes of the Court of Burgesses. Ed. E. H. Kausler, 1839.
    Assizes of the High Court—Jean d'Ibelin. Ed. Beugnot, 1841.
    Assizes of the High Court—Philip of Novara. Ed. Beugnot, 1841.
Atto, Bishop of Vercelli—Migne Patrologia Latina, vol. 134.

Beaumanoir—'Les Coutumes du Beauvoisis.' Ed. A. Salmon, Paris, 1899.
Beno, Cardinal—M. G. H. Libelli de Lite, vol. 2.
Bernald, 'De Solutione Iuramentorum,' M. G. H. Libelli de Lite, vol. 2.
Berno, Abbot of Reichenau—Migne Patrologia Latina, vol. 142.
Berthold of Constance—'Annales,' M. G. H. Scriptores, vol. 5.
Bracton—'De Legibus et Consuetudinibus.' Ed. Woodbine.
Bruno, St, Bishop of Würzburg—Migne Patrologia Latina, vol. 142.
Bruno—'De Bello Saxonico,' M. G. H. Scriptores. vol. 5.

'Consuetudines Feudorum.' Ed. C. Lehmann, 1892.
'Constitutiones,' M. G. H. Legum, sect. iv.
'Couronnement de Louis.' Ed. E. Langlois, 1888.

Damian, Peter—'Liber Gratissimus,' M. G. H. Libelli de Lite, vol. 1.
—— 'Disceptatio Synodalis,' M. G. H. Libelli de Lite, vol. 1.
—— Opusculum, 50, Migne Patrologia Latina, vol. 145.
—— Epistles, Migne Patrologia Latina, vol. 144.
Deusdedit, Cardinal — 'Libellus contra invasores et symoniacos,' &c., M. G. H. Libelli de Lite, vol. 2.

Ekkehard Uraugiensis—'Chronicon Universale,' M. G. H. Scriptores, vol. 6.

'Etablissements de St Louis.' Ed. P. Viollet, 1881-1886.

Fulbert, Bishop of Chartres—Epistles, Migne Patrologia Latina, vol. 141.

Gerbert (Silvester II.)—Epistles, 983-997. Ed. J. Havet, 1889.

Gerhoh of Reichersberg—M. G. H. Libelli de Lite, vol. 3.

'Gesta Pontificum Cameracensium,' M. G. H. Scriptores, vol. 7.

Glanvill—'De laudibus et consuetudinibus Regni Angliæ.' Ed. J. Rayner, 1780.

Gregory VII. (Hildebrand)—'Registrum.' Ed. Jaffé.

Gregory of Catino—'Orthodoxa defensio imperialis,' M. G. H. Libelli de Lite, vol. 2.

Hermann of Reichenau—'Chronicon,' M. G. H. Scriptores, vol. 5.

Herrand, Bishop of Halberstadt—Epistola, M. G. H. Libelli de Lite, vol. 2.

Honorius Augustodunensis—'Summa Gloria,' M. G. H. Libelli de Lite, vol. 3.

Hugh, Monk of Fleury—'Tractatus de regia potestate et sacerdotali dignitate,' M. G. H. Libelli de Lite, vol. 2.

John of Salisbury—'Policraticus.' Ed. C. C. I. Webb, 1909.

'Jostice et Plet.' Ed. Rapetti and Chabaille, 1850.

Lambert of Hersfeld—'Annales,' M. G. H. Scriptores, vol. 5.

Manegold of Lautenbach—'Ad Gebehardum,' M. G. H. Libelli de Lite, vol. 1.

'De Ordinando Pontifice,' Auctor Gallicus, M. G. H. Libelli de Lite, vol. 1.

Othloh of St Emmeran, 'Dialogus de Tribus questionibus,' Migne Patrologia Latina, vol. 146.

Pierre de Fontaines, Le Conseil de. Ed. M. A. J. Marnier, 1846.

Quedlinburgenses—Annales, Continuatio, M. G. H. Scriptores, vol. 3.

Rahewin—'Gesta Friderici.' Ed. Simson, 1912.

Ratherius, Bishop of Verona—Migne Patrologia Latina, vol. 136.

'Raoul de Cambrai.' Ed. P. Meyer and A. Lognon, 1882.

Roger of Hoveden—'Chronicle.' Ed. Stubbs.

'Sachsenspiegel.' Ed. C. G. Homeyer, 1861.

'Schwabenspiegel.' Ed. H. G. Gengler, 1875.

Sigebert of Gembloux — 'Leodicensium Epistola Adversus Paschalem Papam,' M. G. H. Libelli de Lite, vol. 2.

Silvester II. (Gerbert)—Papal Epistles, Migne Patrologia Latina, vol. 139.

'Statuta et Consuetudines Normaniæ.'   Ed. E. J. Tardif in 'Coutumiers de Normandie,' vol. 1, 1881.

'Summa de Legibus Normanniæ.'   Ed. E. J. Tardif in 'Coutumiers de Normandie,' vol. 2, 1896.

'Tractatus Eboracenses,' M. G. H. Libelli de Lite, vol. 3.

' De unitate ecclesiæ conservanda,' M. G. H. Libelli de Lite, vol. 2.

Wenrich of Trier—Epistola, M. G. H. Libelli de Lite, vol. 1.

William, Abbot of St Benignus—Epistles, in Rodolphus Glaber, Hist. iv. 1, M. G. H. Scriptores, vol. 7.

Wippo—'Vita Chunradi,' Migne Patrologia Latina, vol. 142.

——— 'Panegyricus Heinrici Regis,' Migne Patrologia Latina, vol. 142.

INTRODUCTION.

In the last volume we endeavoured to determine the nature of the influence of the ancient world on the political theory of the Middle Ages, as it is represented in the systems of mediæval Roman and Canon law. It seemed well to consider these elements of mediæval theory first, because in order to appreciate rightly the nature or characteristic developments of political thought, we must first consider carefully how much had been inherited from the ancient world, and also because with the help of these more or less systematic works we can distinguish more easily between the normal opinions of men and abnormal or eccentric views.

We must now face the task of trying to determine what were the characteristic political theories of those centuries of the Middle Ages during which all ideas were in a state of ferment, during which nothing was fixed or systematic, but every day as it brought new conditions so also it brought new theories, new ideas, often in such bewildering abundance as to make it difficult to estimate their value.

We turn in this volume first to the consideration of the characteristic conceptions of feudalism and their influence on the development of political ideas, and we have found that in order to deal with this effectively we must carry our study down to the end of the thirteenth century. For the rest we deal with the political theory as illustrated in general literature only to the end of the twelfth century, for in the thirteenth century the great schoolmen began to reduce the world of ideas

A

and theories to a systematic form. The work of these great systematic thinkers was indeed often admirable and enlightened, and we propose in later volumes to deal with this, but there has been in our judgment some tendency to misunderstand mediæval thought, because it has been studied too exclusively in these systematic writers. There has been a tendency to conceive of it as representing a completely articulated system of fixed principles and logical deductions from them. This is true, strictly speaking, only of the thirteenth century, and even then only of the great schoolmen. The literature of the centuries from the tenth to the twelfth century represents no such systematic mode of thought ; the men of these times had indeed in the writings of the Christian Fathers a great body of theories and principles which had a constant influence upon them, while their habit of life and feeling was grounded in the traditions of the new Teutonic societies, but in neither of these had they an ordered and articulated system of political thought, but rather a body of principles, significant indeed and profound, but not always easily to be reconciled with each other. The history of the social and political ideas of these centuries is the history of the continual discovery of the relation of the traditions and principles which men had inherited to the actual circumstances of the time.

Our main difficulty in handling the matter is due not to the want of materials, for there is almost an over-abundance of these, but rather to the variety and complexity of the materials, and to the difficulty necessarily inherent in the attempt to set out in some systematic terms the conceptions of men who were not systematic thinkers, while they were acting and thinking energetically and often audaciously. And if the materials are abundant, the political ideas themselves are somewhat bewildering in their complexity. It has sometimes been thought that the political theory of the Middle Ages was simple and clear, because it was dominated by the principle of the unity of the world under the supremacy of the spiritual power. But the real truth is very different. We do not doubt that these conceptions had a real importance, but there were other aspects of the theory of society which were at least equally important, and which were more permanent in their importance. We cannot rightly apprehend the character of mediæval civilisation if we conceive of it as something isolated from the continuous movement of Western life, for indeed as it was in a large measure founded upon the civilisation of the ancient world, so also it contained the elements of the modern.

Let us try to sum up briefly the general characteristics of the political ideas with which the men of the Middle Ages set out.

It is evident to any student of the political thought of the Middle Ages that it was immensely influenced by the traditions of the Christian Fathers—it is from them that it directly and immediately derived the forms under which it expressed its own conceptions. The formal political theory of the Middle Ages is dominated by the contrast between nature and convention ; to the Fathers and to the great majority of mediæval writers, until St Thomas Aquinas and the recovery of the Aristotelian Politics, all the great institutions of society are conventional and not natural. Men are, in this view, by nature free and equal, and possess the world and the things in it in common, while coercive government and slavery and private property are conventional institutions which were devised to correct the vices of human nature when it lost its first innocence. These great formal conceptions indeed control the terms of political theory until the end of the eighteenth century, until Rousseau and Burke and the beginnings of the modern historical method. In the first volume of this work we have endeavoured to set out in detail the characteristics of this mode of thought, and we can here only refer the readers to this.

If, however, we are rightly to appreciate the relations of mediæval thought to that of the ancient world, we must remember that although these theories came to the Middle Ages primarily through the Christian Fathers, they were not distinctively Christian conceptions, but rather the commonplaces of the later philosophical schools, and the Fathers learned them in the schools and universities where they were educated. The forms of the political theory of the Middle Ages represent therefore an inheritance from the Stoics and other philosophical schools of the Empire.

We must consider a little more closely the character of these theories. To the Stoics and the Christian Fathers the institutions of society were conventional, not natural, and they understood the natural as being in the first place the primitive. But the natural was to them something more than the primitive, it represented something which was also essential and permanent. It was necessary for the due order of human life that men should rule over each other, and the Fathers added to this the conception that in some sense slavery was a punishment as well as a remedy for human vice. But both philosophers and Fathers maintained that the freedom and equality of human nature continued to be real. Their conception of human nature was radically distinct from that which is represented by the Aristotelian philosophy. To them there was no such thing as a naturally servile person, for the soul of man was always free. This principle is indeed the exact reverse of that of Aristotle. He found the ground and justification of slavery in his judgment that only some men were in the full sense rational and capable of virtue, while others were not properly and fully possessed of reason, and could not therefore in the strict and complete sense of the word possess virtue. Whatever may have been the foundation of this judgment, the judgment had disappeared before the Christian era, and Cicero had in a famous passage, summing up the philosophical judgment of his time, repudiated it in the strongest terms.[1] Seneca, a hundred years later, repeats the judgment in a memorable phrase. Men's bodies, he says, may be enslaved, the mind is free.[2] These principles are also those of the Christian faith. To St Paul slavery is a merely external and accidental condition, the slave is just as capable of the highest life, the life of communion with God, as the freeman. His great words, " There can be neither Jew nor Greek, there can be neither bond nor free, there can be no male and female : for ye are all one in Christ

[1] Cf. vol. i. p. 8; Cicero, ' De Legibus,' i. 10, 12.

[2] Cf. vol. i. p. 21; Seneca, ' De Beneficiis,' iii. 20.

Jesus," represent the principle of all Christian writers.[1] We have in the first volume pointed out how emphatically these principles are restated in the literature of the ninth century,[2] and in the second volume how they are repeated by the Roman jurists and the Canonists of the Middle Ages.[3]

It is not, however, only slavery which was held to be conventional, the same thing applies also to private property. In the primitive and innocent conditions of human life there was no such thing as private property, but all things were common. Private property is the result of man's greed and avarice, and is justified only as a limitation of this. Private property is indeed lawful, but it is the creation of the State, and is determined and limited by its authority ; and while the institution is lawful under the sinful conditions of human nature, the good things which God has given men through nature are still intended for the use of all. When the rich man assists the poor he is doing an act of justice, not of charity.[4]

The institution of government is also conventional, and not natural. To the Stoics and the Fathers the coercive control of man by man is not an institution of nature. By nature men, being free and equal, were under no system of coercive control. Like slavery, the introduction of this was the result of the loss of man's original innocence, and represented the need of some power which might control and limit the unreasonable passions and appetites of human nature. This was the doctrine of the Christian Fathers, but it was also the doctrine of the Stoics as represented by Seneca,[5] and it is impossible to understand the mediæval theories of government if we forget this. It was not till Aristotle's Politics were rediscovered in the thirteenth century that St Thomas Aquinas under their influence recognised that the State was not merely an institution devised to correct men's vices, but rather the necessary form of a real and full human life.[6] The formal conceptions of the Middle Ages were, however, on this point little affected by St Thomas. It is

[1] Cf. Gal. iii. 28 ; vol. i. p. 84 ; and pp. 111-124.
[2] Cf. vol. i. pp. 199-209.
[3] Cf vol. ii. pp. 34-40, 117-135.
[4] Cf. vol. i. chaps. 4, 8, 12 ; vol. ii.

Part I. chap. 5 ; Part II. chap. 6.
[5] Cf. vol. i. pp. 23, 24, 125-131.
[6] Cf. St Thomas Aquinas, 'De Regimine Principum,' I. i. ; and 'Summa Theologica,' I. Q. 96. 4.

evident that the conception of the conventional and "unnatural" character of the state was too firmly fixed to be shaken even by his authority, and that it passed with little alteration into the political theory of the sixteenth, seventeenth, and eighteenth centuries, and that, as we have said, it was not until Rousseau in the ' Contrat Social ' recovered the organic conception of the state,[1] and till the rise of the historical method of studying institutions, that this mode of thought passed away ; and it lingered on in the nineteenth century in the form of the "police theory" of the state, of Herbert Spencer and the English radicals.

The formal theory of nature and convention in the Middle Ages represents the principles of the post-Aristotelian philosophy, as mediated by the Christian Fathers. We must refer the reader to the second volume of this work for a discussion of the place of these conceptions in the Roman and Canon law of the twelfth century.

So far, then, we have been dealing with conceptions which dominate the theories of the Middle Ages, and which had come to them through the Fathers, but which were not strictly speaking distinctively Christian, but rather represented the general principles of the post-Aristotelian philosophy. The political theory of the Middle Ages was also however profoundly affected, or rather controlled, by certain conceptions which were distinctively Christian in their form, if not in their origin.

The first of these is the principle of the autonomy of the spiritual life, which in these ages assumed the form of the independence of the spiritual authority from the control of the temporal. We have endeavoured in the first volume to give some account of the nature and early forms of this conception. It finds characteristic and permanently important expression in the phrases of the letters and tractates of Pope Gelasius I., in which he lays down the great principle that the spiritual and the temporal authority each derives its authority from God, and that each is independent of the other within its own sphere, while each is dependent in the sphere of the other.[2]

---

[1] Cf. Rousseau, ' Contrat Social,' i. 8.

[2] Cf. vol. i. Part III. chap. 15 ; and   Pope Gelasius I., Tract. iv. 11, and Ep. xii. 2.

We have in the second volume endeavoured to give some account of the treatment of this principle by the Civilians and Canonists of the twelfth and thirteenth centuries.[1] We shall have to consider in detail the relation of these principles to the theory and structure of mediæval society. We shall have to deal with the theory and the practical nature of the relations of the spiritual and temporal powers in the Middle Ages, to plunge into the great conflict of the Papacy and the Empire, to try to disentangle the real and vital significance of that great dispute whose clamour fills these centuries.

But before we do this we must remind ourselves of the real nature of the problem, the real and fundamental principle which lies behind the confused noise of factions. Behind the forms of the great conflict we have to recognise the appearance in the consciousness of the civilised world of principles new and immensely significant. For behind it all there lies a development of the conception of individuality or personality which was unknown to the ancient world. We cannot here pretend to measure fully the gulf which lies between the Platonic and Aristotelian philosophy and that of the Stoics, and the other later philosophical systems, but it cannot be doubted that the gulf is profound. The phrases, for instance, in which Seneca describes the self-sufficiency of the wise man may be exaggerated and overstrained. No one, he says, can strictly be said either to benefit or to injure the wise man, for he is, except for his mortality, like God himself ; he is indeed bound to the service of the common good, but if the conditions of life are such as to make it impossible for him to take part in public affairs, he can withdraw into himself and still serve the same cause by developing his own nature and character.[2] The phrases may be overstrained and rhetorical, but they represent a sense of individual personality which is immensely significant, an apprehension of aspects of human life which are sacred and inviolable, independent of the authority, and, in his view, even of the support of society.

[1] Cf. vol. ii. Part I. chap. 8 ; Part II. chaps. 10 and 11.

[2] Cf. Seneca—'Ad Serenum,' viii. ; De Clementia,' i. 3. 2 ; 'De Otio,' iii., and vol. i. pp. 25-29.

The changes which can be traced in the history of Western thought can be observed with equal clearness in the Semitic literature of the Old Testament. There are few sayings more significant than those indignant words in which Ezekiel repudiates the traditional conceptions of Israel. "The soul that sinneth, it shall die. The son shall not bear the iniquity of the father, neither shall the father bear the iniquity of the son : the righteousness of the righteous shall be upon him, and the wickedness of the wicked shall be upon him."[1] The solidarity of the primitive and ancient group was giving way before the development of a new apprehension of individuality.

It is this apprehension to which a new impulse and force was given by our Lord and his disciples. To them the soul of man has an individual relation with God which goes beyond the control of the society. The principles of the Christian religion represent, on this side, the same development as that of Ezekiel and the Stoics, and it is on this foundation that the civilisation of the mediæval and modern world has grown up. This does not mean that religion has no social aspect, or that the political societies have no moral or spiritual character, but it does mean that men have been compelled to recognise that the individual religious and moral experience transcends the authority of the political and even of the religious society, and that the religious society as embodying this spiritual experience cannot tolerate the control of the State. There are aspects of human life which are not and cannot be under the control of the laws or authority of the State.

It is true that the great individualist development has often been misinterpreted and exaggerated, and the greatest task of the modern world is to recover the sense of the organic unity of human life, that sense of unity which to the Christian faith is equally vital with the sense of individuality. The recovery of that sense of unity by Rousseau and Burke does indeed represent a great moment in the development of human apprehension, and separates the political thinking and action of the nineteenth century by a great gulf from that of the preceding centuries. We are once again Aristotelian, but

[1] Ezekiel xviii. 20.

with a great difference, for the apprehension of individual personality remains with us.

It is these convictions which lie behind the great struggles of the spiritual and temporal powers in the Middle Ages, the greatness of the conflict is some measure of the immense difficulties which beset then, and even now, the attempt to disentangle the sphere of religion from those aspects of life which are under the control of the State. For it must not be supposed that this was an easy thing to do. In the first volume we have endeavoured to point out how in the ninth century, while men clearly recognised in principle the distinction between the sphere of the two great authorities, yet in actual practice the two authorities constantly overlapped.[1] These difficulties became far greater in the centuries which followed, and we cannot measure the significance of the events which took place, or estimate the real character of the theories which were put forward, unless we continually take account of this.

The political theory of the Middle Ages then inherited a great conception of the independence of the Church, and we have here the first conception which was distinctively Christian, at least in form.

There is, however, another conception which the Middle Ages inherited from the ancient world which is also distinctively Christian in form if not in substance. This is the principle of the divine nature and origin of political authority. We have dealt with the origin and nature of this conception in the first volume,[2] and have in the second volume examined the treatment of the subject by the Civilians and Canonists of the twelfth century,[3] and it is unnecessary to say more about it here, as we shall have to consider its significance very carefully in this volume. But we must be under no misapprehension, whatever may have been the precise significance of St Augustine's treatment of the nature of secular authority, and the extent of its influence, the tradition which had come down to the Middle Ages was substantially clear and emphatic, and that was that

[1] Cf. vol. i. pp. 253-292.
[2] Cf. vol. i. pp. 89-98, 147-160, 211-218.
[3] Cf. vol. ii. pp. 76-78, 143-150.

the secular power is a divine institution and derives its authority from God.

This conception had been interpreted by some of the Fathers, and notably by St Gregory the Great, as meaning that the authority of the secular ruler was in such a sense divine that it was irreligious and profane to resist, or even to criticise it.[1] The theory of the " Divine Right " of the King is a patristic conception whose influence in the Middle Ages we shall have to consider, although it was not till the period of the Renaissance that it can be said to have received its full development, and it was then related to the development of the absolute monarchy in Europe.

Such, then, are in general outline the principles of political theory which the Middle Ages inherited by direct and continuous tradition from the ancient world, and these influences must be clearly and sharply distinguished from those which came to them in the twelfth century through the revived study of the Roman jurisprudence, and in the thirteenth century through the rediscovery of Aristotle's Politics. We have dealt with the former of these influences in the second volume, the latter we must leave till we can deal with the thirteenth century in a later volume. It was in the main through the writings of the Fathers that the continuous tradition came, but, as we shall have occasion to see, it was reinforced throughout these centuries by the energetic study of the Latin authors whose works had survived. We have seen that in many most important aspects this continuous tradition represents rather the general political ideas of the last centuries of the ancient world than distinctively Christian conceptions.

We must now observe that the order of society in Western Europe was based largely upon principles which belonged to the new societies. There has been and there still is much controversy on the exact degree of the independence of the Teutonic constitutions and political principles. The great constitutional historians of the middle of the nineteenth century, like Waitz and Stubbs, assumed that the ancient world had little or no

[1] Cf. vol. i. pp. 147-160.

influence in determining the characteristic forms and principles of the government of the Teutonic state. In the latter part of the nineteenth century a very learned and capable body of historical scholars, of whom the chief were, on the Continent, Fustel de Coulanges, and in England, Seebohm, argued that in reality much which had been thought to be Teutonic was merely an adaptation of the forms and principles of the provincial administration of the later empire. We do not need for our purpose to attempt a dogmatic decision of the controversy, though we cannot conceal our own conviction that the balance of historical research and discussion has turned strongly against the Romanist view. For our purpose it is enough that we should observe the nature of the principles which were implicit in the structure of the new societies, and which found a large measure of reasoned expression in the literature especially of the ninth century.

Some of these principles are of great significance. The first and fundamental principle implicit in the organisation of the new societies is the supremacy of the law or custom of the community over all its members, from the humblest free man to the king. And the second is that there could be no succession to kingship without the election or recognition of the community. There is here indeed an obvious parallel, but also an obvious divergence in the structure of the Teutonic societies, as compared with that of the Roman empire. It was indeed the fundamental principle of the Roman jurists that the source of all political authority was the Roman people, that the emperor held his authority only because the Roman people had been pleased to confer it upon him.[1] But there was this far-reaching difference between the Roman legal theory and the principles of the Teutonic societies, that the Roman theory was a theory of origins, while the Teutonic principles were those of actually existing conditions. It was not merely that the Teutonic king required the consent or recognition of the community for his accession to power, but that he was not over the law, nor its creator, but under it. The Roman doctrine of the legislative authority of the emperor has no counterpart in

[1] Cf. vol. i. pp. 63-70.

the principles of the Teutonic societies, the law was the law of the community, not of the king. It is true indeed that in the earlier Middle Ages there was normally no such thing as legislation in the modern sense, the law, strictly speaking, was nothing but the traditional custom of the community, and legislative acts were, properly speaking, nothing but authoritative declarations of custom. As the changing conditions of mediæval life finally made deliberate modification of these customs inevitable, such action was taken, though reluctantly, but could only be taken with the assent, expressed or tacit, of the community.

Here are indeed political principles or ideas of the highest moment, derived not from the traditions of the ancient world and empire, but rooted in the constitutional practice of the new societies. We have endeavoured to set out the evidence for the predominance of these conceptions in the first volume,[1] but their significance cannot be fully appreciated without a study of the more important works on the constitutional history of the various European countries in the early Middle Ages.

It is in relation to these principles that we have to study the appearance of the doctrine of the social contract ; that is, the conception of an agreement or bargain between the people and the ruler. In the popular mind this conception is supposed to belong to the seventeenth and eighteenth centuries, but the real truth is that it is a mediæval conception, and that it arose primarily out of conceptions and circumstances which were characteristic of mediæval society. This principle or theory has some place in ancient literature, especially in Plato's ' Laws,' [2] and a phrase of St Augustine's has been sometimes quoted as related to it, though probably without any sufficient justification,[3] but there is no evidence that there is any continuity between the Platonic theory and that of the Middle Ages. We have in the first volume pointed out the circumstances out of which we think it arose,[4] and, as we shall have to deal with it in detail in this volume, we need only here say that it seems to us clear that its origin is to be traced to the promises of

[1] Cf. vol. i. chaps. 19 and 20.
[2] Cf. vol. i. p. 17.
[3] St Augustine, ' Confessions,' III. 8. 2.
[4] Cf. vol. i. pp. 240-252.

obedience to the law, and of good government taken by the king on his accession. It was in the eleventh century that the conception found a formal expression, but the principles which lay behind the formal expression were already in existence, and were firmly rooted in the constitutional order of the early Middle Ages.

In approaching the subject of the nature of the political theory of the great central period of mediæval civilisation, from the tenth to the thirteenth centuries, we must then first be careful to observe the nature of the general principles which the men of that time had inherited. These principles were complex, and no complete or systematic treatment of them was made until the thirteenth century. It may indeed be doubted whether the various elements were capable of being brought into an organic relation with each other, but we must not here anticipate the discussion which belongs to later volumes. Whether in the end these various conceptions were capable of being fused into an organic whole or not, we must recognise that they all have a real and significant place in mediæval theory. (The great formal conception of the distinction between nature and convention, which came from the post-Aristotelian philosophy in which the Christian Fathers were trained ; the principle of the equality and freedom of men which arose out of this and the Christian tradition ; the immensely significant conception of the necessary freedom of the spiritual life and the spiritual authority which specially represents this ; the conviction of the sanctity of the political order ; the principle of the supreme authority of the law or custom of the community, and of the King as responsible to govern according to the law, —these conceptions or principles dominated the sentiment and the theory of all mediæval society.)

Our present task is to consider the development of these conceptions under the actual circumstances of European society from the tenth to the thirteenth centuries, and to inquire how far they may have been modified or superseded by other principles. For the new times brought new conditions, new and important forms of political and social relations. We shall

have especially to consider how far the development of feudal
ideas, and the organisation of European society on the basis of
feudal tenure, may have modified or overlaid earlier principles ;
how far again in the great conflicts between the spiritual and
the temporal powers the conception of the sanctity and
autonomy of either may have been questioned or denied. The
development of mediæval society was very rapid, and the
intellectual development was even more rapid than that of
the organisation of society. The greatest difficulty indeed with
which the historian has to contend, in trying to interpret the
Middle Ages to the modern world, is the impression that the
civilisation of these times was stationary and rigid, that the
mediæval world was unlike the modern, specially in this, that it
was unchanging, while we perpetually change. This tradition
is primarily derived from the ignorance and prejudice of the
men of the new learning and the Renaissance, and lingers
on, not in serious history, but in the literary tradition, and in
the prejudices which arose naturally enough out of the great
struggles of the Reformation and the Revolution. If we are to
study the Middle Ages intelligently, if we are to appreciate
their real relation to the modern world, we must dismiss from
our minds these notions of a fixed and stereotyped society, we
must rather recognise that there have been few periods in the
history of the world when the movement of thought and of
life was more rapid than in the twelfth and thirteenth
centuries.

When we attempt to trace the history of political ideas
in the Middle Ages, we are at once confronted with the fact
that, after the active political reflection which is represented in
the literature of the ninth century, there follows a considerable period from which very little indeed of political theory
has survived in literature. From the end of the ninth century
till the middle of the eleventh the references to the principles
or ideas of politics are very scanty indeed. We have indeed to
remember that it is probable that a great deal of literature,
especially in the vernacular languages, has disappeared, but it
is at least a probable conclusion from what has survived that

there was not much reflection upon social and political questions, and that it was not till the middle of the eleventh century that the great political agitations in Germany, and the development of the great conflict between the Papacy and the Empire, compelled men to question themselves as to the principles which underlay the order of society.

This does not mean that during this time no important changes were taking place in the structure of European society; on the contrary, in some respects the period was one of great and significant development. It was during these years that feudalism was taking shape and form, establishing itself as a system of social and economic and military organisation, and in some degree affecting the structure of government. How far the growth of feudalism affected the principle or theory of political organisation is the first important question which we have to consider.

It was during these years that European civilisation was being rescued from a second great wave of barbarism, which threatened for a time to overwhelm it. For upon the confused faction fights which distracted Western Europe while the great empire of Charlemagne was breaking up, there fell the torrent of the second barbaric invasion. The Norsemen on the North and West, the Magyars on the East harried and plundered, and for a time it seemed as though the work of the preceding centuries would be completely undone; and indeed Europe very nearly relapsed into anarchy, and Church and State were almost overwhelmed in a common destruction. But the victory of Alfred over the Danes, of Otto the Great at the Lechfeld over the Magyars, and the limits within which the Norse invasion of France was finally contained, mark the fact that the new civilisation was stronger than the forces which attacked it, that the new barbarians had to reckon with a civilisation which was not worn out like that of the Western Empire which the forefathers of the Franks and the Englishmen had overthrown five centuries earlier, but with one which was living and powerful and capable of a rapid recovery and growth. The new invasions did indeed leave profound traces behind them, but the greatest and most powerful of the invaders, the Normans who settled in

North-Western France, proved rapidly that they were capable not merely of conquest, but that they could contribute greatly to the progress of the very civilisation which for the moment they had shaken.

The development of feudalism was in great measure the result of the downfall of the Carolingian civilisation, but the effects of this can also be traced in the relations of the Papacy and the Empire. The breaking up of the Empire of Charlemagne might indeed seem to have set the Papacy at liberty, but actually it left it under the tyranny of the barbarous factions of the Roman nobles, and its degradation was even deeper than that of the State. It was rescued from this in the tenth century by the Ottos, and in the eleventh by Henry III., but the conditions of its deliverance held in themselves the seeds of disaster. The emperor exercised, and for the time with excellent results, a very large measure of control over the Church, and especially over the appointment of its chief ministers, but it was impossible that the Church should in the long run acquiesce in this. The principle of its necessary independence was too firmly rooted in its history, and it was the attempt to recover and vindicate this which led to the great conflict of the Papacy and the Empire, of the spiritual and temporal powers in the various European countries. This conflict in its turn contributed a great deal to compel men to consider and make explicit the fundamental principles of the structure and organisations of society, and thus to produce those energetic and audacious developments in political theory which we have to consider.

We have, then, to deal with three great subjects—first, the nature of the principles implicit in feudalism, and the effect of these principles upon political ideas ; second, the characteristic political conceptions of the eleventh and twelfth centuries as related to the development of the general political and social structure of Western civilisation ; and thirdly, the forms and theories of the relations of the temporal and spiritual authorities. It is indeed true that we cannot isolate these various aspects of mediæval life and thought from each other, but they do in some measure really represent the operation of different forces, and we have to consider how far it may be true that they tended to give rise to different conceptions or principles. We shall have to make the effort finally to bring our reflections upon them together, and to form some unified view of their effect upon the principles of mediæval life, but for the time being we have found ourselves driven to deal with them separately.

We have found that the adequate treatment of the subjects has required so much space that we have decided to deal with feudalism and the general political ideas in this volume, and with the relations of the temporal and spiritual powers in the next.

We deal with feudalism first, not because it was in our judgment the most important element in the structure of mediæval society, but because it has often been thought to have been so, and because this at least is true, that whatever its influence may have been, it represented a new element in civilisation. In dealing with it we shall be obliged to transcend the limits of time which we have set to the general scope of this volume. For the significance of feudalism in relation to political theory cannot adequately be discussed without taking into account the great feudal law books of the thirteenth century ; and, what is more important, the system of feudalism represents an organic development culminating in the latter years of the thirteenth century, which cannot be understood unless we take account of the whole process of its development. We are, of course, aware of the risk that we run of reading back the conceptions of the thirteenth century into the eleventh and twelfth, and we shall do our best to guard against this risk.

PART I.

THE INFLUENCE OF FEUDALISM ON POLITICAL THEORY.

CHAPTER I.

PERSONAL LOYALTY.

THERE is perhaps no subject in mediæval history which is so difficult as that of feudalism. Its origins are still obscure and controverted, its development belongs largely to the tenth century, and there are few periods of mediæval history where the sources of our information are so scanty and so fragmentary, and in the literature which has survived there is only a little that can be said to bear directly upon feudalism. And, finally, its real nature and essential characteristics have been so confused by the laxity of literary usage that it is difficult to say what is meant by the word.

Feudalism is a system of personal relations, of land tenure, of military organisation, of judicial order, and of political order. It affected the life of every class in the mediæval community, from the villein to the king or emperor, and it even affected profoundly the position of at least the greater clergy, the bishops and abbots. There are, indeed, few aspects of mediæval life which were not touched by it, and it is therefore natural that it should be thought that it must have profoundly modified both the institutions and the political ideas of the Middle Ages.

It is not our part here to deal with the first of these

subjects, the influence of feudalism on the institutions of the Middle Ages, its direct effects upon the forms of the great constitutional development which culminated in the Parliament of Edward I. and the States-General of Philip the Fair, and the parallel developments in other European countries. We cannot even attempt to summarise the results of the work of the constitutional historians, for any summary would probably mislead rather than illuminate. But it is possible to say that while feudalism left for centuries deeply marked traces on the social and political structure of European society, and while the great systems of national organisation did indeed take into themselves elements which belonged to feudalism, they also represented principles which in their essential nature were independent of and even contradictory to some specific characteristics of the feudal system. In the end the king or the parliament, or both, came to be directly related to all the individuals who compose the State, and in their authority the local and personal authorities and jurisdictions of feudalism were finally lost. The royal justice at last absorbs all feudal justice, in the administrative authority of the crown all the areas of feudal administration are merged, and the legislative authority of parliament asserts itself as supreme over all feudal traditions and customs. The king and the parliament represent the nation, and the unity of the nation finally transcends all the separatist tendencies of feudalism.

It may even be said that the best example of this can be found in that country where at first sight feudalism might seem to have triumphed, for the unity of the German kingdom was finally destroyed, and the great fiefs became practically autonomous provinces. But it was not feudalism which triumphed, but territorialism. In the territorial areas there developed the same centralised authority and administration as in England or France, and it was no doubt that very fact which accounts for the failure of the constitutional movement of the close of the fifteenth century.

We have to deal here not primarily with institutions, but with the question how far feudalism affected the political ideas of the Middle Ages, how far its influence coincided with the traditions which they inherited, and furthered the development of social and political ideas which were already present, or how far it may have tended to neutralise or modify them. We must be prepared to find that the influence of feudalism was very complex, and that it may have tended in different directions.

We begin by pointing out what may seem a paradox, that feudalism represents two principles which in their ultimate development may seem contradictory, but which yet affected the minds of the men of the Middle Ages at the same time. The first principle is that of personal loyalty and devotion, the second is that of the contractual relation.

The first principle is that which is represented especially in the poetic literature of the Middle Ages, and which has thus passed naturally enough into the literary as distinguished from the historical presentation of the Middle Ages in modern times. We are all familiar with the romantic representation of mediæval life as dominated by the sentiment of chivalrous loyalty and devotion. How much of exaggeration there is contained in this we shall presently see, but there are elements of real truth in it. And, more than this, these sentiments have a real and permanent importance in political as well as in social life. Human life in its deepest and largest terms cannot be lived upon principles of utility and contract. Whether in the family or in the nation the actual working of human life is impossible without the sense of loyalty and devotion.

This is the first principle of feudalism, and the second may well seem contradictory to it. For nothing could seem further apart than the conception of personal loyalty and the conception of bargain or contract as the foundation of human relations. And yet there is no escape from the conclusion that in the last resort feudal relations were contractual relations, that the vassal was bound indeed to discharge certain obligations, but only on the condition that the lord also discharged his obligations to the vassal. Here again it is evident that we are dealing with a principle which is reasonable and just, for in the long run human relations are impossible unless there is some reasonable recognition and fulfilment of mutual obligations.

The principles may seem contradictory, and indeed they were hard to reconcile, but it is also true to say that they were not only held together and constantly reconciled in practice, but also that the political thinkers of the Middle Ages were aware of certain great rational principles which lie behind these conceptions, and in which they found a reasonable reconciliation of them.

For this is the truth about feudalism. At first sight it seems very strange and unintelligible. We find it difficult to understand how men could think and act thus, but if we are a little patient we find it becoming intelligible, and finally we see it not as wholly unnatural and abnormal, but as representing a phase of social and political development which lies indeed behind us, but whose conditions we can understand, and we shall see that in a measure these apparently strange principles have a continuing significance even among ourselves.

The difficulty of understanding feudalism has been immensely increased by the habit of conceiving of it as a homogeneous system, complete and perfect at some definite time and place. It becomes much more intelligible when we begin to see that under the one term there are contained ideas which were very different from each other, and that as it had slowly grown up, so it was perpetually developing and changing. The feudal idea as it is presented to us in the epic or romantic poetry is something quite different from that which is represented by such a characteristic set of law books as those which make up the Assizes of Jerusalem, or by Beaumanoir, and when we look a little more closely we begin to understand this, and to see that the conceptions of the epics and romances of the twelfth and thirteenth centuries represent sometimes the tradition of the past, sometimes an elaborate and artificial convention rather than the actual reality.

There has indeed often been a very serious misunderstanding even among scholars as to the value of the artistic representation of manners and customs. In some poetry, as for instance in the earlier mediæval epic, the picture of external life and manners of men and women, is highly realistic, and supplies us with very valuable information as to the conditions of contemporary society. In other forms of literature, and especially in the romance of the twelfth and thirteenth centuries, it is evident that we are dealing with an art which is in great part, in its relation to the circumstances of life, conventional and traditional, and which even in its essential sentimental or emotional interest represents an abstraction of human life, valuable indeed and profoundly moving and significant, but still an abstraction rather than a realistic treatment. The great fighting man of the epic literature, and the frank, high-hearted, and sometimes implacable woman, upon whom often the whole movement of the story depends, these are real figures of men and women, and they live in the real world. But the romantic hero or heroine, absorbed in their emotions, far removed from the actual circumstances of daily life, are placed in a world which is mainly unreal and conventional. The transition from the Beowulf or the Icelandic Sagas to the Arthurian romance is the transition from idealised and heroic reality to an elaborate convention.

It is necessary to use the evidence of mediæval poetry with great caution, and to make careful distinctions between the value of different forms of it as illustrating the customs and ideas of any one time.

We cannot here attempt to discuss in detail the origin of feudalism, the subject has been handled with great learning by a number of historians,[1] but we can say with great confidence that its origin was extremely complex. Comitatus, Commendatio, and Beneficium, these are the main elements of the relation of lord and vassal, and each of these had an important part in the development of the whole system. From the Comitatus there came the devotion of the band of followers to their leader in war, the almost indissoluble tie which united the "companion" to his chief in faith and loyalty, and this may have been the first, as it was certainly among the most important, of the elements out of which the feudal relation grew. It

---

[1] Cf. *e.g.*, Waitz, Brunner, Fustel de Coulanges, Flach, &c.

is this aspect of the relation that we find specially illustrated in the epics and romances, while its influence can also be traced in certain principles of the feudal law books. The process of Commendation by which a hitherto independent person became dependent on some powerful man or ruler in return for the protection that he could afford to him, was probably the means by which the feudal relation was most widely extended. The gradual transformation of a relation, which was originally almost wholly personal, into a great system of land tenure on the basis of military or of " base " service, which in its turn became a system of political relations, this is connected with the Beneficium. It is out of these complex and incoherent elements that the feudal system was gradually formed ; something of each goes to make up the whole system as we see it from the tenth to the thirteenth centuries, and they are all represented in the literature and legal systems of these times.

It is not necessary to deal at length with the conception of personal loyalty and devotion, it will be sufficient to indicate its nature by means of an example from the literature of the twelfth century.

One of the most interesting illustrations of the influence of the conception is to be found in the French Chanson de Geste, the ' Raoul de Cambrai,' which belongs probably to the latter part of the twelfth century. When Raoul is knighted he takes as his squire Bernier, the illegitimate son of Ybert of Ribemont. Raoul obtains from the King of France a grant of the lands of Vermandois, which had belonged to Ybert's family, and invades the country in spite of the protests of Bernier. He sacks and burns the town of Origny with its monastery, and Bernier's mother perishes in the fire. Bernier vows revenge, and joins his father ; and, in the battle which follows, kills Raoul. But the significant thing is the reluctance with which he turns against Raoul ; in the first flush of his passion over his mother's death he does indeed refuse all Raoul's attempts to make amends, but afterwards he endeavours to make peace, and when he has given him the fatal wound he weeps and laments that he should have turned against him who had knighted him, and, in spite of his grievous wrongs, he can find no joy in his vengeance.[1]　Through all his life the thought of what he had done haunts him, and there is a tragic fitness in his end, for after many years Raoul's uncle kills him near the place where long before he had killed Raoul.

Nothing can illustrate more vividly the essential character of the traditional feudal conception as it is expressed in the poetry of the Middle Ages.　In spite of the dreadful wrongs of which Raoul had been guilty, in spite of his brutal and overbearing character, in spite of the wanton murder of his mother and the other nuns of Origny, Bernier feels that he has committed an unheard-of crime in turning against his lord, to whom he feels himself bound by ties even more sacred than those of nature.[2]

Illustrations of the personal loyalty and devotion of vassal to lord could be indefinitely multiplied from the mediæval poets, but no useful purpose would be here served by doing this.　Only it is important to remember that they do not represent a principle peculiar to France, but rather a universal and highly significant aspect of the organisation of European society in the Middle Ages.　[The feudal relation was not one of mere dependence, or of mere advantage, but one of faith and loyal service, and the whole conception is admirably summed up in the famous phrases of the letter of Fulbert of Chartres written in 1020 A.D. to the Duke of Aquitaine.　He that swears fidelity to his lord must have in his mind these

[1] 'Raoul de Cambrai,' 3132—

" B. l'oï, le sens quida changier
Desoz son elme commence a larmoier ;
A haute voiz commence a huchier :
' E ! R., sire, fix de franche mollier,
Tu m'adoubas, ce ne puis je noier ;
Mais durement le m'a puis vendu chier.
Ma mere arcis par dedens j. monstier,
Et moi fesis la teste peçoier.
Droit m'en ofris, ce ne puis je noier ;
De la vengance ja plus fain ne qier.' "

[2] I wish here to express my great obligation to the extremely valuable and suggestive discussion of this aspect of feudalism, as it is presented in the French epics, by M. Flach, in an essay entitled, " Le Compagnonnage dans les Chanson de Geste," which he afterwards embodied in his work entitled, ' Les Origines de l'Ancienne France.' I do not know that I am convinced by his very interesting and ingenious attempt to show that the feudal relation finds its ultimate source in the conception of adoption into a new family or blood brotherhood, but M. Flach has admirably illustrated and classified the principles of the feudal relation as seen especially in the mediæval poetry of France.

six words, "Incolume, tutum, honestum, utile, facile, possibile," he must do what he can to keep his lord's body unharmed, to keep his secrets and strongholds, to maintain his rights of jurisdiction and all his other dignities, to keep his possessions safe, to see that he does not make that difficult or impossible to his lord which is now easy and possible. Fulbert adds that these obligations are mutual, and we shall have more to say upon this point presently.[1]

These conceptions were not merely traditional or merely ideal, and we should observe that they have their place also in the more technical expression of feudal principles in the law books, and as late as the thirteenth century.

We have in the Assizes of Jerusalem a very full treatment of the mutual obligation of vassal and lord to which we shall constantly have to recur ; for the moment we can fix our attention on one passage in the work of Jean d'Ibelin, which forms a very important part of the Assizes. In this passage he has described the mutual nature of the obligations of lord and vassal, and then points out that there are some obligations which are peculiar to the vassal. The vassal owes his lord reverence as well as faith, and must do some things for him which the lord is not bound to do. He must be ready to act as a hostage to deliver his lord from prison, and if in battle he sees his lord disarmed and unhorsed he must if necessary give him his own horse in order to enable him to escape from

---

[1] Fulbert of Chartres, Ep. 58 : "Qui domino suo fidelitatem jurat, ista sex in memoria semper habere debet : incolume, tutum, honestum, utile, facile, possibile : videlicet, Incolume, ne sit domino in damnum de corpore suo. Tutum, ne sit ei in damnum de secreto suo, vel de munitionibus per quas tutus esse potest. Honestum, ne sit ei in damnum de sua iustitia, vel de aliis causis quæ ad honestatem eius pertinere videntur. Utile, ne sit ei in damnum de suis possessionibus. Facile vel possibile, ne id bonum quod dominus suus leviter facere poterat, faciat ei difficile : neve id quod possibile ei erat, reddat ei impossibile.

Ut autem fidelis hæc nocumenta caveat justum est sed non ideo sacramentum meretur.

Non enim sufficit abstinere a malo, nisi fiat quod bonum est. Restat ergo ut in eisdem sex supra dictis consilium et auxilium domino fideliter præstet, si beneficio dignus videri vult, et salvus esse de fidelitate quam iuravit.

Dominus quoque fideli suo in his omnibus vicem reddere debet : quod si non fecerit, merito censebitur malefidus : sicut ille si in eorum prævaricatione vel faciendo vel consentiendo, deprehensus fuerit, perfidus et perjurus."

danger, and again he must be ready to act as security for his lord's debts to the extent of the value of his fief.[1] The lord must indeed in his turn do all that he can to help and deliver his vassal who has thus imperilled himself for him, and to compensate him for the losses he may have suffered ; but there is a real and marked difference in the nature of the obligations, they are indeed mutual, but they are not quite the same, and the element of reverence, which the vassal owes, is distinctive and important. It is noteworthy that both Glanvill and Bracton, while describing the feudal obligations as mutual, both treat the element of reverence which the vassal owes as distinctive.[2]

The principle of personal devotion and fidelity to the lord forms, then, a very important part of the tradition of mediæval society, and we must take careful account of it in trying to estimate the characteristic conceptions of the Middle Ages with respect to the nature of political association. And we must also observe that we have here something quite different from those principles of political relation and obligation which we have so far considered. These sentiments of personal

[1] Assizes of Jerusalem—Jean d'Ibelin, 196 : "Mais que tant que l'ome deit au seignor reverence en totes choses, et chascun deit garder sa fei l'un vers l'autre fermement et enterinement, chascun en dreit sei, por sa fei et s'onor garder et sa leauté et sa bone renomée : et l'ome deit tant plus au seignor par la fei que il li est tenus, que le seignor à l'home : que l'om deit entrer en ostage por son seignor geter de prison, c'il l'en requiert ou fait requerre par certain message. Et chascun qui fait homage à autre est tenus par sa fei, ce il treuve son seignor en besoin d'armes, à pié, entre ses enemis ou en leuc que il soit en perill de mort ou de prison, de faire son leau poeir de remontir le et geter le de cel perill, et c'il autrement ne le peut faire, il li doit doner son cheval ou sa beste sur quei il chevauche, c'il la requiert, et aider le à metre sur, et aider

le à son pooir à son cors sauver. . . . Et chascun qui tient fié d'autre de quei il est son home, est tenus à son seignor d'entrer por lui en tel point en hostage por dette on en plegerie de tant vaillant come le fié que il tient de lui, et de quei il est son home, vaudreit raisnablement à vendre par l'assise."

[2] Glanvill, ix. 4 : "Mutua quidem debet esse dominii et homagii fidelitatis connexio, ita quod quantum homo debet domino ex homagio, tantum illi debet dominus ex dominio præter solam reverentiam."

Bracton, ' De Legibus et Consuetudinibus Angliae,' ii. 35. 2 (fol. 78) : " Est itaque tanta et talis connexio per homagium inter dominus et tenentem suum, quod tantum debet dominus tenenti, quantum tenens domino, præter solam reverentiam."

loyalty must not be confused with the principles of political society either in the form in which they had come down from the ancient world through the Fathers, or as they were implicit in the political structure of the Teutonic societies, so far as we have considered them hitherto. It is no doubt true that in the Teutonic societies, as distinguished from the developed political organisations of the ancient world, there survived traditions and sentiments which were related to the conception of the chieftainship of a tribe, and one of the chief difficulties in dealing with the history of feudalism is to disentangle the tribal from the feudal sentiment. In some mediæval states, and especially in the German kingdom, the influence of tribal sentiment and tribal loyalty is difficult to measure, and it is probably true to say that the feudal relation only partially overlaid it.

However this may be, these sentiments of personal loyalty and devotion to the immediate lord to whom a man had sworn his faith and service constitute a new element in the tangle of ideas and organisations, out of which there slowly emerged the national state of modern times. And it was an element which was very difficult to reconcile with the national idea and the national constitution. The loyalty of the vassal to his immediate lord was one of the most characteristic elements of the chaos of the tenth century, and it was only very slowly that this loyalty was transferred to the national king.

If we turn back again to the French epics of the Middle Ages we sometimes find that they represent alongside of the profound devotion of the vassal to his immediate lord an almost unmeasured contempt for the king or overlord, and we can find an illustration of this in the same Chanson de Geste, the ' Raoul de Cambrai,' which we have already cited. The death of Raoul, which we have already described, is followed by a long conflict between his house and that of Bernier, until, after a long struggle, Gautier, the nephew of Raoul, and Bernier are reconciled with each other. The King of the French is vexed at the reconciliation, and both parties then turn on the King and denounce him as the real author of the feud. When the King threatens to take his father's lands from him, using many violent words, Bernier flatly defies him, and there follows a long war between the nobles and the King, who is represented throughout as playing a mean but unsuccessful part. The nobles do indeed hold their hand when the King is defeated, because he is their lord, but in the main nothing is more emphatically marked than the difference between the deep sense of obligation and loyalty of the vassals or companions to their immediate lords, and the loose and uncertain deference which they owe to the overlord or King.[1]

Enough has been said to indicate the nature of feudalism conceived of as finding its principle in the sense of personal loyalty, of an almost unlimited obligation of the vassal towards his lord. This conception has a place even in the technical legal works of the Middle Ages, but it is especially emphasised in the poetry, in the epics and romances. It is to a large extent upon this that there has grown up the literary tradition of mediæval society as based primarily upon the conception of an unswerving loyalty, a romantic personal devotion which overrides all other obligations and principles. But the whole truth is very different from the literary tradition. When we turn from the poetry to the law books we find ourselves in another world, we find a conception of society which is much nearer to the actual conditions and ideals of the Middle Ages.

---

[1] 'Raoul de Cambrai,' line 5368. Guerri of Cambrai—

" B. frere, por Dieu venez avant.
Cis roi est fel . . .
Iceste guerre, par le cors S. Amant
Commença il, se sevent li auquant.
Faisons li guere, franc chevalier vail
　　lant."

Id., line 5412. Bernier—

" Sire asez poez plaidier
Qe par celui gi tot a a baillier
Ja vos secors ne li ara mestier
Qe ne li face toz les membres trenchier."

Id., line 5425. Guerri—

" Cest coart roi deit on bien essilier,
Car ceste guerre nos fist il commencier."

CHAPTER II.

JUSTICE AND LAW.

WE have dealt with that aspect of feudalism which would seem to present a conception of social or political relations very different from those which we have hitherto considered, and we must recognise that we have here a principle which has exercised and still exercises a great influence in the actual working of political and social relations. When, however, we set out to examine the structure of feudal society more completely, we find that this principle of personal obligation and fidelity is only one of many principles, and that the normal conditions of mediæval society were not determined by such considerations alone. No doubt the feudal system as a whole did materially affect the development of the method of government in the Middle Ages, but our own impression is that it did not really alter the conception of the nature of political society to the extent which might be supposed, and that in the end its influence was in the main to strengthen the normal tendencies in the development of constitutional order.

There is still a vulgar impression that in the Middle Ages men looked upon authority as irresponsible, that they conceived of the ruler as a person who exercised a capricious and almost unlimited authority over his subjects, and that men had little knowledge of, or care for, any rational principles of social organisation.

We have endeavoured in the first volume to point out how wholly incorrect such an impression proves to be when confronted with the energetic and abundant literature of political thought in the ninth century, and in the last volume we have

dealt with the carefully considered theories of government of
the Civilians and Canonists, especially of the twelfth century.
It may be imagined that while this is true, the feudal system,
in its insistence upon the merely personal element in social
relations, had undermined these reasoned judgments, and had
diverted the attention of practical men from the consideration
of the principles of political order. It is no doubt true that
the compilers of the feudal law books were primarily practical
men, trying to set down the details of the customs and regulations of mediæval society, and not theorists in jurisprudence or
politics ; but this in some ways only brings into sharper relief
the fact that the system which they were describing embodied
very important and more or less determinable principles, and
that they were in a large measure conscious of these principles
and tenacious in maintaining them. As we shall see, so far
from its being true that they conceived of authority as something arbitrary and capricious, they conceived of it as a thing
very sharply defined and very severely limited. The truth is
that the characteristic defect of the system of mediæval society
was not that it left too much liberty for arbitrary and capricious
action, but that it tended to fix both rights and obligations to
such an extent as to run the risk first of rendering government unworkable, and secondly of rendering the movement
and growth of life impossible.

It is of course perfectly true that mediæval society often
seemed to oscillate between an uncontrollable and arbitrary
despotism, and an anarchical confusion, but this was due, not
to the want of a clear conviction of the rights and duties of
rulers and subjects, but to the absence of an effective instrument of government. The history of mediæval society constantly impresses upon us the conviction that the real difference
between a barbarous and a civilised political system lies in the
fact that the latter has an almost automatically working
administrative and judicial machinery, while the former is
dependent upon the chance of the presence of some exception-
ally competent and clear-sighted individual ruler.

The truth is that the men of these times were in no way
inferior to us in their sense of reverence for law, or in respect

for the great principles of human life, of which law is the
embodiment, but that they had no efficient civil service and
police to secure the smooth execution of law. They appre-
hended very clearly the principles of political and social order,
but it has taken all these centuries to work out an adequate
instrument for giving them practical effect.

To the men of the Middle Ages, as to every serious thinker
upon politics, the principle which lies behind every form of
the authority of the state is the principle of justice.   The
justification of authority is that it represents the principle
of justice ; the purpose of it is to maintain justice.   There
is a passage in one of the French epics of the twelfth
century which is very characteristic of the temper and judgment of the Middle Ages. The purpose of God, the writer
says, in making the king, is not to satisfy his appetite or
to enable him to rob the poor, but that he should tread
down all wrongs under his feet, and that he should hearken to
the complaint of the poor man and do him right.[1]

This judgment that authority stands for the maintenance and
vindication of righteousness lies behind the whole structure
of feudal law.   It is admirably expressed in a phrase of the
Assizes of the Court of Burgesses of Jerusalem : " La dame
ni le sire n'en est seignor se non dou dreit," and " mais bien
sachiés qu'il n'est mie seignor de faire tort." [2]   The authority
of the lady or lord is only an authority to do law or justice
—for the phrase implies both—they have no authority to
behave unjustly.   Here is a great principle stated with a
certain epigrammatic force.   It is true that this principle
was not novel, but corresponds with the traditions of the
Roman and Canon law, and no doubt arose directly out of

---

[1] " Le   Couronnement   de   Louis,"
line 174—

" Filz Looïs, a celer ne te quier,
Quant Deus fist rei por peuples justicier
Il nel fist mie por false lei jugier,
Faire luxure, ne alever pechié,
Ne eir enfant por retolir sen fie,
Ne veve fame tolir quatre deniers ;
Ainz deit les torz abatre soz ses piez,

Encontreval et foler et pleissier.
Ja al povre ome ne te chalt de tencier ;
Se il se claime ne t'en deit ennoier
Ainceis le deis entendre et conseillier,
Por l'amor Deu de son droit adrecier ;
Vers l'orgoillos te deis faire si fier
Comme liepart qui gent vueille man-
         gier."

[2] Assises de la Cour des Bourgeois, 26.

those political principles of the Teutonic societies which we
have already considered, as they are expressed in the writers
of the ninth century.[1] But, though the principle was traditional, the whole contents of the Assizes show very clearly
that it was no merely formal tradition, but rather that the
organisation of such a typical feudal state as the kingdom of
Jerusalem represented the effort to secure its reality.

It is worth our while to consider the character of the whole
passage from which these words are taken. If any man or
woman, knight or burgess, has obtained a judgment of the
court, and the king or queen endeavours to prevent its
execution, this is a sin against God and their oath. For the
king has sworn to maintain the good usages and customs of
the kingdom, to protect the poor as well as the rich in the
enjoyment of their rights. If he now breaks his oath he
denies God, and his men and the people should not permit
this, for " la dame ni le sire n'en est seignor se non dou
dreit." [2]

Here is indeed an admirable summary of the principles of
government, and of the relations of rulers and subjects ; we
shall presently consider this more closely under the terms
of the place of law in the political principles of feudalism,
but in the meanwhile it is important to observe how clear

[1] Cf. vol. i. chaps. 5, 18 ; vol. ii.
Part I. chaps. 1, 2 ; Part II. chaps.
2, 3.

[2] 'Assises de la Cour des Bourgeois,'
26 : " S'il avient que un homme ou
une feme seit jugé par la cort, qui que
il seit, ou chevalier ou borgés, et le roi
ou la rayne, de cuy est la terre, ne le
veut laisser desfaire au juise ou il est
jugé par droit, il fait tort, et si vait
contre Dieu et contre son sairement ;
et il meysmes se fauce et ne peut ce
faire par droit. Car le roi jure tout
premier, sur sains, de maintenir tous
les dons des autres rois ; après jure de
maintenir les bons hus et les bones
coustumes dou reaume ; après jure de
maintenir et de garder à dreit, contre
tous homes, à son poer, auci le povre

comme le riche et le grant comme le
petit ; après jure de maintenir ces
homes liges à dreit contre toutes per-
sonnes, segont l'us de sa cort, par ces
homes liges. Et c'il avient puis, en
aucune maniere, que il vaise contre ses
sairemens, il fait tout premier tort et
renée Dieu, puis que il fauce ce que il
a juré. Et ne l'deivent soufrir ces
homes ni le peuple ; car la dame ne le
sire n'en est seigneur se non dou dreit,
et de ces homes faire son comandement, et de reseivre ses rentes par tout
et ces dreitures. Mais bien sachiés
qu'il n'est mie seignor de faire tort,
car se il le faiseit, donc n'i avereit il
desous lui nul home qui droit deust
faire ne dire, puis qui le sire meyme se
fauce por faire tort."

and well defined is the general conception of the nature of political authority. The feudal lawyers do not generally discuss abstract principles, but it is easy to see that behind the detail of regulations there lay the assumption that these represented some principles of what was reasonable and equit-able, that political authority represented moral and religious as well as purely legal obligations.

Some of the law books, and especially the Assizes of the Court of Burgesses, were strongly influenced by the revived study of the Roman law, and in these we find a more definite attempt to deal with the abstract nature of justice. These Assizes begin with a paraphrase of the first title of the Institutes of Justinian, and it is interesting to see how the compiler blends religious and legal conceptions to express his meaning.[1]

The whole conception of the feudal lawyers is summed up in a very important and significant passage in Bracton's treatise on the laws of England. The king, he says, must, at his corona-tion, swear three things—first, that he will do what lies in him to secure that the Church and all Christian people may have peace in his time ; secondly, that he will forbid rapine and wrong-doing among all classes of the people ; thirdly, that in all his judgments he will ordain equity and mercy as he hopes for mercy from God. The king is indeed elected for this very purpose, that he should do justice to all men, and that through him God may distribute His judgments, for it would be useless to make laws if there were not some one to enforce them. The king is God's vicar upon earth, and it is his duty to

---

[1] ' Assises de la Cour des Bourgeois,' 1 : " De justise et de dreiture le cou-mencement de se livre devons dire. Tout premièrement devons querre jus-tise, por son dreit douner a chascun homme et a chascune feme : car en Latin justise se descrive enci : ' Jus-titia est constans et perpetua voluntas ius suum cuique tribuendi.' ' Con-stans,' ce est, ferm doit estre en fei et en justise, car celuy qui est ferm en fei et en justise, cil vit et non mora mie. Car ce dit l'Escriture en la lei : ' Justus ex fide vivit ' ce est, le juste home si vit par fei. Encement justise deit estre eternel, c'est a dire parmable, car David dist : ' Justitia Dei manet in seculum seculi,' c'est a dire la droiture de Dieu est a touz jours per-durable. Donc de fei et de justise devons aver matiere tout premiere-ment, si que par fei et par justise puissons rendre son dreit a chascun home et a chascune feme."

divide right from wrong, the equitable from the inequitable, that all his subjects may live honestly, and that no man should injure another.

In power, indeed, he should excel all his subjects, for he should have no equal nor superior, specially in administering justice. For the king, inasmuch as he is God's vicar and servant, can do nothing except that which he can do lawfully. It is indeed said that what pleases the prince has the force of law, but at the end of this law there follow the words, " cum lege regia, quae de imperio lata est," &c., that is, not everything is law which may be thought to be his will, but only that which is determined upon with the intention of making laws, with the authority of the king, with the counsel of his magistrates, and after due deliberation and discussion.

The authority of the king is the authority of law (or right), not of wrong. The king, therefore, should use the authority of law (or right) as being the vicar and servant of God on earth, for that alone is the authority of God ; the authority of wrong belongs to the devil, and not to God, and the king is the servant of him whose work he does. Therefore when the king does justice he is the vicar of the eternal King, but the servant of the devil when he turns aside to do wrong. For the king has his title from the fact that he governs well, and not from the fact that he reigns, for he is a king when he governs well, but a tyrant when he oppresses the people entrusted to him. Let him therefore restrain his authority by the law, which is the bridle of authority, let him live according to law, for this is the principle of human law that laws bind him who makes them, as it is said, " digna vox maiestate regnantis est legibus se alligatum principem profiteri," and again, " Nihil tam proprium est imperii, quam legibus vivere," and " maius imperio est legibus submittere principatum," and " merito debet retribuere legi, quia lex tribuit ei, facit enim lex quod ipse sit rex." [1]

<hr/>

[1] Bracton, ' De Legibus et Consuetudinibus Angliæ,' iii. 9. 2 (fol. 107): " Debet enim in coronatione sua, in nomine Jesu Christi præstito sacramento, hæc tria promittere populo sibi subdito. Imprimis, se esse præcepturum et pro viribus opem impensurum, ut ecclesiæ Dei et omni populo Christiano vera pax omni suo tempore observetur. Secundo, ut

Bracton's words are an admirable summary of the principle
that all authority represents some essential principle of justice
and equity, that an unjust authority is no authority. We shall
frequently have occasion to refer to this passage, for it contains
much which requires comment. It is obvious that his phrases
represent many influences besides that of feudal tradition and
custom, he is well acquainted with some important passages

rapacitates et omnes iniquitates omnibus gradibus interdicat. Tertio, ut
in omnibus iudiciis acquitatem præci-
piat et misericordiam, ut indulgeat
ei suam misericordiam clemens et
misericors Deus, et ut per iustitiam
suam firma pace gaudeant universi.
3. Ad hoc autem creatus est rex et
electus, ut iustitiam faciat universis,
et ut in eo Dominus sedeat, et per
ipsum sua iudicia discernat, et quod
iuste iudicaverit sustineat et defendat,
quia si non esset, qui iustitiam faceret,
pax de facili posset exterminari, et
supervacuum esset leges condere, et
iustitiam facere, nisi esset qui leges
tueretur. Separare autem debet rex
(cum sit Dei vicarius in terra) ius ab
iniuria, æquum ab iniquo, ut omnes
sibi subiecti honeste vivant, et quod
nullus alium laedat, et quod unicuique
quod suum fuerit, recta contributione
reddatur. Potentia vero omnes sibi
subditos debet præcellere. Parem
autem habere non debet, nec multo
fortius superiorem, maxime in iustitia
exhibenda, ut dicatur vere de eo,
magnus dominus noster, et magna
virtus eius etc. Licet in iustitia recipienda minimo de regno suo comparetur, et licet omnes potentia præcellat,
tamen (cum cor regis in manu Dei
esse debeat), ne sit effrenata, frænum
apportat temperantiæ, et lora moder-
antiæ ne cum effrenata sit, trahatur
ad iniuriam. Nihil enim aliud potest
rex in terris, cum sit Dei minister et
vicarius, nisi id solum quod de iure
potest, nec obstat quod dicitur, ' quod
principi placet, legis habet vigorem,'
(Dig., i. 4. 1), quia sequitur in fine

legis, ' cum lege regia, quæ de imperio
eius lata est,' id est non quicquid
de voluntate regis temere præsumptum
est, sed quod magnatum suorum consilio, rege auctoritatem præstante,
et habita super hoc deliberatione et
tractatu, recte fuerit definitum. Potestas itaque sua iuris est, et non
iniuriæ, et cum ipse sit auctor iuris,
non debet inde iniuriarum nasci
occasio, unde iura nascuntur, et
etiam qui ex officio suo alios prohibere
necesse habet, id ipsum in propria
persona committere non debet. Exercere igitur debet rex potestatem
iuris, sicut Dei vicarius et minister in
terra, quia illa potestas solius Dei est,
potestas autem iniuriæ diaboli et non
Dei, et cuius horum opera fecerit rex,
eius minister erit, cuius opera fecerit.
Igitur dum facit iustitiam, vicarius est
regis æterni, minister autem diaboli
dum declinet ad iniuriam. Dicitur
enim rex a bene regendo, et non a
regnando, quia rex est dum bene regit,
tyrannus dum populum sibi creditum
violenta opprimit dominatione (cf.
Isidore, Etym., ix. 3). Temperet igitur
potentiam suam per legem, quæ frænum
est potentiæ, quod secundum leges
vivat, quod hoc sanxit lex humana,
quod leges suum ligent latorem, et alibi
in eadem : ' digna vox maiestate regnantis est legibus scilicet alligatum
se principem profiteri ' (Cod., i. 14. 4),
Item, ' nihil tam proprium est imperii,
quam legibus vivere,' et ' maius imperio
est legibus submittere principatum '
(Cod., i. 14. 4), et ' merito debet retribuere legi, quia lex tribuit ei, facit
enim lex quod ipse sit rex.' " (unde ?)

in the Roman law, either by direct knowledge of the Corpus Juris, or through the intermediary of great civilians like Azo, and he is also much influenced by certain aspects of the patristic tradition, and especially by reminiscences of St Isidore of Seville. But his position is fundamentally that of all feudal law ; whatever may have been the importance of the principle of personal loyalty and devotion in mediæval society, it was no part of the thought or feeling of serious and practical men that these obligations were independent of reason and justice.

No doubt the adjustment of these principles to each other has always proved and will always prove difficult, and, as we shall see, a good deal of the complexity of feudal law arises from the difficulty of finding an adjustment of traditional sentiments with the practical needs of an organised and civilised community, but this had to be effected, and it was found in the gradual transference of the conception of loyalty from the individual lord to the nation and its head.

" La dame ni le sire n'en est seignor se non dou dreit." Here is the whole principle of government in a phrase, but the phrase itself suggests to us that this is not a merely abstract principle, that the conception of right or justice is not a merely abstract principle but that it had also a practical embodiment. To the mediæval mind the law was the practical form of justice, and it is in the due maintenance of law that men found the security for justice and for all good in life. There is an excellent statement of this conception in the prologue to one of the Norman law books, the ' Summa de Legibus,' which is thought to belong to the middle of the thirteenth century. The author looks upon law as created in order to restrain men's unbridled desires and the conflicts which these would cause if unchecked ; it is God, the lover of justice, who has created princes in order that they may restrain the discord of men by definite laws.[1]

[1] ' Summa de Legibus,' Prologue—
" Cum ineffrenatæ cupiditatis malicia humanum genus ardore suo insaciabili teneat irretitum, discordias generans ac dissensiones, a finibus hominum pacem et concordiam penitus proscripsisset, si non eius anxios impetus, legum freno constrictis faucibus, iuris severitas refrenasset ; quam ob rem rex pacificus, iustus dominus et

To the feudalist, indeed, law is in such a sense the foundation of authority, that where there is no law there is no
authority. In the terms of a famous phrase of Bracton,
"There is no king where will rules and not law."

Bracton is indeed careful to maintain that all men are under
the king, while he is under no man, but only under God ; but he
is under the law, for the law makes the king. And he is under
the law precisely because he is God's vicar, for Jesus Christ
whom he represents upon earth willed to be under the law that
he might redeem those who were under the law ; and thus the
blessed Virgin Mary, the mother of the Lord, did not refuse to
submit herself to the ordinances of the law. The king should
do likewise, lest his authority should be unrestrained ; there is
no one greater than the king in administering justice, but he
should be as the least in receiving the judgment of the law.[1]

We shall have to recur to this passage, and to deal with some
sentences which follow those we have here cited, as well as

amator iusticie, in terris principes
regnare voluit, ut iuris semitas certis
legibus limitantes contentiones singulas,
quas inimica pacis discordia parturivit,
iudicii calculo diffinirent."

[1] Bracton, 'De Legibus et Consuetudinibus Angliæ,' i. 8. 5 (fol. 5b) :
"Sunt etiam sub rege liberi homines,
et servi, et eius potestati subiecti, et
omnes quidem sub eo, et ipse sub
nullo, nisi tantum sub deo. Parem
autem non habet rex in regno suo, quia
sic amitteret præceptum, cum par in
parem non habeat imperium. Item nec
multo fortius superiorem, neque potentiorem habere debet quia sic esset inferior sibi subiectis, et inferiores pares
esse non possunt potentioribus. Ipse
autem rex non debet esse sub homine
sed sub deo et sub lege, quia lex facit
regem. Attribuat igitur rex legi, quod
lex attribuit ei, videlicet dominationem
et potestatem, non est enim rex ubi
dominatur voluntas et non lex. Et
quod sub lege esse debeat, cum sit dei
vicarius, evidenter apparet ad similitudinem Jesu Christi, cuius vices

gerit in terris. Quia verax dei misericordia, cum ad recuperandum
humanum genus ineffabiliter ei
multa suppeterent, hanc potissimam
elegit viam qua ad destruendum opus
diaboli non virtute uteretur potentie,
sed iustitie ratione. Et sic esse voluit
sub lege, ut eos, qui sub lege erant
redimeret, noluit enim uti viribus
sed iudicio. Sic etiam beata dei
genitrix, virgo Maria, mater domini,
quæ singulari privilegio supra legem
fuit, pro ostendendo tamen humilitatis exemplo legalibus subdi non
refugit institutis. Sic ergo rex, ne
potestas sua maneat infrenata. Igitur
non debet esse maior eo in regni suo
in exhibitione juris, minimus autem esse
debet, vel quasi, in iudicio suscipiendo,
si petat."

Cf. id., ii. 24. 1.

Cf. also 'Jostice et Plet,' i. 2. 3 :
"Li prince n'est pas sus la loi, mès la
loi est sus le prince ; quar il li donerent
tiel privilige comme il avoient." (Cf
Cod., i. 14. 4.)

with other passages related to this matter. In the meanwhile it is sufficient to observe the emphatic assertion that kingship is impossible without law, and that the king is not only under God but also under the law. It may perhaps be suggested that the evidence of Bracton as to the principles of feudalism cannot be accepted without much caution, for his work belongs to that time when feudal relations were giving way before national. Caution is no doubt necessary, but in this case we need have no scruple in taking Bracton's phrases as representative of the general system of feudal law, for these are precisely the principles which are set out in all the earlier feudal law books.

It is this principle which is emphatically expressed in the forms attendant on the coronation of the mediæval king. We have in the first volume dealt at some length with the great significance of the coronation oath in the earlier mediæval societies ;[1] it was equally important in the feudal State. Jean d'Ibelin describes at length the circumstances attendant on the succession to the kingdom of Jerusalem. The king is to swear that he will help the Patriarch of Jerusalem and protect the liberties of the Church, that he will do justice to widows and orphans, that he will maintain the ancient customs and assizes of the kingdom, and that he will keep all the Christian people of the kingdom according to their ancient and approved customs, and according to the assizes of his predecessors in their rights and " justises," as a Christian king and a faithful servant of God ought to do. And what the king swears all the men of the kingdom are also to swear, that they will hold and maintain the good usages and customs of the kingdom.[2]

---

[1] Cf. vol. i. chap. 20.

[2] 'Assizes of Jerusalem,' Jean d'Ibelin, vii. : " Je tel . . . promet à tei mon seignor tel, patriarche de Jerusalem . . . que je de cest jour en avant, serai ton feel aideor et defendeor de ta persone contre toz homes vivant el reiaume de Jerusalem. Les possessions et les franchises de la sainte yglise de Jerusalem ma mere et de totes les yglises apartenant à li principaument . . . en mon tens maintendrai à elles, as veves et as orfenins justise ferai ; les privileges des beneurés reis mes devanciers et les assises dou roiaume et dou rei Amauri et dou rei Baudoyn son fiz, et les anciennes costumes et assises dou roiaume de Jerusalem garderai ; et tot le peuple crestien dou dit roiaume, selonc les costumes anciennes et aprovéez de ce mesme roiaume, et selonc les assises des devant dis rois en lor dreis et en lor justises

This principle of the loyal observance of the law is well expressed in another place where Jean d'Ibelin says that the kings and nobles of Jerusalem should be wise, loyal, and good administrators of justice : they must be loyal, for they must loyally keep and govern themselves and their people, and must not do or suffer to be done disloyalty or falsehood ; they must be good administrators of justice, for they must uphold the rights of every man in their several courts and lordships.[1]

The same principle is again tersely expressed in one of the Norman law books. When the Duke of Normandy is received as Duke he must swear to serve the Church of God, and to keep good peace and justice according to law ; [2] and again, in the most important of the feudal law books of Germany, the 'Sachsenspiegel,' when the king is elected he is to swear to uphold the law of the kingdom, according to his power.[3]

We have already dealt with the important passage in which Bracton sets out the same principle in relation to the coronation oath of the King of England,[4] and Bracton is only commenting on the immemorial customs attendant on English coronations, customs which had not been in any way interrupted by the Norman Conquest.

garderai, si come roi crestien et feil de Dieu le doit faire en son roiaume."

Id. id., cxi. : " Et toz les homes dou roiaume de Jerusalem deivent jurer ausi de garder les assizes, et les bons us et les bones coustumes dou reaume de Jerusalem et tenir et maintenir."

[1] Id. id., viii. : " Le chief seignor dou roiaume de Jerusalem, seit rei ou autre, et toz les barons et seignors dou dit roiaume, qui ont court et coins et justise. deivent estre sages, loiaus, droituriers et bons justisiers . . . loiaus, qui il loiaument teignent, mainent, mainteignent et gouvernent eaus et lor homes et lor peuple, et que il ne facent à lor escient ni ne sueffrent à faire à leur pooir en lor seignorie des-

loiauté ne fauceté ; dreituriers, que il teignent et mainteignent dreiture dreitement à chascun en lor cours et en lor seignories, selonc ce qu'il est en droit soi."

[2] 'Statuta et Consuetudines Normaniæ,' i. 1 : " Quando dux Normanniæ in ducem recipitur, sacramento tenetur ecclesiam Dei deservire et ea, que ad eam pertinent, et bonam pacem tenere et legalem iusticiam."

[3] 'Sachsenspiegel,' iii. 54. 2 : " Als man den Koning küset, so sal he deme rike hulde dun, unde sveren dat he recht sterke, unde unrecht krenke, unde it rike voresta an sime rechte, als he künne unde moge."

[4] See p. 34.

CHAPTER III.

THE SOURCE OF LAW.

THE law is then to the feudal jurist the expression of the principle of justice, and it is supreme in the state, the king himself is the servant of the law.

What is then the source of law, what is the authority which it represents ? It is here perhaps that it is most difficult for the modern to understand the Middle Ages, while it is to the failure to do this that we may attribute most of the mistakes which have been made with regard to the nature of the mediæval State and the conception of government in the Middle Ages.

Above all things we must, if we are to make our way at all, discard the common conception of sovereignty, the conception that a law represents the mere command of a lawgiver, or even of a community. This conception, whose value in regard to modern times we cannot here discuss, is wholly foreign to the Middle Ages. To them the law was not primarily something made or created at all, but something which existed as a part of the national or local life. The law was primarily custom, legislative acts were not expressions of will, but records or promulgations of that which was recognised as already binding upon men. The conception of legislation had perhaps already appeared in the ninth century, but if so it had in the main died out again in the tenth and eleventh.[1]

Bracton, indeed, in a well-known passage based on Glanvill, claims that while other countries use " leges " and " jus scrip-

[1] Cf. vol. i. p. 235.

tum," England alone uses unwritten law and custom.[1] His phrase probably is related to the fact that there were people in some parts of Europe who lived under Roman law, and possibly to the great development of the influence of the Roman jurisprudence since the rise of the law school of Bologna in the twelfth century. While, however, we can in part explain Bracton's saying, and while it was no doubt correct about England, it is a curiously inaccurate view of the nature of law in the other European countries.

If we turn from Bracton to his great contemporary, Beaumanoir, in France, we find that he asserts boldly that all pleas are determined according to custom, and that the great feudatories like the Count of Clermont, and even the King of France himself, are bound to keep them, and cause them to be kept ; and Beaumanoir states the two tests by which it can be determined whether a custom is legally binding. The first is that the custom is general, and has been observed without dispute as far as man's memory goes, the second is that there has been a dispute about the matter and that there has been a judgment of the Court about it.[2]

---

[1] Bracton, i. 1. 2 (fol. 1): "Cum autem fere in omnibus regionibus utatur legibus et iure scripto, sola Anglia usa est in suis finibus iure non scripto et consuetudine. In ea quidem ex non scripto ius venit, quod usus comprobavit."

Cf. Glanvill, Prologue.

[2] Beaumanoir, xxiv. 682 : "Pour ce que tuit li plet sont demené selonc les coustumes, et que cest livre generaument parole selonc les coustumes de la conteé de Clermont, noz dirons en cest chapitre briement quele chose est coustume, tant soit ce que nous en aions parlé especiaument en aucuns chapitres, selonc ce qu'il convenoit es cas de quoi nous parlions. . . .

Coustume si est approuvee par l'une des II voies, dont l'une des voies si est, quant elle est generaus par toute la contée et maintenue de si lonc tans comme il peut souvenir a home, sans debat ; si comme quant aucuns hom de poeste connoist une dete, on li fet commandement qu'il ait paié dedens VII jours et VII nuis, et au gentil home dedens XV jors : ceste coustume est si clere que je ne la vi onques debatre. Et l'autre voie que l'en doit connoistre et tenir pour coustume si est quant debas en a esté, et l'une des parties se vout aidier de coustume, et fu approuvee par jugement si comme il est avenu mout de fois en parties d'oirs et en autres quereles. Par ces II voies peut on prouver coustumes, et ces coustumes est li cuens tenus à garder et a fere si garder a ses sougèis, que nus ne les corrumpe. Et se li cuens meismes les vouloit corrompre ou soufrir qu'eles fussent corrumpues, ne le devroit pas li rois soufrir, car il est tenu a garder, et a fere garder les coustumes de son roiaume."

Perhaps, however, the most illuminating view of the place of custom in mediæval law may be found in the account of the origin of the Assizes of Jerusalem which is given by Jean d'Ibelin and Philip of Novara. The story is historically very improbable,[1] but it is none the less important for us, for it represents in a very vivid fashion the conceptions of these jurists. Jean d'Ibelin tells us that when Godfrey of Bouillon had been elected as head of the newly conquered state of Jerusalem, he, with the advice of the Patriarch and princes and barons, and the wisest men whom he could find, appointed a certain number of wise men to inquire of those who were in Jerusalem what were the customs of their various countries, and to put these into writing. When this had been done the collection was brought before Godfrey and the Patriarch and notables, and he then with their counsel and consent selected such of the customs as seemed good to him, and made Assizes and usages, by which he and all the people of the kingdom were to be governed.[2] He relates further how the Kings of Jerusalem with the same advice and consent added from time to time other Assizes and altered the old ones, after inquiring from those who came to the Holy Land about their customs and usages, and how several times the Kings of Jerusalem sent to other countries to inquire directly about their customs.[3]

We have here a very suggestive account of what these jurists

---

[1] Cf. G. Dodu, 'Histoire des Institutions Monarchiques dans le Royaume Latin de Jerusalem,' pp. 36-61.

[2] Jean d'Ibelin, i. : "Il . . . eslut par le conseil dou patriarche de la sainte cité et yglise de Jerusalem, et par le conseill des princes et des barons, et des plus sages homes que il lors pot aveirs, sages homes à enquerre et à saveir des genz de diverses terres qui là estaient les usages de leur terres ; et tot quanque ciau que il ot eslu à ce faire en porent saveir ne aprendre il mirent et firent metre en escrit, et aporterent cel escrit devant le duc Godefroi ; et il assembla le patriarche et les autres avant dis, et lor mostra et fist lire devant eaus cel escrit ; et après, par leur conseill et par leur acort, il concuilli de ciaus escrits ce que bon li sembla, et en fist assises et usages que l'on deust tenir et maintenir et user ou roiaume de Jerusalem, par les quels il et ses genz et son peuple et totes autres manieres de genz alanz et venans et demorans en son reiaume fussent gouvernés, gardés, tenus, maintenus, et menés et justisés à droit et à raison el dit roiaume."

[3] Jean d'Ibelin, iii. ; cf Philip of Novara, xlvii.

looked upon as a great legislative action. The circumstances indeed were unparalleled in mediæval history, for the Kingdom of Jerusalem represented the establishment of a Western and Christian state in an alien and infidel country, while the Crusaders were not a homogeneous body, but were drawn from many different Western countries. They were therefore, as the authors of the Assizes thought, compelled to create a system of law for themselves, to proceed to a large and comprehensive effort of legislation. It is the more significant that in doing this they, according to the tradition, endeavoured scrupulously to ascertain the customary laws of the various national societies from which the Crusaders came, and formed their own laws by a process of selection and conflation from them.

The whole story illustrates very vividly the fact that the mediæval conception of law was dominated by custom, for even when the jurists thought that the Crusaders had to legislate for a new political society, they conceive of them as doing this by the process of collecting existing customs, only selecting and modifying as far as was necessary to bring them into some sort of harmony with each other. The Assizes of Jerusalem were, in their estimation, primarily written customs. And it is of interest to observe that when, as they thought, the great compilation was lost, when Saladin conquered Jerusalem, and when therefore they could no longer consult the text of the written customs, they at once fell back upon the unwritten customs and the decisions of the courts.[1]

We have so far been dealing with the Assizes of the High Court of Jerusalem, but there has also come down to us a collection of the Assizes of the Court of Burgesses. It is noticeable that these are influenced in a high degree by the Corpus Juris Civilis : no doubt this seems to indicate that the population of

[1] Jean d'Ibelin, cxi. : "Les assises deivent estre tenus fermement en totes choses ; et de ce de quei l'on ne sera certain qui seit assise, deit l'on tenir selonc l'usage et la longue acostumance. Et de ce que court aura fait esgart ou conoissance ou recort qui seit assise, deit estre tenu et maintenu come assise : car les assises ne pevent estre en pluisors choses provées, que par le lonc usage, ou por ce que l'on l'a veu faire et user, comme assise ; et ce est maniere de lei, et deit estre et est tenu ou reiaume de Jerusalem et en celui de Chypre miaus que leis ne decrés ne decretales."

the towns was drawn in large measure from those countries like
the south of France, and some parts of Italy, in which there were
many who lived under Roman law. Our text of these Assizes
dates from a much earlier time than the works of Jean d'Ibelin
and Philip of Novara, it is indeed generally thought to belong
to some time between 1173 and 1180. It is not quite clear
whether the statement of Jean d'Ibelin with regard to the origin
of the Assizes of the High Court refers to them also, but there
seems no substantial reason to doubt it. It is also deserving
of notice that there was established in Jerusalem a court for
the native Syrian population, and that this administered a
justice based upon their own customs.[1]

The first element in the conception of feudal law is that it
is custom, that it is something not made by the king or even
by the community, but something which is a part of its life.
We can, however, see that at least as early as the thirteenth
century there began to reappear the conception of laws as
being made, not that the idea of custom as law disappears, but
that there gradually grew up alongside of this the conception
that laws could be made under certain conditions and by
suitable authority. It is difficult to say how far the development of this was due to the pressure of circumstances com-
pelling men deliberately to make new laws, or to modify old
ones, how far it may have been facilitated by the revived and
extended study of the Roman jurisprudence, and by the systematic development of the Canon law, which in this matter
represents the same principles as the Roman law, and was
indeed no doubt greatly influenced by it. Whatever may have
been the circumstances which produced this great change, it is
of the first importance in the history of political theory to
observe the fact of the change.

We have here arrived at the beginnings of the modern
conception of sovereignty, that is, of the conception that there
is in every independent society the power of making and un-
making laws, some final authority which knows no legal limits,
and from which there is no legal appeal. We cannot here
consider how far, and in what sense, this conception was

[1] Jean d'Ibelin, iv.

present to the political thinkers of the ancient world. Still less can we here consider what is the real character of the modern theory, how far indeed it has been thought out completely and adequately, how far it still represents a somewhat crude and inorganic conception of society, a somewhat crude and partial apprehension of certain elements in the nature of the state.

It is at any rate quite certain that the modern conception as a whole was not only unknown to the Middle Ages, but that it would have been to them almost unintelligible. For to them the law of any particular state represented, in the first place, the customs of the community, which had not been made, but were part of the life of the community; and, in the second place, so far as they reflected upon the principles which lay behind these customs, they conceived of them as related to and determined by the rule of justice ; and, if and so far as they went further, they conceived of the law of the state as subservient to the natural law and the law of God.

It remains true that at least in the thirteenth century the conception of definite legislative action begins to appear, and we must therefore now consider the terms or forms of this legislative action as it is presented to us by the feudal jurists.

We begin with a phrase of Glanvill which bears upon its face the influence of the revival of Roman law, and which is yet also clearly mediæval in its principle. The laws of England, he says, though unwritten, may properly be called "laws," for the law says that whatever the Prince pleases has the force of law ; that is, we may properly call these "laws" which have been promulgated on doubtful matters with the counsel of the chief men and the authority of the prince.[1] We may put beside this some sentences from the Norman 'Summa de legibus' of the middle of the thirteenth century. "Consuetudines" are customs observed from ancient times, approved by the prince, and maintained by the people, which

Glanvill, Prologue :   "Leges namque anglicanas, licet non scriptas, leges appellari non videtur absurdum, (cum hoc ipsum lex sit, 'quod principi' placet, legis habet vigorem " (Dig., i. 4. 1)), "eas scilicet, quas super dubiis in consilio definiendis, procerum quidem consilio, et principis accedente authoritate, constat esse promulgatas."

determine to whom any thing belongs. Laws (leges) are institutions made by the prince and maintained by the people of the province, by which every dispute is decided. And again, laws and institutions were made by the Norman princes with great industry, by the counsel and consent of the prelates, counts, barons, and other prudent men, for the wellbeing of the human race.[1]

In these passages the conception of the authority of law is related first to custom, but the writers are aware that there are forms of law which have an immediate origin of a different kind, which have been made after due deliberation. The force of these laws is derived from the authority of the prince, the counsel and consent of the great men, and the observation, or reception, or maintenance of them by the people : it is difficult to find an exact rendering for the phrase " a populo conservati."

This conception of law is characteristic of the whole mediæval tradition. It is for the prince or king to issue or promulgate laws, and without his authority this cannot be done ; but to make his action legitimate he must consult the great and wise men of the nation ; and the people or whole community has its place, for they have to receive or observe the law. This is the conception which we find in the political writers and in the legislative documents of the ninth century,[2] and it is evident that it continued to be the conception of the feudal lawyers of the twelfth and thirteenth centuries. It may have some relation to the definition of law by Papinian.[3] It is possible that the terms of the phrases which describe the part of the people in legislation may be related to the principle laid down by Gratian, that no law is

---

[1] ' Summa de Legibus,' x. 1 : " Consuetudines vero sunt mores ab antiquitate habiti, a principibus approbati et a populo conservati, quid, cuius sit, vel ad quem pertineat limitantes. Leges autem sunt institutiones a principibus facte et a populo in provincia conservate, per quas contentiones singule deciduntur ; sunt enim leges quasi instrumenta in iure ad contentionum declarationem veritatis."

Id., Prologue : " Quoniam ergo leges et instituta, que Normannorum principes non sine magna provisionis industria, prelatorum, comitum, et baronum necnon et ceterorum virorum prudentium consilio et consensu, ad salutem humani generis statuerunt."

[2] Cf. vol. i. pp. 229-239.

[3] Dig., i. 3. 1.

valid, by whomsoever promulgated, unless it is accepted by
the custom of those concerned[1] A similar doctrine was held
by some at least of the civilians of the twelfth and thirteenth
centuries.[2]

The same principles, again, are stated by Bracton in the
passage of which we have already cited the first words. While
in almost all other countries men follow the laws (leges) and a
written " jus," England alone uses not written law but custom ;
it is not, however, absurd to call the English laws " leges," for
that has the force of law (legis) which has been justly determined and approved, with the counsel and consent of the great
men, the approval (sponsione) of the whole commonwealth and
the authority of the king. And again, in another place, he says,
that such English laws and customs, by the king's authority,
sometimes command, sometimes forbid, and sometimes punish
transgressors, and inasmuch as they have been approved by the
consent of those who are concerned with them (utentium), and
confirmed by the oath of the king, they cannot be changed or
abolished without the common consent of all those by whose
counsel or consent they were promulgated, although they may
be improved (in melius converti) even without this consent, for
to improve is not to destroy.[3]

There is one great feudal lawyer whose position requires
some special examination, and that is Beaumanoir. For his
phrases are, at least at first sight, a little ambiguous. In some

---

[1] Gratian, ' Decretum,' D. iv., after
3. Cf. vol. ii. p. 155.

[2] Cf. vol. ii. pp. 61-63.

[3] Bracton, ' De Legibus,' i. 1. 2 (fol.
2) : " Cum autem fere in omnibus regionibus utatur legibus et iure scripto,
sola Anglia usa est in suis finibus iure
non scripto et consuetudine. In ea
quidem ex non scripto ius venit, quod
usus comprobavit. Sed absurdum
non erit leges Anglicanas, licet non
scriptas, leges appellare, cum legis
vigorem habeat, quicquid de consilio et
de consensu magnatum et reipublicæ
communi sponsione, authoritate regis
sive principis præcedente, iuste fuerit

diffinitum et approbatum."

Id. id., i. 2. 6 : " Huiusmodi vero
leges Anglicanæ et consuetudines
regum auctoritate, iubent quandoque,
quandoque vetant, et quandoque judi-
cant et puniunt transgressores ; quæ
quidem, cum fuerint approbatæ consensu utentium, et sacramento regum
confirmatæ, mutari non poterunt nec
destrui sine communi consensu eorum
omnium, quorum consilio et consensu
fuerunt promulgatæ. In melius
tamen converti possunt, etiam sine
eorum consensu, quia non destruitur
quod in melius commutatur."

passages he would seem to say simply that the king is the legislator, and if this stood alone, we might conclude that to him the authority of law was derived simply from the king's will. It is indeed possible that Beaumanoir represents some tendency which was peculiar to the French monarchy, and it is more than probable that his conceptions of the nature of the power of monarchy were strongly influenced by the revived study of the Civil law, and its conception of the legislative authority of the Emperor, and we might therefore incline to the conclusion that his position was different from that of the feudal lawyers whose principles we have so far examined. In order then that we may rightly estimate his position we must examine briefly his conception of the origin of kingship.

In an important passage, which we shall have to consider again later, Beaumanoir says that in the beginning all men were free, and of the same freedom, for we all are descended from one common parent, but as the number of men increased strife arose, and those who desired to live in peace recognised that this was impossible while every man thought himself as good as others. They therefore elected a king, and made him head over them, and gave him power to judge their misdeeds, and to make commandments and "establissemens" over them.[1] The phrases of the passage suggest very strongly the influence of the Roman jurisprudence ; the conception of the original equality of men, the appearance of war and its consequent confusions and crimes, the conception of the people creating a king and giving him authority to make laws, these may have come directly to Beaumanoir by many channels, but it is at least very probable that they represent the traditions of the Institutes and Digest.[2]

[1] Beaumanoir, xlv. 1453 : " Comment que pluseur estat de gent soient maintenant, voirs est qu'au commencement tuit furent franc et d'une meisme franchise ; car chascuns set que nous descendimes tuit d'un pere et d'une mere. Mes quant li pueples commenca a croistre, et guerres et mautalent furent commencié, par orgueil et par envie, qui plus regnoit lors et fet encore que mestiers ne fust, le communetés du peuple, cil qui avoient talent de vivre en pes, regarderent qu'il ne pourroient vivre en pes tant comme chascuns cuideroit estre aussi grans sires l'uns comme autres ; si eslurent roi, et le firent seigneur d'aus, et li donerent le pouoir d'aus justicier de lor mesfés, de fere commandemens et establissemens sur aus."

[2] Cf. Digest, i. 1. 4. 5 ; 2. 11 ; 4. 1; Institute, i. 2. 2.

The phrases are remarkable both for their democratic conception of human nature, and of the source of authority, and for their sharply marked conception of the legislative power of the king, and if they stood alone we might have to conclude that Beaumanoir's theory of the nature of law was different from that which we have so far seen to be characteristic of the feudal jurists. But the phrases do not stand alone, and in order to form a complete judgment upon his theory we must examine some other passages in his work. The first is one in which Beaumanoir is careful to point out that while every baron is "souverain" in his own barony, the king is "souverain" in all the kingdom, and has thus the general care of the whole kingdom, and therefore he can make such " establissemens " as he thinks well for the common good.[1] The words represent an important development of the conception of the national monarchy, and they attribute the supreme legislative power to the king ; but it should be noticed that he holds the power because he is responsible for the care of the whole kingdom, and exercises it not for his own ends, but for the common good. The last phrase is important, and is constantly repeated, the legislative power must be used for the common good.[2]

In other passages we find, however, phrases which add another principle to these. The king may make " establissemens " only for his own domain, and in this case they do not concern his barons, who must continue to administer their lands according to the ancient customs. When, however, the " establissemens " are general, they are in force throughout the kingdom. But such " establissemens " are made " par tres grant conseil,"

---

[1] Beaumanoir, xxxiv. 1043 : "Pour ce que nous parlons en cest livre, en plusours lieus, du souverain, et de ce qu'il peut et deit fere, li aucun porroient entendre, pour ce que nous ne nommons conte ne duc, que ce fust du roi, mais en tous les lieus que li rois n'est pas nommés, nous entendons de ceus qui tienent en baronie, car chascuns barons est souverain en sa baronie. Voirs est que li rois est souverains par dessus tous, et a de son droit, la general garde de tout son roiaume, par quoi il pot fere teus establissemens comme il li plest pour le commun pourfit, et ce qu'il establist doit estre tenu. Et si n'i a nul si grant dessous li que ne puist estre tres en sa court par defaute de droit ou pour faus jugement, et pour tous les cas qui touchent le roi."

[2] Cf. id., xlix. 1512 : "Mes li rois le peut bien fere quant il li plest et quant il voit que c'est li communs pourfis."

and for the common good.[1] Again, in another place ; the
king may indeed make new " establissemens," but he must
take great care that he makes them for reasonable cause, for
the common good, and " par grant conseil." [2]

Beaumanoir does not anywhere explain what precisely he
means by the words " par grant conseil " ; but it would seem
most natural to understand them as referring to the need of
consultation with some body of persons qualified to advise the
king. We must then at least correct our first impression of
Beaumanoir's theory of legislation. He would seem to place
the royal authority in a more isolated position than is general
in the feudal jurists, he may be more influenced than they are
in general by the newly recovered conception of the legislative
power of the emperor in the Roman law, and may possibly,
though on this we can express no opinion, represent some
conception of monarchy which was developing specially in
France at that time. But, on the other hand, in his insistence
upon the need of reasonable cause, on the " grant conseil,"
and on the principle that legislation must be for the common
good, he comes very near to the general principles of the other
feudalists.[3]

We are therefore justified in the conclusion that the feudal
conception of law is first that of custom ; and secondly, that
so far as men began to recognise the necessity of actual legislative action, they conceived of the law as deriving its authority
not from the will or command of the ruler alone, but also from
the counsel and consent of the great or wise men, and the
assent of the whole community.

---

[1] Id., xlviii. 1499 : " Mais quant li
Rois fet aucun establissement espe-
cieaument en son demaine, si baron
ne lessent pas pour ce a user en leur
terres, selonc les anciennes coustumes.
Mes quant li establissemens est
generaus, il doit courre par tout
le roiaume. Et nous devons croire
que tel establissement sont fet par

tres grant conseil et pour le commun
pourfit."

[2] Id., xlix. 6 : " Tout soit il ainsi
que li Rois puist fere nouveaus establissemens, il doit mout prendre garde
qu'il les face par resnable cause, et
pour le commun pourfit, et par grant
conseil."

[3] Cf. p. 154 (note 4).

CHAPTER IV.

THE MAINTENANCE OF LAW.

THE feudal jurists held clearly and maintained emphatically that the relations of men to each other are determined by the principles of justice, that the law is the form and expression of justice, and that it is in the strict observance of the law that men find the security for the maintenance of justice. The principle is clear, but it may be said that this was little more than formal, that the king might indeed swear to administer justice and to maintain the law, but there was no method by which this obligation could be enforced. How far this was from being true we shall see as we examine more closely the principles of the structure of feudal society.

We shall do well to remind ourselves of a very noticeable phrase in that passage in the Assizes of the Court of Burgesses of Jerusalem which we have already quoted. If the lord should break his oath and refuse to minister law and justice to his people, they are not to permit this.[1] This is a blunt expression of the principle which underlies the structure of feudal society, and the relations of lord and vassal. But feudal law did more than recognise the principle, it provided a carefully constructed machinery for carrying it out.

We must turn from the principle of the supremacy of law to the method of its determination and enforcement. That is, we must examine the nature of the feudal court, and the relation of lord and vassal to this, and we begin by examining these questions as they are presented in the

[1] See p. 33.

Assizes of Jerusalem. Jean d'Ibelin draws out with great
care the nature of the mutual obligations of lord and vassal.
He expresses in the highest terms the fidelity which the
vassal owes to his lord, the service and help which he must
render to him, the secrecy which he must maintain about
his counsels, and the respect which he owes to his wife and
daughter,[1] and he enumerates those distinctive obligations
which the vassal owes to his lord, which we have already
mentioned,[2] but at the same time he insists that the lord is
bound to his vassal by the same faith which the vassal owes to
him, and that he may not touch his vassal's body or his fief
except by the judgment of the court.[3]

These are the principles of the relation between lord and
vassal, but they are not mere abstract principles, they are
legally enforceable. If the vassal fails to discharge his obligations, and the lord can establish this by the judgment of the
court, the vassal will lose his fief, and the lord can treat him as
a traitor, and as one who has broken his faith.[4] On the other
hand, if the lord breaks his faith to the vassal, the vassal can
bring the matter before the court, and if the court decides in
his favour, it will declare him to be free from his obligations,
and he will hold his fief without service for his lifetime.

[1] Jean d'Ibelin, 195.

[2] See p. 26.

[3] Jean d'Ibelin, 196 : " Le seignor
ne doit metre main, ne faire metre
main el cors ni el fié de son home,
si ce n'est par l'esgart ou par la
conoissance de sa court ; et est tenus
à son home, se me semble, par la
fei qui est entri'aus de totes les
choses avant dittes de quei home est
tenus à son seignor ; car entre seignor
et home n'a que la fei, et la fei deist
estre coneue et gardée entre caus ès
choses avant dites."

[4] Id. id.: " Et qui faut vers son
seignor d'aucunes des avant dittes
choses, il ment sa fei vers lui ; et se le
seignor l'en peut prover par recort de
court, il pora faire de lui et de ses
choses come d'ome ataint de fei

mentie. . . . Et qui defaut à son
seignor, je crei que il perdreit à sa vie
le fié que il tient de lui."

Id. 206 : " Se home ment sa fei vers
son seignor ou le seignor à son home
. . . et de laquel des choses dessuz
dittes que l'un mesprent vers l'autre,
il ment sa fei vers l'autre. Et se le
seignor en ataint son home, il est
encheu en sa merci de cors et de fié et
de quanque il a, et se il en viaut aveir
dreit et il le requiert à sa court qu'elle
li conoisse quel dreit il en deit aveir, je
cuit que la court conoistra qu'il en peut
de son cors faire justise, selonc ce que
le mesfait sera, de trayson ou de fei
mentie, et que il peut son fié et totes
ces autres choses prendre et faire en
come de choze de traïtor ou de fei
mentie."

Neither lord nor vassal can take the matter into his own hands, but must submit his complaint to the court, and abide by its judgment.[1] It is the court which is the judge in all cases of dispute about the relative rights or duties of lord and vassal.

It is thus important to ask what was the composition of the feudal court. It was the court of the lord, and one might naturally enough think that it was the lord who decided the matters brought before it. But this was not the case ; the court was composed in principle of all the vassals, and the judgment of the court was the judgment of its members. It was even by some disputed whether the lord was properly speaking a member of the court at all. Jean d'Ibelin's work contains a very interesting and significant discussion of this subject. He is dealing with the question how a man is to claim a fief which he, or his ancestors, have held, and says that the man is to appear before the lord and say by his advocate that he, or his ancestors, have held the fief, and that if the lord doubts this he is prepared to prove it " par le recort de partie des homes de vostre court." The lord may reply that proof must be " par privilege ou par recort de court," and that proof " par la recort de partie des homes de la court " is not valid, for there could be no court unless the lord himself or his representative were present. To this the vassal replies that on the contrary the lord may not sit in the court, " as esgars ne as conoissance ne à recors que il font " ; the vassals are to sit without the lord, and when they have arrived at their decision, it is to be reported to the lord as the judgment of the court. Jean d'Ibelin does not formally pronounce a judgment upon the whole question, but he is clear that the presence of the lord is not necessary to constitute a proper court, at least in cases concerning claims

[1] Jean d'Ibelin, 206 : " Et se l'ome ataint son seignor en court que il a mespris vers lui de sa fei, et il en requiert à aveir dreit par esgart ou par conoissance de court je cuit que la court esgardera ou conoistra que l'ome est quiete vers lui de sa fei, et a son fié sans servise tote sa vie. . . . Ne l'un ne peut de ce ataindre l'autre, se n'est par reconoissance qu'il en ait faite en court ou par quei l'un mespreigne vers l'autre en court de aucuns des devant dittes choses : car seignor ne peut prover vers son home aucune chose qui monte à sa fei, ne l'ome vers son seignor, autrement que par le recort des homes de la court don seignor."

to the tenure of a fief.[1] In another passage he describes the
proper procedure of the court when the king or his representative is not present.[2] The court, then, whose duty it is
to enforce upon lord and vassal alike the due observance of

[1] Jean d'Ibelin, 166 : "Et se le
seignor viaut riens dire ou esloignier
celle requeste, il li peut respondre ;
. . . 'Je n'entens que je tel recort
voz déi faire, ne que il voz vaille ne
déi valeir à aveir la saisine que voz
me requerés, tot l'eussés vos enssi
prové come voz dittes, se mei ou mon
ancestre ne fume o les homes de
nostre court, par quei voz volés prover
en dit ou ce fu fait que voz offrés a
prover ; que je n'entens que court
seit, se le seignor et deus de ces
homes ou plus ne sont ensemble, ou
se le seignor n'en establist un homme
en leuc de lui et autres deus o lui
come court a oyr et aveyr ou à dire ce
qu'il lor comande que il en facent come
court ; et que puisque court n'en est
ni ne peut estre sanz seignor ou sans
home qu'il ait establi en son leuc, si
n'entent je por chose que voz aiés ditte
ne offerte à prover, que je voz en dée
faire le recort que voz me requerés,
ne que il voz vaille ne déi valeir à la
saisine aveir que voz me requerés, par
chose que voz aiés dite, se la court ne
l'esgarde : et de ce me met je en
l'esgart de la court, sauf mon retenaill.'
Contre ce peut le requerant dire :
' Sire, à ce que voz dittes que court
n'est que là où le seignor et deus de
ces homes ou plus ne sont, voz dites
votre volenté ; mais je entens que si
est que ensi fuest come vos dites, il
n'aureit jamais esgart ne conoissance
ne recort de court ; car seignor ne
peut ni ne deit estre ne seyr à la court
o les homes de la court as esgars ni as
conoissance ne à recors que il font,
ainz le font il sanz le seignor ; et
quant il les ont fais et il les ont
retrais devant le seignor, ce que la
court a fait, soit esgart ou conoissance

ou recort, celui qui le retrait en la
court dit : Sire la court a ce fait. Et
por ce que la court le fait, si est clere
chose que les homes sont court en
aucun cas sans le seignor, et puisque
il le sont en aucun cas sanz le seignor,
ne il n'est assise ne usage qui vaille
que en tel cas les homes de la court,
dont le fié muet, ne puissent et
deivent recorder en la court ce il on
veu celui qui requiert la saisine dou
fié ou son ancestre saisi et tenant ou
usant de ce que il requiert come de
son fié, ne autrement que par le recort
des homes de celle court ne peut l'on
prover la saisine de lui ou de son
ancestre dou fié que il requiert ; ' . . .
Et selonc ce qui est devant dit, il me
semble que la court devreit esgarder
que le seignor n'a chose dite por quei
il dée demorer que il ne face aveir au
requerant le recort que il li requiert . . .
Que se autrement esteit, moult à
enuis poreit l'on prover nulle saisine
de fié de lui ou de son ancestre, por
quei moult de genz perdreient leur
dreit et leur raison par defaute de
recort de court, laquel chose sereit
contre dreit raison et tort apert."
Cf. p. 65 for discussion of this subject
by Beaumanoir.

[2] Id. 257 : "Et quant cort est ensemble por jugement ou por recort
faire ou por conseill ou por avoiement,
sanz le rei ou sanz celui qui est en son
leuc, il (i.e., the Constable) peut et
deit demander l'avis de chascun, ou
faire le demander au mareschal, ce il
viaut : et peut destraindre chascun
de dire ou de soi aquiter si come il
est usage : et peut comander à retraire
l'esgart ou la conoissance ou le recort ou
l'aveement que la court a fait, auquel
que il vodra de ciaus de la court.

these obligations, is indeed the court of the lord, but its judgment is the common judgment of all those concerned.

It may, however, be urged that this is very well in principle, but what sanction could there be for such a comprehensive control over lord and vassal, what power was there which could enforce the observation of the decisions of the court. This question may seem to us, from our modern standpoint, one of great difficulty, but the compilers of the Assizes of Jerusalem had what seemed to them a perfectly simple and clear answer.

The matter is dealt with both by Jean d'Ibelin and by Philip of Novara, but the treatment of the latter is the more complete. He has set out, in a passage to which we shall have to return later, the relation of the overlord to the sub-vassals, as declared in an Assize of King Amauri, and then explains the position of the mesne vassals in case of dispute between them and the overlord. The king, he says, recognised, when the Assize was established, that all his liegemen, whether they held of him immediately, or of his vassals, were bound in faith to each other, and could demand aid each of all the others,[1] and he draws out the significance of this in detail. If a vassal makes some claim upon his lord and demands that the matter should be brought before the lord's court and the lord refuses, the vassal may call upon all his peers to go to the lord and demand that he should allow the matter to be brought before the court. If the lord refuse to listen to them, they must declare to the lord that they will discharge none of their obligation to him till he has done this. And thus also if the case has been brought before the court and the lord refuses to carry out its judgment, the vassals are to renounce their service to him until this has been done. And again, if the lord or his repre-

---

[1] Philip of Novara, 51: "Vos aveis oi les avantaiges que le chief seignor a en la ligece de ses homes, après orreis l'eschange et l'avantage que les homes lieges ont a l'encontre de ce. Le rei otroia, à l'establissement de l'assise que tous ses homes liges qui tenoient de li ou de ses homes, queis qu'il fussent, grans on petis, fussent tenu de fei l'un à l'autre de ce que est dessus escrit, et que chascun d'eaus peust requerre les autres comes ses peirs en tel endreit. Et les homes en sont tenu l'un à l'autre, aussi au petit come au plus grant, por quei il ne seit entechié d'aucun des vices por quei l'on pert vois en cort. La devise de ce par quei les home liges sont tenu l'un a l'autre, est desus escrite et devisée par chapitres."

sentative should deprive a man of his fief without judgment of the court, the vassal's peers are to help him and give him force to recover his fief.   And Philip adds that he remembered that when the representative of the Emperor (Frederick II.) deprived the lord of Beyrouth and his nephews of their fiefs, this assize was cited in the court, and the court recognised it as valid.[1]

Jean d'Ibelin maintains the same principles, and it is worth while to notice the emphatic phrases he uses with respect to the case of a lord putting his vassal in prison without the judgment of the court.   In such a case his friends and relations may summon all his peers to accompany them to the lord, and to demand his release or the judgment of the court.   If the

---

[1] Philip of Novara, 52 : " S'il avenist que aucun des homes liges venist devant le chief seignor en la Haute Cour, et il feist aucune requeste et le seignor delaiast, et l'ome li requist esgart de cort et le seignor ne li feist aver ou s'en delivrast par esgart de cort meisme ; ou s'il avenist que l'on ne le laissast entrer devant le seignor et aussi le deloiast on de venir à son droit, l'ome peut venir a ses pers là ou il les porra trover, et requerre lor, par la fei que il li doivent, come à lor peir, que il veingent avant li seignor o lui et li requierent que il le maint par sa cort come son home, et se il li a requis esgart, que il le face aver ; il y deivent aler et faire ce que l'ome lor a requis. Et s'il avenist que le seignor ne vosist otroier ne faire lor requeste, il deivent et pevent dire au seignor, que il ne feront riens por lui tant qu'il ait fait lor requeste. Par trei feis li doivent ce dire, et s'il por tant ne le fait outreement, li pevent guagier de lor servises tant que il li ait acomplie lor requeste. Et s'il avenet que la cort ait fait aucun esgart, et le seignor ne le veut tenir, aussi le doivent guagier de lor servises tant que il ait accompli lor esgart. Et se il aveneit que le seignor, ou autre por lui en aichoison de li, dessaissist sans esgart de cort aucun de ses homes de tout ou de partie de son fié, celui qui est dessaissi peut requere ses pers que il li aident à recovrer sa saisine, fornissant dreit au seignor, et se le seignor, ou autre por lui, li seit que demander et il est prest de fornir raison ; les homes en deivent requerre le seignor, se il est au pais, ou le bailli, se le seignor n'i est. Et se il ne fait lor requeste, il pevent et doivent aler à lor per et doner li force et pooir de recovrer sa saisine et les rentes dou tens passé, c'est assaver despuis que il fu dessaisi dou fié sans esgart de court. Et ce meisme vi ge avenir de monseignor de Baruth à Acre, quant le seignor de Saeste dessaisi li et ses nevous et ses amis, par le comandement de l'emperour, de lor fiés que il avoient à Acre. Et adonc fu recordée et retraite l'assise enterinement ; et toute la court dist et otroia que il entendoient que tel estoit l'assise. Et là ot pluisors homes liges qui l'avoient oi retraire autrefeis en cort, por le content qui fu entre le rei Aimeri et messire Rau de Tabarie."

Cf. also Philip of Novara, 40, and Jean d'Ibelin, 202.

lord refuses, they are to rescue their peer by force, unless the lord resists in person ; in that case, as they cannot bear arms against him, they are each and all to renounce all service to him till he has set their peer at liberty, or has submitted the case to the judgment of the court.[1]

The principle of the authority of the court in enforcing their mutual obligations upon lord or vassal is to the compilers of the Assizes of Jerusalem perfectly clear and obvious, and the whole body of the vassals is bound to maintain this authority even against the lord.   This is perhaps even more clearly brought out by Jean d'Ibelin in another passage, in which he maintains that if the court has given a judgment against the lord in the case of a man who is not a vassal, and the lord refuses to carry this out, such a man may lay the matter before the vassals and adjure them to compel the lord to carry out the judgment. The vassals are then to go to their lord and request him to do this, and if he refuses they are to declare to him that they are bound to maintain the honour of the court and the Assizes of the Kingdom of Jerusalem, and that they will renounce all service to him until he has carried out the judgment of the court.[2]

---

[1] Jean d'Ibelin, 201 : " Et se le seignor ne le fait delivrer à leur requeste, ou ne dit chose par quei il ne le deit faire et tel que court l'esgarde ou conoisse, tos les homes ensemble deivent aler là où il sevent que il est aresté et delivrer le à force ou autrement, se le cors de leur seignor ne lor defent as armes, contre le quel il ne pevent ni ne deivent porter armes ne fair chose a force. . . . Et se le seignor le defent contre eaus as armes ou autrement à force, il li deivent dire.

" Sire, voz estes notre seignor, ne contre vostre cors noz ne porteremes armes, ni ne feriens chose a force.   Et puisque voz noz defendés a force à delivrer nostre per qui est pris et emprisonés sanz esgart ne sans conoissance de court, noz voz gajons toz ensemble et chascun par sei dou servise que noz

devons tant que voz aiés nostre per tel delivrer ou fait delivrer, ou dite raison por quei voz ne le devés faire et tel que court l'esgarde ou conoisse."

Cf. Philip of Novara, 59.

[2] Jean d'Ibelin, 244 : " Et por ce que nos somes homes de vostre court et que nos somes tenus de garder et faire garder à nos pooirs l'onor de la court dont noz somes, et de maintenir les assises et les usages dou reiaume de Jerusalem, nos toz ensemble, et chascun par sei, voz gajons dou servise que nos voz devons, tant que vos aiés a tel," et le noment, " tenu et parfait ou fait tenir et parfaire ce que vostre court, dont noz somes homes, a esgardé ou coneu ou recordé, ou dit en la court tel raison que le court esgarde ou conoisse que voz ne le devés faire."

This was then the method by which the authority of the laws and customs of Jerusalem was to be declared and enforced. The court was the supreme judge, and the lord, that is, the King of Jerusalem, had to submit to it ; if he refused to do this the ordinary relations between him and his vassals were for the time suspended, and they were to renounce all their service to him until he submitted to the court and its judgments.[1] The compilers of the Assizes justify their opinion by citing two cases in which, as they say, the vassals of the kingdom of Jerusalem had taken such action.[2]

It may perhaps be urged that the Assizes of Jerusalem represent an extreme and even fantastic development of the principle of the obligation of the king or lord to govern according to law, and that their principle of the supremacy of the court over the king or lord was eccentric and unparalleled. It is indeed true that in their detail they represent a particular and local attempt to create a method of control over the ruler, a method which, however good it may seem in theory, was not likely to produce an effective system of government; and we cannot look upon this method as being more than one of the many experiments in government which were being made in the twelfth and thirteenth centuries. But we are in this work concerned rather with the principle which lay behind such experiments than with the experiments themselves. If we are content to consider them from this standpoint we shall find these experiments immensely interesting, and shall also find that these principles are reflected more or less clearly and completely in many at least of the feudal law books.

In those compilations of the feudal law of Lombardy which are known to us as the ' Consuetudines Feudorum,' and which belong substantially to the twelfth century, the principles of the relation of lord and vassal are set out with great clearness. The obligations of the vassal must be discharged by him, and if he

---

[1] Cf. Jean d'Ibelin, 203, 204, 205, 208, 210, 213, 214, 239 ; Philip of Novara, 41, 42.

[2] Cf. Jean d'Ibelin, 203, 204 ; Philip of Novara, 40, 42.

refuse or fails to carry them out, he will lose his fief.[1] On the other hand, it is laid down with great emphasis that no vassal can be deprived of his benefice except for a definite and proved offence.[2] And it is very clearly maintained that in all cases of dispute about the fief and its tenure between the lord and vassal there is always a proper tribunal to decide, and this tribunal is either the court which is composed of the peers of the vassal or the court of the Emperor.[3] It is noteworthy that the lord has only the same remedy against his vassal as the vassal against him, that is, the appeal to the court, and that the court is, if need be, to compel the lord to make restitution to his vassal or to submit himself to the judgment of the court. If the lord should refuse to do this the vassal can carry the case to the higher authority, that is, clearly to the overlord or Emperor.[4]

[1] 'Consuetudines Feudorum,' ii. : " Quia supra dictum est, quibus modis feudum adquiritur et retinetur, nunc videamus, qualiter amittatur. Si enim prælium campestre habuerit, et vasallus eum (dominum) morantem in ipso praelio dimiserit non mortuum non ad mortem vulneratum, feudum amittere debet. Item si fidelis dominum cucurbitaverit vel id facere laboraverit aut cum uxore eius turpiter luserit vel si cum filia aut cum nepte ex filio aut cum sorore domini concubuerit, iure feudum amittere censetur." Cf. vi. 11.

[2] Id., v. 10 : " Sancimus ut nemo miles sine cognita culpa beneficium amittat, si ex his culpis vel causis convictus non fuerit, quas milites usi sunt vel per laudamentum parium suorum, si deservire noluerint."

C. Lehmann, in his edition of the ' Consuetudines Feudorum,' gives in full the text of two groups of MSS. for Tit. vi., but the differences are not in the case of the passages here quoted of substantial importance for our purpose.

[3] Id., vi. 1 : " Si fuerit contentio inter dominum et fidelem de investitura feudi, dirimatur per pares curtis."

Id., vi. 5. 1 : " Si contentio fuerit

de beneficio inter capitaneos, coram imperatore diffiniri debet. Si vero fuerit contentio inter maiores valvassores et minores de beneficio, iudicio parium diffiniatur."

Id., vi. 13 : " Et si dominus possederit et miles sic dixerit, quod investitus fuerat a domino suo et dominus negaverit, adhibeantur pares illius et per illos inveniatur veritas."

Cf. vii. 3, viii. 23.

The regulations cited in this note and the previous one are founded upon the ' Edictum de beneficiis regni Italici,' of the Emperor Conrad II. (1037 A.D.)

[4] Id., viii. 29 : " Dominus vocat militem qui ab eo feudum possidebat dicendo eum in culpam incidisse per quam feudum amittere debeat. Hic non respondit. Quid domino faciendum sit quæritur. Respondetur : Curiam vocare debet et in ea de milite illo conqueri, quam curiam ter vocare debet spatio eiusdem curiæ arbitrio terminando. Si nec ad tertiam vocationem venit, hoc ipso feudum amittat et ideo debet curia dominum mittere in possessionem. Sed si intra annum venerit, restituitur ei possessio, alioquin et

The ' Sachsenspiegel,' the most important German handbook of feudal law, which was written before 1232, does not describe in detail like the Assizes of Jerusalem the organisation of the feudal court and the method of securing its authority in enforcing the mutual obligations of lord and vassal, but it contains two very significant passages which are related to the position of the vassal and the control of the king.

In the first of these it says that a man may without violation of his fidelity wound or even slay his lord, or the lord the man, if this is done in self-defence.[1] In the second it lays down the principle that the man who feels himself injured by the "richtere" can appeal to the Schultheiss, and that also the Count Palatine is judge over the Emperor.[2]

The work entitled ' Le Conseil de Pierre de Fontaines ' belongs probably to about the year 1253, when its author was Bailli of the Vermandois. Its intention, according to the author, was to record the customs of the Vermandois, and other lay courts,[3] but it consists very largely of citations from the Code and Digest of Justinian, and it has been suggested that it is really a fragment of a French " Summa " of the Code.[4] The author assumes that a vassal has the right to implead his lord in the lord's court, that is, that the court has authority to judge between the lord and the vassal, but he limits the right to

beneficium et possessionem perdit. § 1. Si vero vasallus de domino quæritur, forsitan quia feudum malo ordine intravit, domino perperam respondente, quid vasallo sit faciendum quæritur. Respondetur : Curiam debet vocare et in ea conqueri. Curia debet adire dominum eumque salva reverentia competenter cogere ut vel possessionem restituat et adquiescat vel iudicio curiæ se comittat. Quod si admonitus facere distulerit, tum licet vasallo ad aliam maiorem potestatem ire et sibi consulere."

[1] 'Sachsenspiegel,' iii. 78. 6: "Wundet ok en man sinen herren, oder sleit he ine dot an notwere, oder die herre den man, he ne dut weder sine trüwe nicht, of die not up ine mit

rechte vulbracht wert." Cf. Glanvill, ix. 1.

[2] Id., iii. 52. 3. : " Wenne klaget man over den richtere, he sal antwerden ver deme sultheiten, wen die scultheite is richter siner scult ; als is die palenzgreve over den keiser, unde die burchgreve over den marcgreven."

Cf. iii. 54. 4 : " Also ne mach deme koninge neman an sin lif spreken, ime ne si dat rike vore mit ordelen verdelt." Cf. ' Schwabenspiegel,' 100 and 104.

[3] ' Le Conseil de Pierre de Fontaines,' i. 2.

[4] Cf. P. Viollet, ' Les Etablissements de Saint Louis,' vol. i. p. 83, note 2.

questions concerning the fief and injuries inflicted upon the vassal concerning this.[1]

In the compilation known as the 'Etablissements de St Louis,' we have a more complete treatment of the relations of lord and vassal, which with some important modifications represents the same principles as those of the Assizes of Jerusalem. In the first place, it is very clearly laid down that the obligations of lord and vassal are mutual and must be observed with equal care by both. The vassal who transgresses against this, and is guilty of various offences against his lord, will justly lose his fief ;[2] but then, with equal clearness, it is laid down that if the lord refuses his vassal the judgment of his court, or if he seduces his wife or daughter, then the vassal will be free from his obligation to him and will hold his fief from the overlord.[3]

Again we find in the Etablissements the same principle as that of the Assizes of Jerusalem, that in cases in the king's court on any matter concerning a vassal's inheritance, the

[1] 'Le Conseil de Pierre de Fontaine,' xxi. 27 : "Ceste meismes forme qui devant est racontée de la défaute as ajournez, entent-je que l'en doit regarder en la défaute al home qui ses sires pleidoie en sa cort meismes, et quant li homs pleidoie à son seignor en sa cort meismes. . . . 28. Mès ge ne croi pas que li homs puisse son seigneur, ne ne doie, apeler de défaute, fors que del mesfait qu'il li auroit fet puis l'omaige, en son propre fié qu'il tient de lui, ou en ses propres choses qui seroient del fié. . . . Mes del mesfet que li sires feroit à son home en son propre cors, ou en ses propres choses qui ne seroient mie del fié, ne qu'il ne tendroit mie de lui, n'en feroit-il jà son home riche, s'il ne voloit, ne droit en sa cort ne requerroit, s'il ne voloit ; car li home de sa cort n'ont mie pooir de jugement fère seur le cors lor seignor, ne de nul de ses torz fais se ce n'est del fié ou de mesfait que i apartient."

[2] 'Etablissements de St Louis,' i. 54 : "Hom qui fait esquousse à son seignor si pert ses meubles ; ou se il met main à son certain aloé (avoé) par mal respet, ou se il li escout autresi ; ou se il desmant son seignor par mal respit, ou se il a mise fause mesure en sa terre ; ou se il va defuiant son seignor par mal respit ; ou se il a peschié en ses estanz, au dessaü de lui ; ou se il a amblé ses conins en ses garennes ; ou se il gist o sa fame, ou o sa fille, par coi ele soit pucele, il em pert son fié, par quoi il en soit provez. Et dreiz et costume s'i accorde."

[3] Id., i. 56 : "Quant li sires vëe à son home le jugemant de sa cort, et il en puisse estre prové, il ne tendra jamais riens de lui, ainz tendra de celui qui sera par desus son seignor. Et einsi seroit il se il gisoit o la feme son home ou o sa fille, se ele estoit pucele ; ou se li hom avoit aucune de ses parentes et ele estoit pucele, et il l'aüst bailliée a garder à son seignor, et il la despucelast, il ne tenroit jamais rien de lui."

decision belongs not to the king personally, but to the court including the vassal's peers.[1] The Etablissements do not indeed contain the same elaborate machinery for the enforcement of the judgments of the court as do the Assizes, but the compiler did not scruple to maintain that in the last resort the vassal, if the King of France refuses to do him justice in his court, has the right to make war upon him, and is entitled to summon his sub-vassals to follow him. Before they obey the summons they must indeed first go to the king and ask whether it was true that he had refused their lord the judgment of the court; if the king denied this and said that he was willing to discharge his lawful obligations, they can refuse to follow their lord, but if his complaint proved to be true, they must then follow him to war, even against the king.[2]

If we now turn to the greatest of the French feudal lawyers, that is to Beaumanoir, we find that his conceptions of the relation of lord and vassal, while they differ in detail, are substantially the same as those which we have hitherto considered. In the first place, he sets out very clearly the principle that the

[1] Id., i. 76 : " Se li bers est apelez en la cort le roi d'aucune chose qui apartaigne à heritage, et il die : ' je ne vueil pas estre jugiez fors par mes pers de ceste chose,' adonc si doit l'en les barons semondre à tout le moines jusque à III., et puis doit la joutise feire droit o ces et o autres chevaliers." Cf. ' Jostice et Plet,' xvi. 1 : " Uns des peres de France s'otroia à jugier pardevant le roi, par ceus qui jugier le doivent, et dit que li rois, ne si consenz, ne le doivent pas jugier : mès il ne dit pas bien. Mès li rois, ne son conseil, sanz autres, ne le puet pas jugier c'est a dire que si pers doivent estre."

[2] Id., i. 53 : " Se li bers a son home lige et il li die : ' venez vous en o moi, car je vueil guerroier encontre le roi mon seignor, qui m'a veé le jugemant de sa cort,' li hom doit respondre en tel meniere à son seignor : ' sire, je irai volentiers savoir au roi s'il est einsinc come vous le me dites. Adonc il doit venir au roi et li doit dire.' ' Sire, mes sires m'a dit que vous li avez veé le jugement de votre court ; por ce en sui je venuz à vos por savoir en la vérité : car mes sires m'a semons que je aille en guerre encontre vous.' Et se li rois die : ' je ne ferai ja à vostre seignor nul jugemant en ma cort,' li hom s'en doit tantost retorner à son seignor ; et li sires le doit porveoir de ses despens. Et se il ne s'an voloit aler o lui, il en perdroit son fié par droit. Et se li rois li avoit respondu : ' je ferai droit volantiers à vostre seignor, en ma cort,' li hom devroit venir à son seignor et dire : ' sire, li rois m'a dit qu'il vous fera volentiers droit en sa cort,' et se li sires dit : ' je n'anterrai jamais en sa cort, mais venez-vous en o moi, si come je vous ai semons,' adonques porroit bien li hom dire : ' je n'i irai mie.' Il n'en perdroit ja par droit nule riens de son fié."

obligations of lord and vassal are mutual, as the vassal owes
faith and loyalty to his lord, so also the lord owes these to the
vassal, and the penalty for a violation of these obligations is the
same, in extreme cases the lord will forfeit the homage of his
vassal, just as the vassal will lose his fief.[1]

In the next place, Beaumanoir lays down as clearly as the
other feudal lawyers that these reciprocal obligations are pro-
tected by a suitable judicial machinery. In cases of dispute
between the whole body of the vassals and their lord, Beaumanoir holds that the court of vassals cannot be judge, as they
are all parties to the dispute, but they should demand justice of
the lord and his council, and if the lord refuses this they should
go to the king, as overlord. In the case, however, of a dispute
between a single vassal and the lord, the case is decided by the
court of the vassal's peers.[2] There is always a court which is
competent to decide upon disputes as to feudal duties and rights,

[1] Beaumanoir, lxi. 1735 : "Nous
disons, et voirs est selonc nostre coustume, que pour autant comme li hons
doit a son seigneur de foi et de loiauté
par la reson de son homage, tout autant
li sires en doit à son homme."

Id., lxii. 1786 : "Et avec la foi, il i
a grant peril d'avoir damage, car se
li sires est atains de la defaute, il pert
l'homage et chiet en grant amende, si
comme nous avons dit alieurs en cel
chapitre meismes, et se li hons ne
l'en puet ataindre, il pert le fief et
est aquis au seigneur."

Id., ii. 65 : "Et quant il faillent a
leur seigneur en tel besoing, il deservent à perdre leur fief."

[2] Id., i. 44 : "Il avient aucunes fois
que ples muet entre le conte et tous
ses hommes, si comme quant aucuns
des hommes requiert sa court d'aucun
cas dont il ne la doit pas ravoir,—ou il
dit qu'il a aucune justice en sa terre
par la reson de son fief, que li cuens
ne li connoist pas, ains dit qu'ele
apartient à li par reson de resort. . . .
En tous tes cas ne doit pas li
baillis metre le plet ou jugement des
homes car il meisme sont partie, si

ne doivent pas jugier en lor querele
meisme. Donques se teus ples muet
entre le conte et les hommes, et li
homme requierent droit, il doivent
prendre cel droit par le conte et par
son conseil. Et si li cuens leur refuse
à fere droit ou il lor fet mauvès
jugement, trere le puent par l'une
des II. voies par devant le Roi, comme
par devant souverain."

Id., i. 45 : "Des ples qui muevent
entre le conte d'une part et aucuns
de ses homes singulierement de l'autre
part, dont tuit li home ne se puent
pas fere partie,—si comme d'aucun
heritage ou d'aucune forfeture, ou
d'aucune querele, des queles il convient que jugemens soit fes selonc la
coustume du pais,—en tel cas puet
bien li baillis prendre droit pour le
conte par les hommes. Car aussi
comme il convient les hommes le
conte mener leur hommes par le
jugement de lor pers, aussi doit li
cuens mener ses homme par le jugement de ses autres hommes, qui
sont leur per, es quereles dout tuit
li homme ne font pas partie contre
lui, si comme il est dit dessus."

and this court is in the first place the court of the lord, but the judgment in the court belongs to the vassals. Until the vassal has demanded justice in the court he cannot appeal to the overlord, and Beaumanoir mentions a famous case of his time in which the men of Ghent had tried to bring a case against their lord, the Count of Flanders, before the King of France ; their suit was refused on the ground that they had not first taken the case to the court of the Count of Flanders.[1]

The important matter is that the feudal court is not one in which the judgment is dependent upon the caprice or self-interest of the lord, but one in which, as it administers the custom and law of the district or country, so also the decisions are given by all those who are concerned to maintain them. The true character of the court is well brought out when Beaumanoir says in another place that when a lord brings a case in his court against one of his vassals he can take no part in considering what should be the judgment of the court, it is the vassals who determine this ; if the lord is dissatisfied with the judgment he can appeal against it, and the appeal goes to the court of the overlord. Beaumanoir seems to maintain that in the Beauvosis the lord was in no case a judge in his own court, but only the vassals.[2] We have dealt with the discussion of the place of the lord in his court in the Assizes of Jerusalem,[3] it is very important to compare with this the opinion of a jurist of the caution and sagacity of Beaumanoir. Finally, it should be observed that Beaumanoir holds that in the last resort a vassal who feels himself wronged by his lord can renounce his homage

[1] Id., lxi. 1779.

[2] Id., lxvii. 1887 : " Quant li sires plede en sa court contre son homme meismes, il n'est pas juges ne ne doit estre au conseil, en sa cort, du juge-ment. Et quant li homme rendent le jugement, s'il le font contre li, apeler en puet comme de faus jugement, et doit estre li apeaus demenés en la court du seigneur de qui li sires tient les homages de ceus de qui il apela du jugement."

Id., lxvii. 1883 : " Nus par nostro

coustume ne puet fere jugement en sa court ne en sa querele, pour deus resons : la premiere resons, pour ce qu'uns seus hons, en sa persone, ne puet jugier ; aincois en convient ou II., ou III., ou IV., au meins, autres que le seigneur ; la seconde resons, pour ce que la coustume de Beau-voisins est tele, que li seigneur ne jugent pas en leur court, mais leur homme jugent."

[3] Cf. pp. 54, 55.

and his fief and challenge his lord, and in the same way the lord can renounce his right to homage and can then challenge his vassal.[1]

The great English jurist Bracton, as we have already seen, lays down the general principles of the relation of authority to justice, and to law as the embodiment of justice, in broader terms than any of the other lawyers whose work we have been considering. His work also illustrates very specially a movement of mediæval society which we have not yet had the opportunity to consider, that is, the gradual supersession of the feudal system of government by that of the national monarchy.

We have already noticed his statement of the reciprocal nature of feudal obligations.[2] Disputes about these are decided in the court of the lord, and if that does not do justice the case is to be taken to the county court, and finally, if the king consents, can be taken to the "great court." [3] We have here

[1] Beaumanoir, lxi. 1734 : "Encore par nostre coustume, nues ne puet apeler son seigneur, à qui il est hons de cors et de mains, devant qu'il li a delessié l'homage et ce qu'il tient de li. Donques, se aucuns veut apeler son seigneur d'aucun cas de crime, ou quel il chiee apel, il doit ains l'apel venir à son seigneur, en la presence de ses pers, et dire en ceste maniere. 'Sire, j'ai esté une piece en vostre foi et en vostre homage, et ai tenu de vous teus heritages en fief. Au fief, et à l'homage, et à la foi, je renonce, pour ce que vous m'avés mesfet, du quel mesfet j'entent à qerre venjance par apel.' Et puis cele renonciacion, semondre le doit fere en la court, de son souverains, et aler avant en son, apel ; et s'il apele avant qu'il ait renoncié au fief et à l'homage, il n'i a nul gage, ains amendera à son seigneur la vilanie qu'il li a dite en court, et a la court aussi, et sera chascune amende de lx. lb."

Id., lxi. 1735 : "Nous disons, et voirs est selonc nostre coustume, que

pour autant comme li hons doit à son seigneur de foi et de loiauté par la reson de son homage, tout autant li sires en doit à son homme, et par ceste reson pouons nous veoir que puis que li hons ne peut apeler son seigneur tant com il est en son homage, li sires ne puet apeler son homme devant qu'il ait renoncié à l'homage. Donques, se li sires veut apeler son home, il doit quitier l'homage en la presence du souverain devant qui il apele et puis puet aler avant en son apel."

Cf. Summa de legibus, lxxxiii. 1.

[2] See p. 27.

[3] Bracton, 'De legibus et consuetudinibus Angliae,' iii. 7. 1 (fol. 105) : "Nunc autem dicendum ubi terminandæ sunt actiones civiles, quæ sunt in rem vel in personam. Et sciendum quod earum quæ sunt in rem, sicut rei vendicationes per breve de recto, terminari debent in curia baronum vel aliorum, de quibus ipse petens clamaverit tenere, si plenum rectum ei tenere voluerit vel possit vel

the same principles as those which we have already considered, with the important modification that the case is to be taken from the court of the lord to the county court, not to a feudal court.

It is, however, in his treatment of the relation of the king to the law that Bracton is most interesting. We have already cited some of the most important passages in which he sets out what he considered the most essential principles of king-ship, and the relation of the king to justice and law. We must now consider some aspects of these in detail.[1]

There is no king, Bracton says, where there is no law,[2] and the phrase has an immense constitutional and philosophical breadth, and warns us how short-sighted is the judgment of those who imagine that the Middle Ages had no philosophical conception of the State. For here we have no mere isolated phrase, but the summary expression of a principle which is illustrated in the whole constitutional structure of mediæval society, and not least in its feudal aspect. Where there is no law there is no king, and the king is under God and the law, for it is the law which makes the king.[3] The phrase may possibly be influenced by a reminiscence of the words of Theodosius and Valentinian in the ' Code,' " our authority depends upon the authority of law,"[4] but the phrase is not the less remarkable, for Bracton, who is constantly influenced by the Roman jurisprudence, must have been aware that the Roman law books also contained the doctrine that the emperor was " legibus solutus,"[5] and he selects from the Roman tradition that which suits his purpose.

The king is under the law, and is to obey the law himself. The king is indeed the minister and vicar of God, but this is

---

sciverit. Si autem noluerit vel non possit vel nesciverit, tunc probato a tenente quod curia domini sui ei de recto defecerit, transferri poterit placitum ad comitatum, ut vicecomes rectum teneat, et sic a comitatu trans-ferri poterit ad magnam curiam, ex certa causa, si dominus rex voluerit, et ibi terminari."

[1] Cf. pp. 34, 38.

[2] Id., i. 8. 5 (fol 5b): " Non est

enim rex, ubi dominatur voluntas et non lex."

[3] Id., i. 8. 5 (fol. 5b): " Ipse autem rex non debet esse sub homine, sed sub deo et sub lege, quia lex facit regem. Attribuat igitur rex legi quod lex attribuit, ei, videlicet dominationem et potestatem."

[4] Code, i. 14. 4: " Adeo de auctori-tate iuris nostra pendet auctoritas."

[5] Cf. Digest, i. 3. 31.

only a further reason why he should obey the law, for being
God's minister his authority is only that of law (right), not of
wrong (*iniuriæ*), for this only is the authority which comes
from God, the authority of wrong (*iniuriæ*) is of the devil, and
the king is the servant of him whose works he does—the vicar
of God when he does justice, the minister of the devil when he
does wrong.[1] Just so far as the king is to be the vicar of God
he must follow the example of Jesus Christ and the blessed
Virgin, who submitted themselves to the law.[2] It is very
significant that Bracton—while maintaining in its highest form
the conception of the divine authority of the ruler, as we have
just seen, he calls him the vicar of God—should use this not
as an argument for an unlimited and uncontrolled authority,
but rather as an additional reason for maintaining that the
king is under the law, and must govern according to law.
Bracton does not hesitate to call the law " fraenum potentiæ,"
the bridle of power.[3]

And now lest we should imagine that this means little,
because the king is himself the source and author of law,
Bracton is careful to warn us against a perversion of the
doctrine of the Roman jurisprudence. He was familiar with
Ulpian's phrase that the will of the prince has the force of law

---

[1] Bracton, iii. 9. 3 (fol. 107) : " Nihil
enim aliud potest rex in terris, cum sit
Dei minister et vicarius, nisi id solum
quod de iure potest. . . . Potestas itaque
sua iuris est, et non iniuriæ, et cum
ipse sit auctor iuris, non debet inde
iniuriarum nasci occasio unde iura nascuntur, et etiam qui ex officio suo alios
prohibere necesse habet, id ipsum in
propria persona committere non debet.
Exercere igitur debet rex potestatem
iuris, sicut Dei vicarius et minister in
terra, quia illa potestas solius Dei est,
potestas autem iniuriæ diaboli et non
Dei, et cuius horum opera fecerit rex,
eius minister erit, cuius opera fecerit.
Igitur dum facit iustitiam, vicarius est
regis æterni, minister autem diaboli
dum declinet ad iniuriam."

[2] Id., i. 8. 5 (fol. 5b) : " Et quod sub
lege esse debeat, cum sit Dei vicarius,

evidenter apparet ad similitudinem
Jesu Christi cuius vices gerit in terris.
Quia verax Dei misericordia cum ad
reparandum humanum genus ineffabiliter ei multa suppeterent, hanc
potissimam elegerit viam, qua ad destruendum opus diaboli non virtute
uteretur potentiæ, sed iustitiæ ratione.
Et sic esse voluit sub lege, ut eos,
qui sub lege erant redimeret. Noluit
enim uti viribus sed iudicio. Sic
enim beata Dei genitrix, virgo Maria,
mater domini, quæ singulari privilegio supra legem fuit, pro ostendendo tamen humilitatis exemplo
legalibus subdi non refugit institutis.
Sic ergo rex, ne potestas sua maneat
infrenata."

[3] Id., iii. 9. 3 (fol. 107b) : " Temperet
igitur potentiam suam per legem quæ
fraenum est potentiæ."

and evidently felt that this might mislead men, and he therefore lays it down that not everything which it may be thought that the king wills has the force of law, but only that which is promulgated by the king's authority, with the counsel of his great men, and after due deliberation.[1] Again, in other passages which we have already quoted,[2] in which he sets out the great importance of unwritten and customary law in England, he says that it is reasonable to call the English laws, though unwritten, " laws," for that has the force of law which is set out and approved with the counsel and consent of the great men, and the general approval of the commonwealth, by the authority of the king.[3]

And again, when these laws have been approved by the custom of those concerned, and by the oath of the king, they cannot be abrogated or changed without the consent of all those by whose counsel and consent they were made.[4] The law is not something which the king makes or unmakes at his pleasure, but rather represents an authority which even the king cannot override.

The king is indeed the supreme administrator of law, and

[1] Id., iii. 9. 3 (fol. 107) : " Nihil enim aliud potest rex in terris, cum sit Dei minister et vicarius, nisi id solum quod de iure potest, nec obstat quod dicitur, quod principi placet, legis habet vigorem, quia sequitur in fine legis, ' cum lege regia quæ de imperio eius lata est,' id est non quicquid voluntate regis temere præsumptum est, sed animo condendi iura, sed quod magnatum suorum consilio, rege auctoritatem præstante, et habita super hoc deliberatione et tractatu, recte fuerit diffinitum."

Cf. Dig., i. 4. 1 (Inst. i. 2. 6).

[2] Cf. pp. 41, 42, 48.

[3] Id., i. 1. 2 (fol. 1) : " Cum autem fere in omnibus regionibus utatur legibus et iure scripto, sola Anglia usa est in suis finibus iure non scripto et consuetudine. In ea quidem ex non scripto ius venit, quod usus comprobavit. Sed non erit absurdum

leges Anglicanas, licet non scriptas, leges appellare, cum legis vigorem habeat quidquid de consilio et de consensu magnatum et reipublicæ communi sponsione, auctoritate regis sive principis præcedente, iuste fuerit diffinitum et approbatum."

Cf. Papinian in Digest, i. 3. 1.

[4] Id., i. 2. 6 (fol. 1b) : " Huiusmodi vero leges Anglicanæ et consuetudines, regum auctoritate iubent quandoque, quandoque vetant, et quandoque vindicant et puniunt transgressores. Quæ quidem, cum fuerint approbatæ consensu utentium, et sacramento regum confirmatæ, mutari non poterunt nec destrui sine communi consensu eorum omnium, quorum consilio et consensu fuerunt promulgatæ. In melius tamen converti possunt, etiam sine eorum consensu, quia non destruitur quod in melius commutatur."

Bracton uses strong phrases to describe the need of submission to his authority ; but here we come upon a somewhat difficult question of interpretation. We have, in the first place, several passages which seem to state very emphatically that the king has no superior, and that no one can judge his actions. In the first of these Bracton, after enumerating the various classes or orders of men in the State, says that all are under the king, and he is under no man, but only under God ; he has no equal in his kingdom, much less a superior ; the king must be under no man, but only under God and the law, for it is the law which makes him king.[1] In another passage it is said that no one can dispute the king's charters, nor his actions, not even the " justiciarii," nor can any one interpret them except himself,[2] and this corresponds with another passage in which it is said that a complaint against the king can only be made by way of supplication to him, for no writ runs against the king, and if he will not correct or amend what is complained of, he must be left to the judgment of God.[3]

So far we have apparently clear statements of the position of

[1] Id., i. 8. 5 (fol. 5b) : " Sunt etiam sub rege liberi homines et servi et eius potestate subiecti, et omnes quidem sub eo, et ipse sub nullo, nisi tantum sub deo. Parem autem non habet rex in regno suo, quia sic amitteret præceptum, cum par in parem non habeat imperium. Item nec multo fortius superiorem, nec potentiorem habere debet, quia sic esset inferior sibi subiectis, et inferiores pares esse non possunt potentioribus. Ipse autem rex non debet esse sub homine, sed sub deo et sub lege, quia lex facit regem."

Cf. id., iii. 9. 3 (fol. 107) : " Potentia vero omnes sibi subditos debet præcellere. Parem autem habere non debet, nec multo fortius superiorem, maxime in iustitia exhibenda, ut dicatur vere de eo, magnus dominus noster, et magna virtus eius, &c."

[2] Id., ii. 16. 3 (fol. 34) : " De cartis vero regiis et factis regum, non debent nec possunt iusticiarii, nec privatæ personæ disputare, nec etiam, si in illis dubitatio oriatur, possunt eam interpretari. Etiam in dubiis et obscuris, vel si aliqua dictio duos contineat intellectus, domini regis erit expectanda interpretatio et voluntas, cum eius sit interpretari, cuius est condere. Et etiam si omnino sit falsa propter rasuram, vel quia forte signum appositum est adulterinum, melius et tutius est, quod coram ipso rege procedat iudicium."

Cf. Cod., i. 14. 12. 3.

[3] Id., i. 8. 5 (fol. 5b) : " Non debet esse maior eo (*i.e.*, rege) in regni suo in exhibitione iuris, minimus autem esse debet, vel quasi, in iudicio suscipiendo, si petat. Si autem ab eo petatur, cum breve non currat contra ipsum, locus erit supplicationi, quod factum suum corrigat et emendet, quod quidem si non fecerit, satis sufficit ei ad poenam, quod deum expectet ultorem. Nemo quidem de factis suis praesumat disputare, nec multo fortius contra factum suum venire."

Bracton, but the matter is not as clear as it looks. The last passage cited begins with the words, " non debet esse maior eo in regno suo in exhibitione iuris, minimus autem esse debet, vel quasi, in iudicio suscipiendo, si petat," and the same principle is set out in a passage in a later Book, " licet in iustitia recipienda minimo de regno suo comparetur." [1] We have just cited the words which immediately precede this. (The king should have no equal, much less a superior, especially in administering justice, but in receiving justice he is like the humblest in his kingdom.)

In another passage Bracton, in discussing the question against whom the Assize of Novel Disseisin may be demanded, says that this cannot be claimed against the king or prince or other person who has no superior but God ; in such a case there is place only for supplication that he should amend his action, and if he will not do this he must be left to the judgment of God, who says " Vengeance is mine, and I will repay." But then, with a sudden turn of thought, Bracton adds that some may say that in such a case the " universitas regni " and the " baronagium " may and should correct and amend the king's action in the king's court (Curia).[2]

And this brings us to a passage which seems, at first sight at least, wholly inconsistent with the conception of the position of the king presented in those passages which we first cited. We have just considered the first part of this passage, in which it is laid down that no one may dispute the king's charters or

---

[1] Id., iii. 9. 3 (fol. 107). Cf. pp. 35, 36 (note 1).

[2] Id., iv. 10 : " Si autem princeps vel rex, vel alius qui superiorem non habuerit nisi dominum, contra ipsum non habebitur remedium per assisam, immo tantum locus erit supplicationi ut factum suum corrigat et emendet, quod si non fecerit, sufficiat ei pro poena quod dominum expectet ultorem, qui dicit : mihi vindictam, et ego retribuam, nisi sit qui dicat, quod universitas regni et baronagium suum hoc facere possit et debeat in curia ipsius regis."

Cf. Maitland, ' Bracton's Note-Book,' vol. i. p. 29.

I must express my great obligations to Dr Ludwik Ehrlich of Exeter College, Oxford, who very kindly allowed me to read some of his preliminary studies for the treatise on proceedings against the king in mediæval English law which he is preparing. He has drawn my attention to the passage just discussed, and I have found his studies most suggestive and illuminating. Dr Ehrlich's work is now published in vol. vi. of the ' Oxford Studies in Social and Legal History.'

acts, but it continues in a different strain. The king has a superior, that is God, and the law by which he is made king ; and also he has his court, namely counts and barons, for counts are so called as being the king's associates, and he who has an associate has a master ; if therefore the king should be without a bridle, that is without law, they should impose a bridle upon him.[1]

It is certainly difficult to reconcile this statement with those in other passages which we have already considered, in which it is said very emphatically that the king is under no man, that he has no equal or superior, except God and the law.[2] It seems most probable that the passage has been interpolated into the text of Bracton's work ;[3] but while it is difficult to think that Bracton would himself have used these terms, it is not clear whether he would have repudiated the substance of them. It is true that in the passages which we have just cited he says that if the king refuses to do justice, he must be left to the judgment of God,[4] but against this must be set the phrase

[1] Bracton, ii. 16. 3 (fol. 34) : "Item factum regis nec chartam potest quis judicare, ita quod factum domini regis irritetur. Sed dicere poterit quis, quod rex iustitiam fecerit, et bene, et si hoc, eadem ratione quod male, et ita imponere ei quod iniuriam emendet, ne incidat rex et iustitiarii n iudicium viventis Dei propter iniuriam. Rex autem habet superiorem, Deum scilicet. Item legem, per quam factus est rex. Item curiam suam, videlicet comites, et barones, quia comites dicuntur quasi socii regis, et qui habet socium, habet magistrum. Et ideo si rex fuerit sine fræno, i. sine lege, debent ei frænum apponere, nisi ipsimet fuerint cum rege sine fræno. Et tum clamabunt subditi et dicent, 'Domine Jesus, in chamo et fræno maxillas eorum constringe.' Ad quos Dominus, 'Vocabo super eos gentem robustam et longinquam et ignotam, cuius linguam ignorabunt, quae destruet eos, et evellet radices eorum de terra, et a talibus indicabuntur, quia

subditos noluerunt iuste indicare ' ; et in fine, ligatis eorum manibus et pedibus mittet eos in caminum ignis, et tenebras exteriores, ubi erit fletus et stridor dentium."

[2] Cf. esp. pp. 67 and 70.

[3] Cf. Maitland, 'Bracton's Note-Book,' vol. i. pp. 28-33, and vol. i. pp. 252 and 332 of the edition of the text of Bracton which is being brought out by George E. Woodbine, Assistant Professor of History at Yale. Professor Woodbine has come to the conclusion that while the passage is contained in one group of MSS., this evidence cannot be accepted against that of two other groups of MSS. which omit it. Cf., however, Dr Ehrlich's work just mentioned, pp. 202-205. I am glad to have the opportunity of expressing the great satisfaction which students of mediæval law will feel that Professor Woodbine has been able to make such substantial progress with his great enterprise.

[4] Cf. i. 8, 5 ; and iv. 10.

" minimus autem esse debet, vel quasi, in iudicio suscipiendo, si petat," [1] the more general but very emphatic statement that the king is under the law,[2] and the reference to the possibility that the " Universitas Regni " and the " Baronagium " may correct the king's unjust action.[3] It should also be observed that in a passage which also we have already cited, Bracton describes the king as the vicar of God if he does justice, but the minister of the devil if he turns to injustice, and he uses phrases, derived in part from St Isidore of Seville, that the title of king is derived from good ruling, not from mere reigning, for he is a king while he rules well, but a tyrant when he oppresses the people which is entrusted to him.[4] It is indeed impossible to say with absolute confidence what Bracton may have implied in using the designation " tyrant " of the unjust king, but it must be borne in mind that in the common usage of mediæval writers this is generally employed to describe a ruler who either never had, or had ceased to have, any claim on the obedience of his subjects.[5]

We are, however, not so much concerned with the question whether the words represent the opinion of Bracton, or of some other contemporary writer. There seems to be no reason to think that the words, although interpolated, belong to a later time. They are important to us on account of their correspondence with the principles of other feudal jurists. The principle which they represent is the principle of some of the most important of these. The Assizes of Jerusalem set out very clearly that the king is subject to the law, and that the court is the tribunal to which any one who feels himself aggrieved by the king or lord can appeal, that it is responsible for the maintenance of the law, if necessary even against the king, and they cite cases in which this principle had been carried out in action.[6] The ' Sachsenspiegel ' seems definitely to lay down the

---

[1] Cf. iii. 9, 3.

[2] Cf. p. 67.

[3] Cf. iv. 10.

[4] Id., iii. 9. 3 (fol. 107b): " Igitur dum facit iustitiam, vicarius est regis æterni, minister autem diaboli dum declinet ad iniuriam. Dicitur enim rex a bene regendo, et non a regnando, quia rex est dum bene regit, tyrannus dum populum sibi creditum violenta opprimit dominatione." Cf. St Idisore of Seville, Etym., ix. 3.

[5] Cf. Part II. of this volume, chap. v

[6] Cf. pp. 52-59

doctrine that even the king is answerable to one who can judge him.[1] The ' Etablissements of St Louis ' are clear that even in the case of the King of France the vassal can demand justice of him in his Court, and that if the king refuses to give this he can make war upon the king, and can require his sub-vassals to follow him.[2] And though Beaumanoir does not commit himself to any definite statement about the coercion of the king, he does emphatically set out the general principle of the supremacy of the court as determining the mutual obligation of lord and vassal.[3]

It is, we think, clear that the feudal system was in its essence a system of contractual relations, and that the contract was binding upon both parties, on the lord as much as on the vassal. Whatever else may be said about it, one thing is clear, and that is that feudalism represents the antithesis to the conception of an autocratic or absolute government.

[1] Cf. p. 61.
[2] Cf. pp. 62, 63.
[3] Cf. pp. 63-66.

CHAPTER V.

FEUDALISM AND THE NATION.

It may be urged that the tendency of feudalism was really anarchical and disintegrating, that it tended to arrest or retard the development of the conception of the national society or state, that the principle of the loyalty which the vassal owed to his immediate lord was really inconsistent with the conception of the authority of the whole community and its head. There is a great amount of truth in such a contention, and we must therefore consider the matter in some detail, but briefly.

In an earlier chapter attention has been drawn to the contrast, which finds expression in some of the epic poetry, between the personal loyalty and devotion which the vassal owes to his immediate lord and the indifference and even contempt for the overlord or king.[1] There is no doubt that we have here a forcible expression of an anti-national and disintegrating character in feudalism. The truth is that the feudal system, whatever may have been its remoter origins, took shape during those years when the dissolution of the Carolingian empire and the invasions of the Northmen and Magyars reduced Europe to an extreme confusion, and that its characteristics are related to the absence of such a well-organised government as might give the private man adequate protection. In the absence of strong central or national authorities, men had to turn for protection to the nearest power which seemed to be capable of rendering this. At the same time all those jurisdictions, which had once represented the delegated authority of the Carolingian emperors and kings, tended to become heredi-

[1] Cf. pp. 28, 29.

tary. When Europe began to recover from the anarchical confusions of the late ninth century and the early tenth century,
the new conditions were firmly established, and the great
national organisations which gradually formed themselves out of
the ruins of the Carolingian empire were at first rather groups
of semi-independent territories or states than compacted administrative unities. It would be outside of our province to
examine the varieties of these conditions as they present themselves to us in Germany or Italy, in France or England. We
must bear in mind that the conditions varied greatly in detail ;
it is enough for our purpose to recognise that in spite of these
variations the conditions were substantially similar.

It was the characteristic of feudal society that the local and
personal attachments were strong, while the relations to the
central authorities were comparatively weak and fluctuating.
This is the fact which lies behind the weakness of the overlord
or king and the power of the immediate lord. The great
feudatories no doubt owed allegiance to the king or emperor,
but the vassals of the great feudatories had at first probably no
very clearly defined relations to the overlord. We have now to
recognise that while this was true, and while in Germany the
process of national consolidation was overpowered by the territorial principle, in England and France, and ultimately in the
other European states, the national unity triumphed over these
disintegrating forces. The truth is that while feudalism was
based primarily upon the relations between a man and his
immediate lord, the principle of the national state was, though
undeveloped, older, and soon began to reassert itself, so that
at least as early as the eleventh and twelfth centuries the
principle of a direct relation between all free men and the
king began to be firmly established. Students of English
constitutional history will remember the significance of the
action of William the Conqueror in requiring all landowners
to take the oath of fidelity to himself, whosesoever men they
were.[1] We have now to observe that this principle is em-

---

[1] The important passages are cited
in Stubbs's 'Constitutional History of
England,' section 96.

Florence of Worcester : " Nec multo
post mandavit ut archiepiscopi, episcopi, abbates, comites, barones, et vice-

bodied in the feudal law books of the twelfth and thirteenth centuries.

Jean d'Ibelin makes it clear that in the kingdom of Jerusalem it was established as law after the war between Amauri I. and Girard of Seeste (Sidon) that the sub-vassals as well as the tenants-in-chief had to take the oath of allegiance (ligece) to the chief lord, the king, and that he could require the inhabitants of cities and castles held by his vassals to swear fealty to himself.[1] In another passage he lays it down that when any man does homage in the kingdom of Jerusalem to any one else than the chief lord he must not do " ligece," for no one can do " ligece " to more than one man, and all the vassals of the vassals are bound to do "ligece" to the chief lord of the kingdom.[2] In another place again he describes the mode in which the sub-vassal makes allegiance to the chief lord of the kingdom ; he is to kneel and, placing his hands between those of the chief lord, is to say, " Sire, I make you allegiance (ligece) according to the Assize for such and such a fief, which I hold of such and such a person, and promise to guard and protect

comites cum suis militibus, die Kalendarum Augustarum sibi occurrerent Saresberiæ ; quo cum venissent, milites eorum sibi fidelitatem contra omnes homines iurare coegit."

Anglo-Saxon Chronicle : " Thær him comon to his witan and ealle tha landsittende men the ahtes wæron ofer eall Engleland, wæron thaes mannes men the hi wæron, and ealle hi bugon to him and wæron his menn and him hold athas sworon thæt hi wolden ongean ealle othre men him holden beon."

[1] Jean d'Ibelin, 140 : " Et fu celle assise ensi faite et establie, que les homes des homes dou chief seignor dou reiaume feisent ligece au chief seignor dou reiaume, par l'assise, des fiés quils tenoient de ces homes, et que toz ciaus qui avoient fait homage au chief seignor, fust par l'assise ou autrement, fucent tenus les uns as autres, et

aussi les homes de ces homes de chascune court par sei ; et que si le rei voleit aveir la feauté des gens qui estoient manant ès cités, et és chastiaux, et és bors, que ces homes tenoient de lui, que il li juracent toz feauté, et que il li fucent tenus par cette feauté de ce que les homes de ces homes li sont tenus par la ligece faite par l'assise au chief seignor."

Cf. id., 199.

[2] Id., 195 : " Et qui fait homage de chose qui seit ou reiaume à autre que au chief seignor il le deit faire en la maniere dessus devisieé, mais que tant que il ne li deit pas faire ligece ; por ce que nul home ne peut faire plus d'une ligece, et que toz les homes des homes dou chief seignor dou reiaume li deivent faire ligece par l'assise ; et puisque l'on li deit la ligece, l'on ne la peut à autre faire sanz mesprendre vers lui."

you against any who may live or die, as I am bound to do by the allegiance (ligece) made according to the Assize." The chief lord kisses him and replies, " And I receive you in the faith of God and in my own, as I ought to do in accordance with the allegiance (ligece) made according to the Assize." When they have thus made allegiance the sub-vassals are bound to defend and support the chief lord against every one, and even against their immediate lord under certain conditions. If the chief lord has a dispute or war with any one of their lords, the sub-vassals are to remind their lord that they are the liegemen of the chief lord, and to request him to demand that the dispute should be submitted to the judgment of the court. If the chief lord refuses to do justice in his court, they will follow their lord, but if he refuses to take these steps within forty days, or if within that time he takes action against the chief lord, they will forsake him and support the chief lord.[1] Again, Jean d'Ibelin says that if any lord is doing wrong to the chief lord, without his knowledge, the sub-vassals

---

[1] Jean d'Ibelin, 197 : " Quant les homes des homes dou chief seignor dou reiaume font au chief seignor la ligece par l'assise, celui qui la fait deit estre a genoills devant lui et metre ces mains jointes entre les soes, et dire li : ' Sire, je voz fais la ligece par l'assise de tel fié que je tiens de tel,' et nomer celui de qui il tient le fié et dire quels est le fié ; ' et voz promet à garder et à sauver contre totes riens qui vivre et morir puissent, si come je faire le dei de ligece faite par l'assise.' Et le seignor li deit respondre : ' Et je ensi voz receis en Dieu fei et en la meie come je faire le dei de ligece faite par l'assise.' Et baisier le en la bouche en foi. Et quant la ligece est ainsi faite, les homes qui l'ont faite sont tenus ou seignor de garder le et de sauver contre totes riens qui vivre et morir puissent, mais que encontre leur seignor de cui il tienent le fié, por quei il ont faite la ligece par l'assise ; et en tele maniere que ce il avient que le chief seignor ait contens ou guerre à aucun des seignors de ces homes qui li ont fait la dite ligece, ciaus homes deivent venir à leur seignor et dire li : ' Sire voz savés que nous somes homes liges dou chief seignor dou reiaume devont voz ; por quei noz ne devonz estre contre lui, si en lui ne remaint : si voz prions et requerons que voz adressiés vers lui, et que voz li mandés que il voz maint par l'esgart de sa court. Et ce vos ce ne faites dedenz quarante jors, nos vos guerpirons et irons à lui aidier et conseillers contre voz, se en lui ne remaint. Et se voz faites ce que noz voz requeronz, et il voz faut de droit faire par sa court, nos ne voz guerpirons pas. Mais se voz dedenz ceaus quarante jors feissiées chose qui fust contre lui, noz ne le soufririens pas se nos le poriens amender ne destorber son mal ; et se noz ne le porieens destorber, nos voz guerpirieens lors et iriemes à lui et feriens vers lui ce que nos deveriens.' "

Cf. id., 198.

must remonstrate with their lord, and if necessary must join the chief lord against him.[1]　Again, the close relation between the chief lord and the sub-vassal is illustrated by the principle that the chief lord is bound to protect him against his immediate lord, if he acts unjustly and without the authority of his court, and to replace him in his fief if he has been unjustly deprived of it.[2]　These principles are stated in much the same terms also by Philip of Novara.[3]

It is clear therefore that even in a typical feudal constitution such as that of the kingdom of Jerusalem in the twelfth century, the principle of the supremacy of the central or national organisation over the relations between the vassal and his immediate lord was already fully recognised.　It is perhaps scarcely necessary to point out that this principle is clearly set out in Glanvill with regard to England in the twelfth century, but it is worth while to notice that he makes a distinction between the homage which a man may make to different lords for different fiefs, and the liege obligation (ligancia) which he can only make to that lord from whom he holds his " capitale tenementum."　The distinction is not the same as that in the Assizes of Jerusalem, but it is parallel to it.　Glanvill makes it clear that in doing homage to any lord, there must always be reserved the faith which he owes to the king, and that the sub-vassal must follow the king even against his lord.[4]

If we turn to France we find the principle of the reservation

[1] Id., 199.
[2] Id., 200.
[3] Philip of Novara, 51.
[4] Glanvill, ix. 1 : " Potest autem quis plura homagia diversis Dominis facere de Feodis diversis diversorum Dominorum : sed unum eorum opertet esse præcipuum, et cum ligancia factum : illi scilicet Domino faciendum, a quo tenet suum capitale tenementum is qui homagium facere debet. Fieri autem debet homagium sub hac forma, scilicet ut is qui homagium facere debet ita fiat homo Domini sui, quod fidem illi portet de illo tenemento unde homagium suum præstat, et quod eius in omnibus terrenum honorem servet, salva fide debita domino Regi et hæredibus suis.　Ex hoc liquet quod vasallus non potest Dominum suum infestare, salva fide homagii sui : nisi forte se defendendo, vel nisi ex præcepto principis cum eo iverit contra Dominum suum in exercitum."

Cf. 'Summa de legibus,' xiii. 1 : " Fidelitatem autum tenentur omnes residentes in provincia duci facere et servare . . . Omnes enim in Normannia tenentur fidelitatem principi observare.　Unde homagium vel fidelitatem alicuius nullus debet recipere, nisi salva principis fidelitate ; quod eciam est in eorum receptione specialiter exprimendum."

of fidelity to the king is clearly stated in the thirteenth
century by the author of the 'Jostice et Plet.' The king, he
says, must hold of no one : dukes, counts, &c., may hold of
each other, and become each other's men, but always, saving
the dignity of the king, against whom no homage is of any
authority. "Chastelain," "vavasor," citizens and villains are
under others, but all are under the king.[1] Again, Beaumanoir
sets out very distinctly the principle that the obligation of the
vassal to follow his lord in battle does not extend to the case
when the vassal is called upon to follow against the overlord
or the king.[2]

The only writer in whom we have found some suggestion of
ambiguity about the matter is one of the Lombard civilians of
the thirteenth century, who also wrote on feudal law, James of
Ardizone. He seems indeed to agree himself with the jurists
already cited that the sub-vassal is not bound to follow his
feudal superior against the overlord, and that he is rather to be
rewarded if he refuses to follow his lord against the "prince"
and the "patria," for every man is bound to defend the
"patria," and the "prince" is to be preferred to every other
creature ; but he mentions, apparently as a view which was
maintained by some, that a vassal is bound to help his lord
against another superior, and is not to be punished for this.
The phrase is indeed ambiguous, but it leaves upon one's mind
the impression that the "alter superior" is his lord's superior.[3]

---

[1] 'Jostice et Plet,' i. 16. 1 : "Li
rois ne doit tenir de nuil. Duc, conte,
visconte, baron puent tenir li un des
autres et devenir home, sauf la dignité
le roi, contre qui homage ne vaut
riens. Chastelain, vavasor, citaen,
vilain, sont souzmis à cels que nous
avons devant nomez. Et tuit sont
soz la main au roi."

[2] Beaumanoir, ii. 65 : " Cil qui sont
semont pour aidier leur seigneurs
contre leur anemis ou por aidier leur
seigneurs à leur mesons defendre, ne
doivent pas contremander ne querre
nul delai. Et s'il contremandent ne
ne quierent delai, il ne gardent pas

bien lor foi vers leur seigneurs. Et
quant il faillent a leur seigneur en tel
besoing, il deservent à perdre leur fief ;
ne il ne se pueent escuser par essoine,
puis qu'il soient ou pais et que la
guerre ne soit contre celi de qui leur
seigneur tienent leur hommage, ou
contre le conte qui est leur souverains,
ou contre le roi qui est par desseur
tous."

[3] Jacobus de Ardizone—' Summa
Feudorum,' 69 : " Item excusatur si
dominus vult quod eum adjuvet contra
dominum ipsius domini : nam si eum
offenderet, nisi ei satisfaceret, feudo
privaretur, ut in tit. de feu. &

It is easy to recognise that the question here raised was a difficult one, and that it would arise specially under Italian conditions ; but it is important to observe that even in Italy the principle of the reservation of fidelity to the overlord, or to the prince, was very definitely maintained. We must, however, allow for the great influence which the Roman jurisprudence would exercise upon the judgment of James of Ardizone.

There is indeed no doubt that in the judgment of the feudal jurists of the thirteenth century the king has a full jurisdiction over all persons within his kingdom.

The author of the 'Sachsenspiegel' lays down this doctrine with great clearness and emphasis. The king, he says, is the common (ordinary) judge over all men. Every man has his right (law) before the king, all authority is delegated by him. Whenever and wherever the king is himself present all other jurisdictions are superseded, and all prisoners must be brought before him, any person refusing to do this will be put under the ban, and any man who is aggrieved by a judgment can appeal to the king.[1] These phrases are very comprehensive in

benefic. l. imperialem, § illud, et in alienando feudum consensus maioris domini debet intervenire, ut in præ-dicta consti. primo respon. & § primo. Vel dicatur quod bene tenetur vasallus adiuvare dominum contra alterum superiorem, et non puniatur, quia in servitio domini sui facit, argumen. ff. de iniur. l. sed unius, § si justus—in fi. de qua materia notavi supra eadem summa, § item si vasallus vasalli, et § ubi vero plures. Item servus vasalli excusatur, si dominus feudi petat ut eum adiuvet contra dominum servi, in cuius est potestate ; cum servus sequendo dominum non puniatur, cum necessitate potestatis domini excusetur servus parendo domino (ut ff. ad legem Cornelian de fal. l. divus, § item senatus) licet dominus debeat damnari.

. . . .

Excusandus est vasallus et potius

præmio afficiendus, si non servierit domino contra principem vel patriam suam, ut in titulo de feudis et benefi. l. imperialem § ultimo, in titulo de sacra. et forma fide. l. illud. . . . Quilibet enim debet patriam suam defendere, (ut in Lombar. de his qui patriam defen. l. prima et ultima) et non potest pater iure patriæ potestatis resistere, quominus patriæ obsequatur, (ut ff. de muneribus et honoribus, l. honor. § plebei, in fine) et princeps omni creaturæ præferendus, ut in titulo, de maioritate et obedient. c. solite. Magna enim servitia ab universis subditis debentur imperio, ut C. de operibus publicis l. quicumque locus."

[1] 'Sachsenspiegel,' iii. 26. 1 : " Die koning is gemene richtere over al."

Id., iii. 33. 1 : " Iewelk man hevet sin recht vor'me koninge."

Id., iii. 52. 2 : " Den koning küset

their nature, and, while this is not the place to discuss their actual constitutional significance in the administration and judicial organisation of the empire, they are yet of great importance as indicating how far at least in theory the national conception had imposed itself upon the feudal.)

The same principle is set out in the 'Summa de legibus,' one of the Norman law books of the thirteenth century. The prince alone has " plena iurisdictio " over all disputes brought to him,[1] and again in another place, the jurisdiction of the feudal lord is severely limited to certain cases, for all " iusticiatio personarum " belongs in Normandy to the Duke, in virtue of the fealty which all men owe to him; and again, jurisdiction over the bodies of all men, small or great, belongs in Normandy to the Duke, inasmuch as they are bound by fidelity and allegiance to him alone.[2]

man to richtere over egen unde len unde over iewelkes mannes lif. Die keiser ne mach aver in allen landen nicht sin, unde al ungerichte nicht richten to aller tiet, dar umme liet he den vorsten grafscap, unde den greven scultheitdum."

Id., iii. 60. 2 : " In svelke stat des rikes de koning kumt binnen deme rike, dar is ime ledich monte unde toln, unde in svelke lant he kumt, dar is ime ledich dat gerichte, dat he wol richten mut alle die klage, die vor gerichte nicht begunt, noch nicht gelent ne sin. 3. Svenne die koning oc alrest in dat land kumt, so solen ime ledich sin alle vangene uppe recht, unde man sal sie vor ime bringen unde mit rechte verwinnen oder mit rechte laten, so man sie erst besenden mach, seder der tiet dat sie de koning eschet to rechte oder sine boden, to dem manne selven oder to 'me hove oder to 'me huse, dar sie gevangen sin oder hebbet gewesen. Weigeret man sie vore to bringene, sint man sie to rechte geeschet hevet, unde man des getüch an des koninges boden hevet, man dut to hant in de achte alle die sie vengen, unde hus unde lüde, die sie weder recht halden."

Id., ii. 12. 4 : " Schilt man en ordel, des sal man tien an den hogesten richtere, unde to lest vor den koning ; dar sal die richtere sine boden to geven, die dar horen welk ire vulkome vor deme koninge."

Id., i. 58. 1 : " Svenne die greve kumt to des gogrefen dinge, so sal des gogreven gerichte neder sin geleget. Also is des greven, svenne die koning in sime grafscap kumt, dar se beide to antwerde sin. Also is jewelkes richteres, dar die koning to antwerde is, die klage ne ga denne uppe den koning."

[1] ' Summa de legibus,' ii. 4 : " Solus autem princeps plenam habet iurisdictionem de querelis ad ipsum delatis omnibus laicalem."

[2] Id., vi. 8 : " Preter hoc tamen sciendum est quod pro debito principis, elapso termino solutioni deputato, solet in debitores iusticiatio fieri corporis, licet pro nullo alio debito debeat corpus hominis iusticiari ; omnis enim iusticiatio in Normannia ad ducem pertinet personarum propter fidelitatem quam ei debent singuli observare. Ex quo eciam usitatum est in Normannia quod nullus potest ab aliquo homagium recipere nisi salva fidelitate ducis Nor-

The author of the 'Jostice et Plet,' and Beaumanoir, maintain the same doctrine in France. The author of 'Jostice et Plet' is indeed so much influenced by the Roman law that it may be held that he is to be considered rather as a civilian than a feudalist, but his treatment of the subject corresponds in principle with that of the feudal jurists. His phrases are noteworthy. The king has jurisdiction everywhere and always, he has plenary authority in everything, while others have it only in part.[1] Again, the count or duke has " jostice " in his lands, but under the king who is over him, the king must not indeed deprive him of this, so long as he does right, but the king can interfere to secure justice. The king holds of no one ; dukes, counts, viscounts, and barons can hold of each other, and become each other's men, but always, saving the dignity of the king, against whom homage is of no avail, for all are under the hand of the king.[2]

mannie, quod eciam est in receptione homagii exprimendum.

Unde nec aliquis in Normannia hominis sui corpus potest vel debet prisonie mancipare, nisi coram eo de latrocinio fuerit insecutus vel in presenti deprehensus, vel eius serviens fuerit, ut prepositus, molendinarius vel quoquo modo rerum suarum receptor, quos arrestare potest quousque compotum debitum et plegios sufficientes habuerit de eisdem.

9. Ad bosci forisfactum garanne vel aquarum defensarum, vel costume detente, vel bladorum, seu pratorum vel aliorum huiusmodi, possunt homines a dominis feodorum arrestari . . . dum tamen ad presens forisfactum fuerint deprehensi, et tantum detineri quousque namna, vel vadia, vel plegios habuerint de damno illato restaurando et emenda, ubi debeat extorqueri. Si autem aliquo casu alio pro facto criminoso aliquis capiatur, justiciario debet reddi indilate.

10. Si autem dominus homini suo fecerit iniuriam feodi ratione, ad ducem pertinet curia de eodem, nisi dominus, si quis fuerit interpositus, eam re-quisierit, qui iurisdictionem habeat feodalem."

Id., cxiii. 1 : " Cum in Normannia omnium iurisdictio corporum ad ducem tam plebis pertineat quam magnatum, eo quod fidelitate et ligancia soli principi teneantur."

[1] 'Jostice et Plet,' i. 7. 6 : " L'en demande porquoi li rois use par tot et en toz tens de juridiction, cum aucun soit en son règne juridiction qui soie est ? et l'en respont que en roi confermée est le poir de tote la région, s'il ne le done ; et il a plenier poer en tot, c'est à entendre poer de prodome ; et li autre si n'ont que partie de poer, quar il ne sont apelé qu'en partie de la cure, non pas en plenier poer.

Enten que rois confermé est aussi comme se chascuns metoit sa bone volenté en la soie. Enten ci reison, par que rois use en chascuns leu de juridicion."

[2] Id., 13. 1 : " Contes a en ses terres en la conté sa jostice, sau le roi qui est par dessus ; ne li rois ne li doit pas sorbir sa jostice, tant comme il fait droit. Li rois peut ce amender."

Id., 14. 1. " Dus a en sa terre totes

Beaumanoir asserts very emphatically that the king is supreme over all jurisdictions and over all persons. In one passage of great importance which we have already discussed he explains the sense in which he uses the word " souverain," and says that while every baron is " souverain " in his own barony, the king is " souverain " over all, and has the charge of the whole kingdom, and therefore can make " establissements " which are binding everywhere. No one is so great that he cannot be called before the king's court, " pour defaute de droit ou pour faus jugement." [1]

The whole conception is summed up by Bracton in an emphatic passage in which he lays down the principle that the king has the " ordinary " jurisdiction and authority over all men who are in the kingdom, for all laws which belong to the crown and the lay authority and the temporal sword are in his hand ; it is he who holds justice and judgment, that is jurisdiction, so that it is by his jurisdiction, as being the minister and

seignories et totes joutices, sauf le roi, qui est li par desus, à amender le torfet qu'il a fet, et sauf ce que li rois a en la duchée, et autres par jutes causes."

Id., i. 16. 1 : " Li rois ne doit tenir de nuil. Duc, conte, vicomte, baron, puent tenir li un des autres et devenir home, sauf la dignité le roi, contre qui homage ne vaut riens. . . . Et tuit sont soz la main au roi."

[1] Beaumanoir, xxxiv. 1013 : " Pour ce que nous parlons en cest livre, en pluseurs lieus, du souverain, et de ce qu'il puet et doit fere, li aucun pourroient entendre, pour ce que nous ne nommons conte ne duc, que ce fust du roi ; mais en tous les lieus la ou li rois n'est pas nommés, nous entendons de ceus qui tienent en baronnie, car çhascuns barons est souverain en sa baronie. Voirs est que le rois est souverains par dessus tous, et a, de son droit la general garde de tout son roiaume, par quoi il puet fere teus etablissemens comme il li plest pour le commun pourfit, et ce qu'il establist

doit estre tenu. Et se n'i a nul si grant dessous li qui ne puist estre tres en sa court pour defaute de droit ou pour faus jugement et pour tous les cas qui touchuent le roi. Et pour ce qu'il est souverain par desseus tous, nous le nommons, quant nous parlons d'aucune souveraineté qui a li apartient."

Cf. xlviii. 1499 : " Mes quant li Rois fet aucun establissement especiaument en son demaine, si baron ne lessent pas pour ce a user en leur terres, selonc les anciennes coustumes. Mes quant li establissemens est generaus, il doit courre par tout le roiaume, et nous devons croire que tel establissement sont fet par tres grant conseil et pour le commun pourfit."

Cf. also xi. 322 : " Qar toute la laie juridicion du roiaume est tenue du roi en fief ou en arriere fief. Et pour ce puet on venir en sa court, par voie de defaute de droit ou de faus jugement quant cil qui de lui tienent n'en font ce qu'il doivent."

vicar of God, that he gives to every man that which is to be his.[1]

When we now endeavour to sum up the conclusions which arise from the study of the political theory of the feudal law books, it is evident that they represent very different principles from those which have been sometimes thought of as related to feudalism. The conception of personal devotion and loyalty, of an almost unquestioning obedience and fidelity of the vassal towards his lord, was no doubt of great importance, and the conception has left deeply marked traces in the structure and the sentiments of European political society. But it is also clear that the principle of loyalty did not, in the minds of the feudal lawyers, or, as we shall see further in the second part of the volume, in the judgment of mediæval society in general, override other considerations of an ideal and rational kind. The feudal jurists recognised very clearly that all human relations, and not least the relations of lord and vassal, must be controlled by the principles of equity and justice, and that these principles found their embodiment in the law—the law which is the superior of kings and princes, which is the expression not of their will merely, but of justice, and of the custom and consent of the community. It is clear that the feudal jurists conceived of the relations of vassal and lord as being limited and determined by the law, that lord and vassal were equally obliged to obey and to maintain the law, which prescribed the nature and extent of their mutual obligations. The relation of lord and vassal was a contractual relation, the terms of the contract were prescribed

---

[1] Bracton, ii. 24 1 (fol. 55b) : "Nunc autem dicendum erit de libertatibus, quis concedere possit libertatem, et quibus, et qualiter transferuntur, et qualiter possidentur vel quasi, et qualiter per usum retinentur. Quis ? Et sciendum, quod ipse dominus rex, qui ordinariam habet iurisdictionem et dignitatem et potestatem super omnes qui in regno suo sunt. Habet enim omnia iura in manu sua, quæ ad coronam et laicalem pertinent potestatem et materialem gladium, qui pertinet ad regni gubernaculum. Habet etiam iustitiam et iudicium, quæ sunt iurisdictionis, ut ex iurisdictione sua, sicut Dei minister et vicarius, tribuat unicuique quod suum fuerit "

by law, and the obligation of the contract was determined by law.

Again, we have seen that while feudalism, in its great development in the tenth century, was the result of the operation of forces which were anarchical, or which at least tended to disintegrate the larger political organisations of Western Europe, these tendencies were rapidly checked by the growth of the principle that the feudal jurisdictions were subject to the control of the rising national systems, and that beyond the obligations of the vassal to his immediate lord every individual free man owed allegiance to the national sovereign. We have considered the history of this movement as it is reflected in the feudal law books themselves, and have seen that at least as early as the twelfth and thirteenth centuries it was recognised that the royal or national authority was paramount over all other authorities.

It is no doubt true that feudalism left for many centuries deep traces in the structure of Western society, and even on the theory of political relations, but it is also true that, when we consider the subject in the broadest way, feudalism did not counteract the normal development of the political ideas of Western civilisation, but rather that in the end its main influence went to further the growth of the principle that the community is governed by law, and that the ruler as much as the subject is bound to obey the law.

PART II.

GENERAL POLITICAL THEORY IN
THE ELEVENTH AND TWELFTH CENTURIES.

CHAPTER I.

NATURAL LAW AND EQUALITY.

WE now turn to the history of the general development of political ideas from the beginning of the tenth century to the end of the twelfth, that is, we can resume the history of these conceptions at the point where we left them in our first volume. We shall in doing this have occasion from time to time to take account of the influence of the three systems of law which we have considered, the feudal, the civil, and the canon law, but our main task is to trace this development in the general literature of those times, and in the principles expressed or implicit in the constitutional development of Europe. For the time being we shall not discuss directly the questions concerned with the relations of the temporal and spiritual powers. These became during this period so important that we propose to devote a separate volume to them.

In considering the theories of the civilians and canonists we have seen how important was the conception of natural law in the Middle Ages, but we must not look for any detailed discussion of this in the literature which we have now to examine, for these writers were for the most part engaged in considering the principles of political society as they emerged in the actual controversies and conflicts of this time.   On the other hand, there is enough to show us that so far as they reflected upon the matter they all thought under the terms of the contrast between the natural and conventional condition.

This is specially clear in regard to the conception of human nature and its "natural" characteristics.   We are apt to think of mediæval society as governed by the idea of distinctions of blood and birth, and these conceptions were not wholly unimportant.   It is, however, clear that, so far as men reflected upon the matter, they accepted the tradition of the later philosophical system of the ancient world, and of Christianity as handed down by the Christian Fathers and by the civil law, that there are no "natural" distinctions in human nature, and that all differences of rank and condition are conventional or "positive."

We have dealt with the subject as it is illustrated in the writings of the civilians and canonists in the second volume,[1] and we only therefore add one citation from an ecclesiastical writer.   It is, however, specially significant to observe how emphatically the conception of the natural freedom of men is stated by some of the feudal lawyers.

In the tenth century, in a work of that strange and eccentric prelate, Ratherius, Bishop of Verona, we find a passage in which he urges upon Christian men that they should remember that God made all men equal in nature, and that it is quite possible that the subject may be a better man than his lord.   The man who boasts of his noble blood should remember that we are all of one origin and are made of the same substance.   In Christ we are all one, redeemed with the same price, reborn in the same baptism, and those who rend asunder the unity of the brotherhood by setting themselves over others are really denying the common fatherhood and redemption of men.   In the sight of God we are only distinguished from each other so far as our actions are better ; the man who humbly serves is better than the man who arrogantly despises his fellow-men, he is nobler who observes the law of nature and does not repudiate his true origin, than he who violates that

[1] Cf. vol. ii. Part I. chap. 4 ; Part II. chap. 5.

friendship between men which is so great and natural a good.[1]

(The passage is no doubt based mainly upon recollections of earlier writers, of the Fathers, and, probably through them, of Stoic writers like Seneca,[2] but it is representative of the normal judgment of mediæval thinkers)

We may take as our first illustration from the feudal lawyers a very notable passage in the ' Sachsenspiegel.' God, says the author, made all men in His own likeness, and redeemed man by His passion, the poor as well as the rich ; there were no slaves when the forefathers of the Germans first settled in the land ; slavery, or serfdom, began by violence and capture and unrighteous force ; the law of Moses required all slaves to be set free in the seventh year ; and the author holds that it is not in accordance with the truth or the will of God that one man should belong to another.[3])

[1] Ratherius of Verona—' Præloquiorum,' i. 10 : " Attende Deum in principio creationis humanæ dixisse : ' Crescite et multiplicamini,' . . . ut intelligas homines non hominibus, sed volatilibus, bestiis et piscibus esse prælatos, omnesque a Deo natura æquales conditos, sed inæqualitate morum faciente, aliis alios intantum suppositos, ut plerumque aliqui dominentur etiam melioribus. . . . Nota vero tu, quisquis es, qui de fastu alti gloriaris abusive sanguinis ; cum omne hominum genus in terris simili surgat ab ortu, et non ex alia, sed ex eadem massa compositus, ex uno patre, ex eademque, qua servorum quilibet, sis matre creatus. Quia si omnes in Christo quoque unum sumus, uno scilicet pretio redempti, eodemque baptismo renati : quisquis eamdem fraternitatis unitatem cæteris se proponendo scindere nititur, paternitatem sine dubio illius, redemptionem et regenerationem quoque, qua eius filii efficimur, quantum in se est, annullare, et, ut ita dicam, abnegare probatur. Verum si solummodo in hac a Deo parte discernimus, si meliores

aliis in operibus bonis, et humiles inveniamur : convincitur melior esse qui tibi servit humiliter, quam tu, qui eum despicis arroganter ; nobilior, qui tibi, quod promisit, exhibit fideliter, quam tu, qui eum decipis mendaciter ; generosior, qui iura naturæ custodiens, proprium non deserit ortum, quam tu, qui vitiis vitia nutriens vim amicitiæ magnumque et naturale violas bonum."

[2] Cf. vol. i. pp. 20-22, and chap. 10.

[3] ' Sachsenspiegel,' iii. 42. 1 : " Got hevet den man na ime selven gebeldet, unde hevet ine mit sinen martere geledeget, den enen also den anderen, ime is die arme also besvas als die rike. . . .

. . . .

3. Do man ok recht irst satte, do ne was nen dienstman, unde waren al die lude vri, do unse vorderen her to lande quamen. An minen sinnen ne kan ik is nicht upgenemen na der warheit, dat jeman des anderen sole sin ; ok ne hebbe wies nen orkünde. . . .

. . . .

4. . . . Den seveden manet gebot

We may put beside these phrases a passage from Beaumanoir
in which he sets out the same principles, but in different
terms. All men, he says, were at the beginning free, and of
the same freedom, for all men are descended from one father
and mother ; slavery (or serfdom) arose in many ways, such as
that men were taken prisoners in war, or sold themselves into
slavery on account of their poverty, or because they could not
defend themselves against the unjust violence of lords; however
men may have become slaves it is a great act of charity that a
lord should set his slaves (or serfs) free, for it is a great evil that
Christian men should be in the servile condition.[1]

he ok to haldene, unde dat sevede
jar, dat het dat jar der losunge ; so
solde man ledich laten unde vri alle
die gevangen waren unde in egenscap
getogen, mit alsogedaneme gerede als
man sie vieng, of sie ledich unde
vri wolden wesen. Over sevenwerf
seven jar quam dat veftegiste jar, dat
het dat jar der vrouden, so muste
aller manlik ledich unde vri wesen,
he wolde oder newolde.

5. Ok gaf uns got orkündes mer
an enem penninge, dar man ime mede
besochte, do he sprak : latet den
keiser sines beldes geweldich, unde
godes belde gevet gode. Dar bi uns
kundich von godes worden, dat die
mensche, godes belde, godes wesen
sal, unde sve ine anders iemanne to
seget danne gode, dat he weder got
dut.

6. Na rechter warheit so hevet
egenscap begin von gedvange, unde
von vengnisse, unde von unrechter
walt, die man von aldere in unrechte
warheit getogen hevet, unde nu vore
recht hebben wel."

Cf. ' Schwabenspiegel,' 57. 2 : " Wir
han daz von der schrift, daz nieman
sol eigen sin. Doch ist ez also dar
komen mit gewalt unde mit twancsal,
daz es nu reht ist daz eigen liute sin."
Cf. id. 206.

[1] Beaumanoir, xlv. 1453 : " Com-

ment que pluseur estat de gent soient
maintenant, voirs est qu'au commencement tuit furent franc et d'une
meisme franchise ; car chascuns set
que nous descendismes tuit d'un pere
et d'une mere. . . . Et li serf si
sont venu par mout de manieres
d'aquisicions. Car li aucun sont venu
par estre pris de guerre, si donnoient
servitude seur aus et seur lor oirs,
par raençon, ou por issir de prison ;
et li autre sont venu parce qu'il se
vendoient par povreté, ou par con-
voitise d'avoir . . . et li autre sont
venu parce qu'il n'ont eu pouoir d'aus
defendre des seigneurs, qui a tort et
par force les ont atrès a servitude
Et par quelconques manieres qu'il
soient venu, nous pouons entendre
que grant aumosne fet li sires qui
les oste de servitude et les met en
franchise, car c'est grans maus quant
nues crestiens est de serve condition."

Cf. id., xlv. 1438 : " Par toutes tes
choses sont servitudes venues avant,
car selonc le droit naturel chascuns
est frans, mes cele naturele franchise
est corrompue par les acquisicions
dessus dites."

Cf. also Bracton, i. 8. 1 (fol. 5b) :
" Liberorum autem hominum quorum-
cumque nulla est acceptio apud Deum,
nec etiam servorum, quia non est personarum acceptor Deus, quia quantum

It is clear that even the feudal lawyers were profoundly affected by the earlier traditions, and that to them just as much as to the Christian fathers the subjection of man to man as slave or villein was a thing conventional, not natural.

ad Deum, qui maior est fit tamquam minor, et qui præcessor fiat tamquam ministrator. Apud homines vero est differentia personarum, quia hominum quidam sunt præcellentes et prelati, et aliis principantur."

CHAPTER II.

THE DIVINE ORIGIN AND NATURE OF
POLITICAL AUTHORITY.

IN the first volume of this work we have examined the characteristic elements of the theory of the origin and nature of political authority as it is set out in the literature of the ninth century, and we think that enough has been said to make it clear that as soon as we find any literary treatment of political conditions and ideas, we find that there were very clearly fixed in the minds of the men of the new mediæval civilisation some highly important conceptions of political origins and obligations. We have in the last volume endeavoured to examine the relation of the revived Roman law, and of the new system of Ecclesiastical law, to these conceptions, and in the first part of this volume we have considered the bearing upon them of Feudalism. We must now inquire how far these conceptions can be said to have been continuously present to men's minds in the centuries from the tenth to the twelfth, and how far they were modified or developed.

We are entering upon the study of an age in which the structure of society was very rapidly growing and changing, and we have to inquire how far and in what manner men's conceptions of the principles of the political order changed with it. If our interpretation of the political theory of the ninth century is at all correct, the main features of that theory are to be found in three principles—first, that all authority, whether Temporal or Spiritual, is ultimately derived from God ; second, that the supreme authority in political society is that of the law, the law which represents the principle of justice   and third, that the immediate source of all political authority is the community, for law is primarily the custom of the community, and there can be no legitimate authority without the election or recognition of the community. We have to inquire how far these principles continued to control the conception of political society, and in what manner they were modified or developed.

During the tenth century and the earlier part of the eleventh we should infer, from the fragments of the literature which have survived, that there was not very much active political speculation ; we can indeed gather from occasional phrases the general nature of the conceptions which were current, but it may be doubted whether men did generally do much more than repeat the commonplaces of the ninth century tradition. These commonplaces were not, however, unimportant, and in some respects they seem to represent real and intimate convictions.

It was the great constitutional and ecclesiastical conflicts of the latter part of the eleventh century, continued in the twelfth, which compelled men to consider these traditional presuppositions more closely, and from the middle of the eleventh century we have an abundant and important body of literature in which we can discern with great clearness the main features of an energetic and determined political speculation.

We must begin by considering the question how far in the period with which we are now dealing it was doubted or denied that the secular authority was derived from God, and this will lead us on to the closely related question whether the State was or was not conceived of as having a moral function and purpose.

As we have seen, the principles of the divine source of political authority, and of the moral function of government, were most emphatically laid down by the Fathers,[1] and maintained by the writers of the ninth century.[2] It has been suggested that these conceptions were really undermined by the influence of St Augustine, especially as expressed in the ' De Civitate Dei,' and that the effects of St Augustine's mode

---

[1] Cf. vol. i. chaps. 11, 13, 14.   [2] Cf. vol. i. chaps. 17, 18.

of thought are clearly traceable in the Middle Ages. We cannot here discuss the real and complete meaning of St Augustine, the subject has been handled with great care and restraint by Reuter.[1] The question with which we have to deal is whether there was among the political theorists of the eleventh or twelfth centuries any important tendency to think of the secular power as lacking the divine authority, and as representing a principle of evil rather than of good.

The discussion centres round some phrases of Pope Gregory VII. (Hildebrand), their meaning and their influence. Some writers have attached a very great importance to these, and have considered them to be representative of a clear and dogmatic theory, which as they have thought was of great importance in the Middle Ages. And no doubt Hildebrand's phrases are emphatic and startling. The best known of them is to be found in his famous letter to Hermann, the Bishop of Metz (1081) : "Quis nesciat : reges et duces ab iis habuisse principium, qui, Deum ignorantes, superbia, rapinis, perfidia, homicidiis, postremo universis pene sceleribus, mundi principe diabolo videlicet agitante, super pares, scilicet homines, dominari cæca cupidine et intolerabili præsumptione affectaverunt."[2] Beside these words we may put those of an earlier letter written to the same Bishop (1076) : "Sed forte putant, quod regia dignitas episcopalem præcellat. Ex earum principiis colligere possunt, quantum a se utraque differunt. Illam quidem superbia humana repperit, hanc divina pietas instituit. Illa vanam gloriam incessanter captat, hæc ad cœlestem vitam semper aspirat."[3] These are indeed strong phrases, and might well, to the unwary, seem to imply a definite doctrine of the secular power, as representing not the authority of God, but of evil.

In order, however, to arrive at the meaning of Hildebrand's phrases, we must begin by observing that in other places he speaks of the secular power in very different terms. In a letter written to Rudolph, Duke of Suabia, in 1073, he speaks of his hope that the "sacerdotium" and the "imperium" may

---

[1] H. Reuter, 'Augustinische Studien.'   [3] Id. id., iv. 2.
[2] Gregory VII., Registrum, viii. 21.

be united in concord, that, as the human body is ruled by its two eyes, so the body of the Church may be ruled and enlightened when the two authorities agree in the true religion.[1] In a letter of 1074 to Henry IV., he bids him to know that he rightly holds the royal power, if he obeys Christ the King of Kings and defends and restores the Church.[2] In a letter to Sweyn, King of Denmark, in 1075, he prays him to administer the authority entrusted to him, according to God, to adorn the dignity of the royal title with the appropriate virtues, and to make it manifest that that justice, in virtue of which he reigned over his subjects, also ruled in his heart.[3] Again, in writing to Harold, King of Denmark, in 1077, he admonishes him to keep the honour of the kingdom committed to him by God with all diligence, and to make his life worthy of it, in wisdom, justice, and mercy, that God may be able to say of him, " By me this King reigneth." [4]   And again, in writing to Olaf, King of Norway, in 1078, he describes the true function of his royal authority as being to help the oppressed, to defend the widow, and to love and defend justice with all his might.[5]

Perhaps the most notable passage is contained in a letter

[1] Id. id., i. 19 : " Quæ (litteræ) nimirum inter cetera dulcedinis suæ verba illud nobis videbantur consulere, per quod et status imperii gloriosius regitur et sanctæ ecclesiæ vigor solidatur : videlicet ut sacerdotium et imperium in unitate concordiæ conjungantur. Nam sicut duobus oculis humanum corpus temporali lumine regitur, ita his duobus dignitatibus in pura religione concordantibus corpus ecclesiæ spirituali lumine regi et illuminari probatur."

[2] Id. id., ii. 30 : " Et tunc demum regiam potestatem recte te obtinere cognoscas, si regi regum Christo ad restaurationem defensionemque ecclesiarum suarum faciendam dominationis tuæ altitudinem inclinas et verba ipsius dicentis cum tremore recogitas ; ' Ego diligentes me diligo, et honorificantes me honorifico ; qui autem me contemnunt, erunt ignobiles.' "

[3] Id. id., ii. 51 : " Rogamus igitur et sincera te caritate monemus, ut commissa tibi regni gubernacula secundum Deum administrare studeas, et nomen regalis excellentiæ congruæ ac consonanti virtutum proprietate geras, quatenus eam, per cuius principatum subiectis imperas, in corde tuo semper regnare iustitiam ostendas."

[4] Id. id., v. 10 : " Monemus insuper, karissime, ut tibi commissi a Deo regni honorem omni industria, sollertia, peritiaque custodias. Sit vita tua digna, sapientia referta, iustitiæ et misericordiæ condimento saleque condita, ut de te vera sapientia quæ Deus est dicere queat : ' Per me rex iste regnat.' "

[5] Id. id., vi. 13 : " Sit vestræ potentiæ usus et exercitatio : subvenire oppressis, defendere viduas, iudicare pupillis, iustitiam non solum diligere sed etiam tota virtute defendere."

in which Hildebrand urged upon William the Conqueror, in 1080, the duty of obedience to the papal authority, inasmuch as the Pope would have to give account to God for him in the day of judgment ; he prefaced this exhortation to obedience by a very explicit statement that God had appointed two authorities greater than all others to rule the world, the apostolical and the royal.[1]

It is clear that if we are to arrive at a complete and just view of the conception of kingship and secular authority held by Hildebrand, we must not isolate the phrases of the two letters to Hermann of Metz, but must consider them along with the sentiments he expresses at other times. If, then, we examine the circumstances under which the two letters to Hermann were written, we find that the purpose of both was to refute the arguments of those who maintained that it was not lawful or proper for the Pope or any one else to excommunicate the king or emperor. Hildebrand was primarily concerned to demonstrate the absurdity of this view, and he justifies his action by three considerations—first, the general authority of binding and loosing given by Christ to Peter, from which no one is exempt ; second, the precedents which he cites of such excommunications of kings in the past ; and third, by a comparison of the dignity and authority of the temporal

---

[1] Gregory VII., Registrum, vii. 25 : " Credimus, prudentiam vestram non latere : omnibus aliis excellentiores apostolicam et regiam dignitates huic mundo, ad eius regimina, omnipotentem Deum distribuisse. Sicut enim, ad mundi pulchritudinem oculis carneis diversis temporibus repræsentandam, solem et lunam omnibus aliis eminentiora disposuit luminaria ; sic, ne creatura, quam sui benignitas ad imaginem suam in hoc mundo creaverat, in erronea et mortifera traheretur pericula, providit, ut apostolica et regia dignitate per diversa regeretur officia. Qua tamen maioritatis et minoritatis distantia religio sic se movet christiana, ut cura et dispensatione apostolica dignitas post Deum gubernetur regia. Quod licet, fili karissime, tua non ignoret vigilantia, tamen, ut pro salute tua indissolubiliter menti tuæ sit alligatum, divina testatur scriptura, apostolicam et pontificalem dignitatem reges christianos cæterosque omnes ante divinum tribunal repræsentaturam et pro eorum delictis rationem Deo reddituram. Si ergo iusto iudici, et qui mentiri nescit, creaturarum omnium creatori, in tremendo iudicio te sum repræsentaturus, iudicet diligens sapientia tua ; an debeam vel possim saluti tuæ non diligentissime cavere, et tu mihi ad salutem tuam, ut viventium possideas terram, debeas vel possis sine mora non obœdire."

and spiritual powers. It is in this last connection that he discusses the origin of secular authority, and urges that this had its origin in the sinful ambition and love of power of men who desired to make themselves the masters of their equals. That is, Hildebrand in these phrases maintains that the origin of secular authority is related to the vicious or sinful character in human nature.

We have then here one aspect of Hildebrand's conception of the nature of secular authority, stated sharply and without qualification, but in a context which is highly controversial. In the other passages which have been cited we have a very different view. In these he describes secular authority as being derived from God, and as finding its true character in the defence and maintenance of justice, and he hopes that there may be a true concord and agreement between the " sacerdotium " and the " imperium," the two authorities which God has appointed to rule over the world.

These two conceptions may seem at first sight, especially to those who are unfamiliar with the Stoic and Patristic tradition, inconsistent and irreconcilable, but this is merely a confusion. For, in this tradition, government, like the other great institutions of society, such as property and slavery, is the result of sin, and represents sinful greed and ambition, and yet is also the necessary, and, in the Christian conception, the divine, remedy for sin. Men in a state of innocence would neither need coercive government, nor would they claim to rule over their fellow-men ; while in the state of sin and ambition, men desire lordship over each other, but also, in this condition, men need control and restraint if any measure of justice and peace is to be attained and preserved. And thus the institution of government, which is the result of men's sinful passions, is also appointed by God to restrain sin.[1]

No doubt the phrases of Hildebrand in the two letters to the Bishop of Metz express one side of the traditional theory in a very harsh and crude fashion, and we have evidence that

[1] Cf. Seneca, Ep. xiv. 2 ; Irenæus, 'Adv. Hær.,' v. 24 ; St Augustine, 'De Civ. Dei,' v. 19, xix. 15 ; ' De   Doctrina Christiana,' i. 28 ; and vol. i. pp. 24, 126, 129.

they were resented even among those who were not prepared to defend the investiture of bishops with ring and staff by the secular authorities. For instance, Hugh of Fleury, in a treatise addressed to Henry I. of England in the early years of the twelfth century, protests indignantly against the phrases which had been used by Hildebrand in these letters about the origin and character of the royal authority, and maintains that such opinions are absurd, and contrary to the apostolic doctrine that all authority is from God, and that there is a divine hierarchy of authority and obedience not only on earth, but also in heaven.[1]

The phrases of Hildebrand were resented, and, considering their highly controversial context, this is not surprising. Is there now any reason to think that the conception which is expressed in these phrases was maintained by other writers of this period as representing a complete and exclusive theory of the origin and nature of temporal authority ? There are a very few passages in the contemporary literature which deserve our attention.

In a fragmentary treatise written in the middle of the eleventh century by a French churchman attacking the action of the Emperor Henry III. with regard to the Papacy, especially no doubt in view of the deposition of the Popes at the Council of Sutri, the author severely condemns the emperor as having claimed jurisdiction over the Pope, and

---

[1] Hugo of Fleury, 'Tractatus de regia potestate et sacerdotali dignitate,' i. 1: "Scio quosdam nostris temporibus qui reges autumnant non a Deo, sed ab his habuisse principium qui Deum ignorantes, superbia, rapina, perfidia, homicidiis et postremo universis pene sceleribus in mundi principio diabolo agitante supra pares homines dominari cæca cupiditate et inenarrabili affectaverunt præsumptione vel temeritate. Quorum sententia quam sit frivola liquet apostolico documento, qui ait : 'Non est potestas nisi a Deo. Quæ enim sunt a Deo ordinatæ sunt.' Constat igitur hac sententia, quia non ab hominibus, sed a Deo potestas regia in terris est ordinata sive disposita. . . . Unde nobis liquido claret Deum omnipotentem non solum humanum corpus membrorum distinxisse lineamentis, sed et totum mundum certis gradibus ac potestatibus, sicut illa cælestis curia cognoscitur esse distincta, in qua ipse solus Deus pater omnipotens regiam optinet dignitatem, et in qua post ipsum angeli, archangeli, throni et dominationes et quæque cæteræ potestates sibi invicem præesse mirabili et modesta potestatum varietats noscuntur."

Cf. St Gregory the Great, Ep. v. 59, and vol. i. p. 127.

urges that the emperor does not occupy the place of Christ, but that it might rather be said that he holds that of the devil, when he uses the sword and sheds blood.[1]

Again, in a treatise written by a certain Bernald, apparently in the last years of the eleventh century, he urges that if the Popes have authority to depose Patriarchs, they have the same authority over secular princes whose dignity seems to have been created rather by men than by the divine institution.[2] Cardinal Deusdedit, in one of his treatises, speaks of the royal authority as arising from human institution, with the permission indeed of God, but not by His will, and he refers to the demand of the Israelites for a king, as related in 1 Samuel.[3]

The first of these passages is very drastic, and if we had any reason to think that it represented a generally current view, would have considerable significance; but as we shall see presently, some of the strongest papalists take the very opposite view of the use of the temporal sword.[4] The phrases of Bernald and of Deusdedit do not represent anything more than the conception that the temporal power is not derived immediately from God, but is directly the creation of human will and authority.

What was, then, the normal view of these centuries as to the source and nature of secular authority ? There can really be

---

[1] 'De Ordinando Pontifice,' 'Auctor Gallicus' : "Ubi enim inveniuntur imperatores locum Christi obtinere ? Si verius liceat nobis dicere, potius offitio diaboli surguntur (v.r. unguntur) in gladio et sanguine, ut, dum per penitentiam eruantur vitia spirituali resecatione, ipsi insaniant vel in cede vel in membrorum carnali obtruncatione ; quod secundum gratiam apud Deum omnino est abhominabile."

[2] Bernaldus, Libellus xii., 'De Solutione Juramentorum' : "Sicut autem Romani pontifices summos patriarchas deponere possunt, ita et inferiores, utpote mundi principes, quorum utique dignitas potius ex humane adinventione, quam ex divina institutione videtur processisse."

[3] Deusdedit, 'Libellus contra invasores et symoniacos,' iii. 12 : "Nec mirum sacerdotalem auctoritatem quam Deus ipse per se ipsum constituit, in huiusmodi causis regiam precellere potestatem, quam sibi humana prefecit adinventio, eo quidem permittente, non tamen volente. Nam de primo rege populi sui, quem sibi petiit spreto prophetæ principatu, ait ad eumdem : 'Non te,' inquit, 'spreverunt, sed me, ne regnem super eos' (1 Sam. viii. 7). Et iterum : 'Paenitet me, quod constituerim Saul regem'" (1 Sam. xv. ii.)

[4] See p. 103.

no doubt whatever about this to those who are at the pains
to make themselves familiar with the literature of those times.
The writers of these centuries are practically unanimous in
maintaining that the authority of the king or emperor is
derived from God. The principle is clearly expressed by those
who wrote before the development of the great conflict between
the Papacy and the Empire in the latter part of the eleventh
century, but we also find it maintained with equal clearness
during the great conflict both by imperialists and papalists.

In a commentary by Bishop Atto of Vercelli, which belongs
to the second half of the tenth century, we find a very interesting and very emphatic statement of the divine authority of the
secular ruler, whether he was Christian or pagan.[1] Again, in
a report of the sermon of the Archbishop of Maintz at the
coronation of Conrad the Salic, which Wippo gives in his
life of Conrad, the Archbishop is represented as referring to
the same phrases of St Paul, and as speaking of God as the
source of all human dignity, who had appointed Conrad to
be king over his people ; the king is the vicar of Christ.[2]
The same conception is maintained by Peter Damian, one
of the most illustrious of the reforming Italian churchmen
of the middle of the eleventh century. In a letter to Archbishop Anno of Cologne, he speaks of the " regnum " and
" sacerdotium " as being both derived from God, and of

[1] Atto of Vercelli, ‘Exp. in Ep.
Pauli ad Romanos,’ xiii. i. : "Prae-
terea, ne diceret aliquis : Transivi ad
gratiam Evangelii ; liber sum : nulli
subditus esse debeo ; propterea apostolus, ut nihil suis auditoribus deesset,
propter bonum pacis, et concordiæ
subiecit : ‘Omnis anima potestatibus
sublimioribus subdita sit.’ Ab excellentiori parte id est anima, totus homo
designatur ; sublimiores autem potestates dicit imperatores, reges et principes huius sæculi, quibus nos subditos
esse admonet propter bonum pacis, et
concordiæ, ne nomen Dei, aut doctrina
Christi blasphemetur. . . . ‘Quae
autem sunt a Deo ordinatæ sunt,’ a
bono quippe ordinatore nihil inordina-

tum relinquitur. Ostendit ergo his
verbis apostolus manifeste, quoniam
omnis potestas, tam apud paganos
quam apud Christianos, a Deo ordinata
est, sive propitio sive irato."

[2] Wippo, ‘Vita Chunradi,’ ‘De Consecratione Regis,’ ‘Scriptum est enim :
Omnis potestas a Deo est’ : "Is omnipotens rex regum, totius honoris auctor
et principium, quando in principes
terræ alicuius dignitatis gratiam trans-
fundit, quantum ad naturam principii
pura et munda. . . . Dominus qui te
elegit ut esses rex super populum suum,
ipse te prius voluit probare, et post
modum regnare. . . . Ad summam
dignitatem pervenisti, vicarius es
Christi."

the need which each has of the other.[1] In another place
he draws out in some detail the complementary relation
between the spiritual and the temporal authorities. The
duties of the different members of the Church, for they are
both within the Church, are not the same. The duty of the
priest is to nourish and cherish all in mercy, the duty of
the judge is to punish the guilty, to deliver the innocent
from the power of the wicked, to be diligent in carrying
out the law, and in maintaining equity ; he should always
remember the words of the apostle, " Wouldest thou have no
fear of the power ? do that which is good, and thou shalt have
praise of him, for he is God's minister to thee for good. But if
thou doest evil, be afraid ; for he beareth not the sword in
vain " (Rom. xiii. 3, 4).[2] Peter Damian is clear that the
authority of the secular power in administering justice and
punishing crime is derived from God.

The writers whom we have just cited belong to the period

---

[1] Peter Damian, Ep., Bk. iii. 6 :
" Sciebat enim (*i.e.*, the High Priest
Jehoiada) quoniam utraque dignitas
alternæ invicem utilitatis est indiga,
dum et sacerdotium regni tuitione
protegitur, et regnum sacerdotalis
officii sanctitate fulcitur. . . . ut dum
regnum ac sacerdotium optata per vos
pace perfruitur, is, qui utriusque
dignitatis auctor est, pacis æternæ
digna vobis præmia largiatur."

[2] Id., ' Opusculum,' lvii. 1 : " Non
omnia membra Ecclesiæ uno fungun-
tur officio. Aliud nempe sacerdoti,
aliud competit iudici. Ille siquidem
visceribus debet pietatis affluere, et
in maternæ misericordiæ gremio sub
exuberantibus doctrinæ semper uberi-
bus filios confovere. Istius autem
officium est, ut reos puniat, et ex
eorum manibus eripiat innocentes ; ut
vigorem rectitudinis et iustitiæ teneat,
et a zelo sanctionum legalium non
tepescat ; ut ab æquitatis linea non
declinet ; ut legitimi vigoris genium
non enervet. Memineat etiam semper
quod per apostolum dicitur ; ' Vis non

timere potestatem ? fac bonum, et
habebis laudem ex illa. Dei enim
minister est tibi in bonum. Si autem
malum feceris, time, non enim sine
causa gladium portat.' In quibus
utique verbis (datur) intelligi, aliud
esse gladium principis, aliud infulam
sacerdotis. Non enim ad hoc præcin-
geris gladio, ut violentorum mala
debeas palpare vel ungere : sed ut ea
studeas vibrati mucronis ictibus ob-
truncare. Hinc est quod sequitur :
' Dei enim minister est vindex in iram
ei, qui male agit.' "

Cf. id., ' Liber Gratissimus,' 10 :
" Regnum namque et sacerdotium a
Deo cognoscitur institutum, et ideo,
licet amministratoris persona prorsus
inveniatur indigna, officium tamen,
quod utique bonum est, competens
aliquando gratia comitatur. . . . Reges
enim et sacerdotes, licet nonnulli eorum
reprobi sint per notabilis vitæ meri-
tum, dii tamen et christi dici rep-
periuntur propter accepti ministerii
sacramentum."

before the great conflict had broken out, but the same principle is maintained by writers of all shades of opinion during the great struggle. It is needless to cite the declarations of the extreme imperialist writers, for this principle is one of the main foundations of their argument against the papalists, and we shall presently have to consider some of their phrases in detail, when we discuss the conclusions which some of them wished to draw from this principle.

It is, however, very important to observe that this principle was held with equal firmness by writers who did not belong to the imperialist party, and even by the extremest papalists. Gerhoh of Reichersberg, one of the most important writers of the middle of the twelfth century, was certainly no partisan of the secular party, rather, vehemently maintained the liberty and authority of the Church, but he was also very clear in asserting the divine origin and authority of the secular power. In one of his treatises he condemns in the strongest terms any attempt of the ecclesiastic to draw to himself the secular authority, on the ground that this would be to destroy the authority which had been set up by God Himself.[1] Again, no writer of the Middle Ages is clearer than John of Salisbury as to the limits and conditions of the royal authority, and the right of resistance to the tyrant, but he is equally clear that the authority of the prince comes from God, and has the divine sanction.[2]

---

[1] Gerhoh of Reichersberg, 'De Investigatione Antichristi,' i. 72 : "Quin etiam, sicut aliquando cesares quædam pontificalia et ecclesiastica presumebant, ita iste de contra cum sacerdotio quoddam in se cesareum ac supercesareum imaginantur. . . . Hoc autem quid est aliud, quam potestatem a Deo constitutam destruere et ordinationi Dei resistere ? . . . Audiant pontifices precipientem sibi Dominum : 'Reddite quæ sunt cesaris cesari, et quæ sunt Dei Deo,' ut, si regalia æcclesie a regibus tradita tenere volunt, regibus inde iustum ac decentem honorem exhibeant. Audiant item apostolum. 'Deum timete, regem honorificate.'"

[2] John of Salisbury, 'Policraticus,' iv. 1 : "Est ergo, ut eum plerique diffiniunt, principis potestas publica, et in terris quædam divinæ maiestatis imago. Procul dubio magnum quid divinæ virtutis declaratur inesse principibus, dum homines nutibus eorum colla submittunt, et securi plerumque feriendas præbent cervices, et impulsu divino quisque timet quibus ipse timori est. Quod fieri posse non arbitror, nisi nutu faciente divino. Omnis etenim potestas a Domino Deo est, et cum illo fuit semper, et est ante evum. Quod igitur princeps potest ita a Deo est, ut potestas a Domino non recedat, sed ea utitur per subpositam manum, in omnibus doctrinam faciens clemen-

We shall presently have occasion to examine in detail the political theory of Manegold of Lautenbach, the most incisive writer of the investiture controversy, and the most unsparing critic in the Middle Ages of what he conceived to be the illegitimate pretensions of the imperialists. While, however, he emphatically repudiates what he held to be the false interpretation of the apostolic doctrine of the divine nature of secular authority, he traces this error to a confusion between the office of the king, which he evidently conceives to be sacred, and the position of an individual king who may have justly forfeited his authority, and cannot then claim obedience in the name of the apostolic authority.[1] And again in another passage he quotes with approbation a sentence from a letter of Pope Innocent I., which asserted that the exercise of criminal justice by the secular power was founded upon the authority of God Himself.[2]

And again the same principle is maintained by Honorius Augustodunensis. In his treatise entitled 'Summa Gloria,' which is in the main a vindication of the greater dignity of

tiæ aut iustitiæ suae. Qui ergo resistit potestati, Dei ordinationi resistit, penes quem est auctoritas conferendi eam, et, cum vult, auferendi vel minuendi eam."

[1] Manegold, 'Ad Gebehardum,' 43 : " In eo namque quod dicitur : ' Subditi estote regi quasi præcellenti,' et : ' Deum timete, regem honorificate,' et : ' Subditi estote dominis non tantum bonis et modestis,' multum sibi aplaudunt sibique titulos victoriæ ascribunt non intellegentes neque que locuntur neque de quibus affirmant. Rex enim non nomen est naturæ, sed officii, sicut episcopus, presbyter, diaconus. Et cum quilibet horum certis ex causis de commisso sibi officio deponitur, non est quod erat, nec honor officio debitus postea est impendendus. Quisquis ergo amissæ dignitatis postmodum sibi reverentiam impendit, potius prevaricator quam legum servator existit."

[2] Id. id., 39 : " Unde sanctissimus papa Innocentius in decretis suis cap. xxii. hos, per quorum ministerium catholici principes et pravos puniunt et pios defendunt, a reatu immunes ostendit dicens : ' Quesitum est super his etiam qui post baptismum administraverunt aut tormenta sola exercuerunt aut etiam capitalem protulerunt sententiam. De his nichil legimus a maioribus difinitum. Meminerant enim a Deo potestates has esse concessas et propter vindictam noxiorum gladium fuisse permissum et Dei ministerium esse in huiusmodi datum vindicem. Quemadmodum igitur reprehenderent factum, quod auctore Deo viderent esse concessum ? De his igitur ita, ut actenus servatum est, sic habemus, ne aut disciplinam evertere aut contra auctoritatem Domini venire videamur."

The passage is from Innocent I., Ep. 6, and is also cited by various canonists. Cf. vol. ii. p. 147.

the spiritual as compared with the temporal authority, he held
indeed that the authority of man over man was not primitive,
but established to restrain men's sinful passions, but he is
also clear that it was established by God.[1]   And in another
chapter of the same work he sets this out with great emphasis.
The royal authority is indeed inferior in dignity to the priestly,
but the royal authority must, in those matters which belong to
it, be obeyed, not only by the laity, but by the clergy ; and
he quotes St Peter and St Paul as teaching plainly that it
was instituted by God for the punishment of the wicked and
the reward of the good.[2]

[1] Honorius Augustodunensis, 'Summa Gloria,' 26 : "Deus namque non
prefecit primum hominem hominibus,
sed bestiis et brutis animalibus, quia
his qui irrationabiliter et bestialiter
vivunt, iudices tantum prelati sunt,
quatenus eos per timorem revocent ad
insitæ humanæ masuetudinis tenorem.
Unde idem Deus per Noe Sem et Iafeth
peccantis filii posteritati prefecit, quia
nimirum peccantes sacerdotio et regno
subiecit. Unde et in evangelio, cum
discipuli dicerent : 'Domine, ecce duo
gladii hic,' hæc verba sua auctoritate
roboravit, quia ad regimen æcclesiæ
in presenti vita duos gladios necessarios
premonstravit ; unum spiritalem, scilicet verbum Dei, quo sacerdotium utitur ad vulnerandos peccantes, alterum
materialem, quo regnum utitur ad
puniendos in malis perdurantes. Necesse
est enim, ut hos regalis potestas subigat
gladio materiali, qui legi Dei rebelles
non possunt corrigi stola sacerdotali."

[2] Id. id., 24 : "Quamvis igitur sacerdotium longe transcendat regnum,
tamen ob pacis concordiæ vinculum
monet evangelica et apostolica auctoritas, regibus honorem in secularibus
negotiis dumtaxat deferendum. Cum
enim quidam a Domino inquirerent,
utrum censum cesari dari liceret, ait :
'Reddite, quæ sunt cesaris, cesari,
atque quæ sunt Dei, Deo.' Ergo in
his quæ ad regni ius pertinent, oportet
clerum et populum regibus parere, in
his autem, quæ ad ius divinæ legis
spectant, Deo placere. . . . Beatus
quoque Petrus apostolus hortatur
honorem deferre regibus : 'Deum,' inquit, 'timete, reges honorificate.'
Et iterum : 'Subditi estote omni humanæ creaturæ propter Deum, sive
regi quasi præcellenti, sive ducibus ab
eo missis ad vindictam malefactorum,
laudem vero bonorum.' In quibus verbis
considerandum est, quod reges et iudices ob solam vindictam malorum
constituuntur, qui laudem ferre bonis
dicuntur. Justi enim reges et iudices
solos impios et iniquos puniunt, iustos
autem et bonos laudibus extollunt.
Beatus etiam Paulus ad subiectionem
principum hortatur dicens : 'Omnis
anima potestatibus sublimioribus subdita sit.' Et ne putes potestates per
homines casu constitui, subiungit :
'Non est enim potestas nisi a Deo.'
Quia vero aliquando propter peccata
populi mali iudices constituuntur, sicut
in Job legitur : 'Qui regnare facit
ypocritam propter peccata populi,' aliquando autem ob merita quorundam
iusti præficiuntur, addit : 'Quæ autem
sunt, a Deo ordinatæ sunt.' Et ne
putares bonis quidem obediendum,
malis autem resistendum, adhuc pro-
sequitur : 'Itaque qui resistit potestati,
Dei ordinationi resistit ; qui autem resistunt, ipsi sibi dampnationem acqui-

There can really be no doubt whatever as to the normal conceptions of the political theorists of the eleventh and twelfth centuries as to the origin and nature of the temporal power. The phrases of Gregory VII. in his letter to Hermann of Metz are no doubt at first sight startling, and it is not surprising that they have led to some misunderstanding, but it is clear that they only represent one aspect of his own conception of the state, and that an examination of his correspondence makes it clear that he had no intention to deny that political authority was derived from God. And we hope that it is now evident that the political theorists of all schools of thought recognised that, if man in a state of innocence would have needed no coercive authority, man under the actual conditions of human nature requires such an authority both for the suppression of wrong and injustice and for the maintenance of righteousness.

runt.' Et quod iudices ad malos tantum reprimendos, immo puniendos preficiantur, patenter subditur : ' Principes non sunt timori boni operis, sed mali. Vis autem non timere potestatem ? Bonum fac, et habebis laudem ex ipsa.' Eadem et Petrus dixit."

CHAPTER III.

THE MORAL FUNCTION OF POLITICAL AUTHORITY.

THE normal conception of the Middle Ages was then that the temporal as well as the spiritual power derives its authority from God. We must now observe that this principle found its rationale in the moral purpose or end of temporal authority. Such occasional and controversial phrases as those of Hildebrand might leave the impression that secular authority had no other purpose than to minister to the ambitions and to satisfy the desires of the ruler. But this was very far from being the real principle of the Middle Ages ; to these the authority of the king or emperor was divine, because it was his function to secure the establishment and maintenance of justice.

It is true that St Augustine had entangled himself in a position which in some places at least led him to deny that the state must find its essential and distinguishing quality in justice.[1] There is no trace of this conception in the writers of the tenth, eleventh, and twelfth centuries ; the passages in St Augustine's writings which support it are not, as far as we have seen, ever quoted. On the contrary, the constant principle set out by the mediæval writers is that the maintenance of justice is the essential function of the ruler.

We can find this represented first in some references to the beginnings of organised society. Such references are scanty and contain nothing new or important, but, such as they are, they all represent the beginning of the authority of man over man as due to the need of order and of some method of restraint upon men's evil tendencies. Gerbert (Silvester II.), for instance, says that

---

[1] St Augustine, 'De Civitate Dei,' xix. 21, 24. Cf. vol. i. pp. 165-170.

it is certain that when our first parents abused their free will by their transgression, man was set over his fellow-man in order to restrain his unlawful desires, and that thus men are held in check by civil and ecclesiastical laws.[1] Again, Othloh of St Emmeran points out that it is impossible that men should live together in peace unless there is some system by which some are subjected to others.[2] Again, the history of the Bishops of Cambrai, a work which belongs to the eleventh century, commences with a brief account of the beginnings of city life—men, as it was said, at first wandered about like the wild animals, without any government of custom and reason, pursuing blindly the satisfaction of their desires; it was only when they began to come together into cities that they learned to keep faith and to maintain justice, and to live in obedience to each other.[3] These phrases obviously represent formal literary traditions, and are not in themselves of much importance, but they may serve as an introduction to our consideration of the theory of the function or purpose of the state.

We begin by observing that the principle of the just end of the state, which was, as we have seen, very firmly maintained by the

[1] Silvester II. (Gerbert), Ep. xi.: "Cum constat post primorum nostrorum parentum prævaricationem in liberi arbitrii abusionem genus hominum ei sententiæ addictum, ut et homo capitibus aliorum secundum Psalmographi vocem superponatur, ad compescendos scilicet humanæ voluptatis illicitos appetitus, et legibus non modo forensibus, verum etiam ecclesiasticis cohibeamur regulis ac rationibus."

[2] Othloh of St Emmeran, 'Dialogus de Tribus quæstionibus,' 24: "O. Ubi rogo, plures, vel saltim duo homines simul commorantes, pacifici possunt esse umquam, nisi alter alteri subdatur?

H. Nusquam omnino.

O. Unde erat necesse ut homines, etiam primi, redderentur pacifici et subiicerentur alter alteri."

[3] 'Gesta Pontificum Cameracensium,' i. 1: "Urbibus quondam ædificandis ea primum causa ab auctoribus extitisse dicitur, ut homines passim ritu ferarum oberrantes, quibus neque mos, neque cultus ratione magistra regebatur, nichilque divinum aut humanum sapiebant, sed propter errorem atque inscientiam cæca ac temeraria dominatrix animi cupiditas ad se explendam viribus corporis abutebatur pernitiosis satellitibus; illi inquam homines instructis urbium mœnibus in unum convenirent, fidem colere et iustitiam retinere discerent, et aliis parere sua voluntate consuescerent; ac non modo labores excipiendos communis commodi causa, sed etiam vitam amittendam estimarent."

Cf. Alcuin, 'Dialogus de Rhetorica et Virtutibus'; Cicero, Tusc., v. 2; and vol. i. p. 211.

political writers of the ninth century, continued to be held in
the tenth and eleventh. In the ' Collectio Canonum ' of Abbo,
the Abbot of Fleury, which is inscribed to Hugh and Robert,
Kings of the French (*i.e.*, before 997), he quotes as from a
Council of Paris a passage from that treatise ' De Duodecim
Abusivis Sæculi,' which was much used in the ninth century ;
the justice of the king is to oppress no man by force, to judge
without favour of persons, to be the defender of strangers and
children and widows, to put down vice and crime, to maintain
the poor with alms, to set just men over the affairs of the
kingdom, to defend his country against its enemies, and to hold
the Catholic faith.[1]

Ratherius of Verona gives a terse statement of the qualities
which make a true king, and without which he may have
the name but cannot have the reality of kingship ; these are
prudence, justice, courage, and temperance, the man who
possesses these qualities, though he be but a peasant, may not
improperly be said to be a king, while the man who lacks them
though he held the universal monarchy of the world could not

[1] Abbo, Abbot of Fleury, ' Collectio Canonum,' iii. : "Unde ex
libris qui ex conciliis sui temporis
effecti sunt cum subiectione episcoporum, quanta facile est reperiri,
expressim libro II. cap. I. post aliqua.
' Justitia regis est neminem inuste
per potestatem opprimere, sine accep-
tione personarum inter virum et prox-
inum suum iudicare, advenis et
pupillis et viduis defensorem esse,
furta cohibere, adulteria punire, iniquos non exaltare, impudicos et his-
triones non nutrire, impios de terra
perdere, parricidas et peierantes vivere
non sinere, ecclesias defensare, pauperes
ellemosynis alere ; justos super regni
negotia constituere, senes et sapientes et
sobrios consiliarios habere, magorum et
hariolorum pythonissarumque super-
stitionibus non intendere, iracundiam
differre, patriam fortiter et iuste contra
adversarios defendere ; per omnia in

Deo vivere, prosperitatibus non elevare
animam, cuncta adversa patienter ferre,
fidem catholicam in Deum habere, filios
suos non sinere impie agere, certis
horis orationibus insistere, ante horas
congruas non gustare cibum.' "

This passage comes from the 9th
section of the treatise ' De Duodecim
Abusivis Sæculi,' to which reference is
made in vol. i. pp. 222-224. I am glad
to have the opportunity to draw the
attention of English students to the
excellent monograph upon this little
treatise which was published at Munich
in 1908 in ' Texte und Untersuch-
ungen,' 34, 1, by Siegmund Hellmann,
to which my friend Professor Souttar
of Aberdeen has kindly drawn my
attention. Hellmann has not only
provided us with an excellent text, but
has demonstrated the great probability
that it is an Irish work dating from
between 630 and 700 A.D.

rightly be called a king, for the man who governs wrongfully loses his authority.[1]

Wippo, in that life of Conrad the Salic to which we have already referred, represents the Archbishop of Maintz, in crowning him, as urging him to remember that he was the vicar of Christ, and that no one but he who imitated Christ was a true ruler, God required of him above all that he should do justice and seek peace for his country, that he should be the defender of churches and clergy, the guardian of widows and orphans.[2]

These examples will suffice to show that the principles of the political theorists of the ninth century continued to be held until the time of the great conflict between the papacy and the empire. They were not changed by that conflict. Neither the imperialists nor the papalists had any doubt whatever that the true function of the king was to maintain and set forward justice. The papalists might use the principle to justify opposition and resistance to what they conceived to be an unjust authority, and the imperialists to repel attacks upon what they conceived to be the legitimate claims and authority of the temporal ruler, but they were at one in maintaining that this was the true purpose of all authority.

There is an excellent example of the principles of the imperialist writers in the work called ' De unitate ecclesiæ conservanda,' which was written against the Hildebrandine tradi-

---

[1] Ratherius of Verona, ' Præloquiorum,' iii. 1 : " Rex es ? Dignitas, rogo, ipsa te dum delectat, instruat. Sunt quaedam regalis ordinis insignia, quibus sine, et si nomen utcunque, re tamen vera certe non potest consistere dignitas tanta. His ergo utere, his exercere, his exornare. Esto prudens, iustus, fortis et temperatus. . . . 2. Hae quatuor, ita regales proprie noscuntur esse virtutes, ut cum his quilibet etiam rusticus, rex non incongrue dici ; sine his, nec ipse universam pene monarchiam obtinens mundi, quamquam abusive, rex valeat iuste vocari ; male enim imperando, ut ait qui supra, summum

imperium amittitur."

[2] Wippo, ' Vita Chunradi,' ' De Consecratione Regis ' : " Ad summum dignitatem pervenisti, vicarius es Christi. Nemo nisi illius imitator verus est dominator ; oportet ut in hoc solio regni cogites de honore perenni. . . . Cum vero Deus a te multa requirat, hoc potissimum desiderat ut facias judicium et iustitiam ac pacem patriæ, quæ semper respicit ad te ; ut sis defensor ecclesiarum et clericorum, tutor viduarum et orphanorum ; cum his et aliis bonis firmabitur thronus tuus hic et in perpetuum."

tion, in the last years of the eleventh century, possibly by
Waltram, Bishop of Naumburg. The author's treatment of the
questions concerning the relations of Temporal and Spiritual
power is important, and we shall have occasion to deal with
the treatise again in this connection, but for the moment it is
enough to observe that in discussing the nature of the State
he cites those passages from the ' De Civitate Dei,' in which
St Augustine has preserved Cicero's description of law as being
the embodiment of justice, and of the state as that which
exists to maintain law and justice.[1]

[1] ' De unitate ecclesiæ conservanda,'
i. 17: " Res publica enim dicitur,
quod sit res populi, sicut scribit sanctus
Augustinus in ipso xviiii libro de
civitate Dei ; sed populum esse definit
cœtum multitudinis iuris consensu
vel utilitatis communione sociatum.
Quid autem dicat iuris consensum, dis-
putando explicat, per hoc ostendens geri
sine iustitia non posse rem publicam.
'Ubi ergo,' inquit, ' justitia vera non est,
nec ius potest esse ; quod enim iure fit,
profecto iuste fit, quod autem fit
iniuste, nec iure fieri potest ; non enim
iura dicenda vel putanda quælibet
iniqua hominum constituta. Quocirca
ubi non est vera iustitia, iuris consensu
sociatus cœtus hominum non potest
esse, et ideo nec populus ; et si non
populus, nec res populi, sed qualis-
cunque multitudinis, quæ populi
nomine digna non est. Ac per hoc, si
res publica res est populi et populus non
est, qui consensu iuris sociatus non
est, non est autem ius, ubi nulla iustitia
est, procul dubio colligitur, ubi iustitia
non est, non esse rem publicam. Iustitia
porro est ea virtus, quae sua cuique dis-
tribuit.' Et longe supra idem Augustinus in libro ii de civitate Dei introdu-
cens sententiam vel Scipionis vel Tullii
de re publica : ' Sicut in fidibus,'
inquit, ' a tibiis atque cantu ipso ac
vocibus concentus est quidam tenendus
ex distinctis sonis, quem immutatum
atque discrepantem aures eruditæ ferre

non possunt, isque concentus ex dis-
simillimarum vocum moderatione con-
cors tamen efficitur et congruus, sic ex
summis et infimis et mediis inter-
iectis ordinibus, ut sonis, moderata
ratione civitatem consensu dissimilli-
morum dicunt concinere ; et quæ
harmonia a musicis dicitur in cantu,
eam esse in civitate concordiam, ar-
tissimum atque optimum omni in re
publica vinculum incolumitatis, eamque
sine iustitia nullo pacto esse posse.
Populum autem non omnem cœtum
multitudinis, sed cœtum iuris consensu
et utilitatis communione sociatum esse
determinant, et dicunt, tunc esse rem
publicam, id est rem populi, cum bene
ac iuste geritur, sive ab uno rege, sive
a paucis optimatibus, sive ab universo
populo. Cum vero iniustus est rex,
quem tyrannum more Græco appellant,
aut iniusti optimates, quorum consensum dicunt factionem, aut iniustus ipse
populus, cui nomen usitatum non re-
periunt, nisi etiam ipsum tyrannum
vocent, non iam dicunt vitiosam, sicut
prius fuerat disputatum, sed sicut ratio
ex illis definitionibus connexa docuisset
omnino nullam esse rem publicam,
quoniam non esset res populi, cum
tyrannus eam factione capesseret, nec
ipse populus iam populus esset, si esset
iniustus, quoniam non esset multitudo
iuris consensu et utilitatis communione sociata, sicut populus fuerat defini-
tus."

The same conception that the essential character of kingship is to maintain justice is maintained in that treatise of Hugh of Fleury to which we have already referred.[1] He has a very high conception of the nature of the royal authority, he cites both the Pauline doctrine that all authority is from God, and the Gelasian principle that there are two powers by which the world is ruled, the royal and the priestly, while Christ Himself was both King and Priest,[2] and he reproduces the phrases of Ambrosiaster and Cathulfus, that the king has the image of God the Father, while the bishop has that of Christ, and maintains that the king has authority over all bishops in his kingdom.[3] At the same time he maintains very emphatically that the function of the legitimate king is to govern his people in justice and equity, to protect the widows and the poor ; his chief virtues are sobriety, justice, prudence, and temperance.[4]

These illustrations will be sufficient to make it clear that those who belonged to the imperialist party were quite clear that the function or end of the temporal authority was to maintain justice. It is more important to observe that the same principle was firmly maintained by the papalists and anti-imperialists. We have already seen that Manegold of Lautenbach maintained the ultimate divine origin of the temporal power, while, as we shall see presently, he held that it was derived immediately from the community. He was perhaps the most vigorous assailant of Henry IV. and the most

---

[1] See p. 98.

[2] Hugh of Fleury, ' Tractatus de regia potestate et sacerdotali dignitate,' i. 1, 2. Cf. vol. i. pp. 149, 215.

[3] Id. id., i. 3 : " Verumptamen rex in regni sui corpore Patris omnipotentis optinere videtur imaginem, et episcopus Christi. Unde rite regi subiacere videntur omnes regni ipsius episcopi, sicut Patri Filius deprehenditur esse subiectus, non natura, sed ordine, ut universitas regni ad unum redigatur principium." Cf. vol. i. pp. 149, 215.

[4] Id. id., i. 6 : " Porro legitimi regis officium est populum in iusticia et æquitate gubernare et æcclesiam sanc-

tam totis viribus defendere. Oportet etiam eum esse pupillorum tutorem, et viduarum protectorem, et pauperum auxiliatorem, ut cum beato Iob Domino dicere possit : ' Oculus fui ceco et pes claudo, et rem quam nesciebam diligenter investigabam.' Debet proinde Deum omnipotentem, qui multis hominum milibus eum præposuit, toto mentis affectu diligere, et populum sibi a Deo commissum tamquam se ipsum. . . . Debet etiam quattuor principalibus maxime pollere virtutibus, sobrietate videlicet, iusticia, prudentia ac temperantia." Cf. id., c. 7.

radical theorist of the nature of government in the eleventh
century, he had as little respect for the arbitrary king as
any political writer of the seventeenth century or of the French
Revolution. But he founds his opinions, not on the theory that
secular authority was a thing illegitimate or improper, but on
the principle that as the royal authority excelled all other
earthly power in dignity, so it should also excel them all in
justice and piety. He who was to have the care of all, to rule
over all, should possess greater virtue than all, in order that he
might administer his power with the highest equity. The
people had not set him over them that he should act as a
tyrant, but that he should defend them from tyranny.[1] Again
in another passage Manegold urges that the chief distinction
between human nature and that of other living creatures is
that it is possessed of reason, and that therefore men consider
not only what they should do, but why they do it. No man
can make himself king or emperor ; when therefore the people
set one man over them, they do it in order that he should
give to every man his due, that he should protect the good,
destroy the wicked, and administer justice to all.[2]

Berthold of Constance in his Annals expresses the same
principle, but in terms derived ultimately from St Isidore of
Seville. The true king is he who does right, while the king
who does wrong will lose his kingship ; or rather, he is no king,
but only a tyrant.[3] Lambert of Hersfeld, in his account of the

---

[1] Manegold, ' Ad Gebehardum,' 30 :
" Regalis ergo dignitas et potentia sicut
omnes mundanas excellit potestates,
sic ad eam ministrandam non flagitiosissimus quisque vel turpissimus est
constituendus, sed qui sicut loco et
dignitate, ita nichilominus ceteros
sapientia, iusticia superet et pietate.
Necesse est ergo, qui omnium curam
gerere, omnes debet gubernare, maiore
gratia virtutum super ceteros debeat
splendere, traditam sibi potestatem
summo equitatis libramine studeat
administrare. Neque enim populus
ideo eum super se exaltat, ut liberum
in se exercendæ tyrannidis facultatem
concedat, sed ut a tyrannide ceterorum

et improbitate defendat."

[2] Id.id., 47 : " In hoc namque natura
humana ceteris præstat animantibus,
quod capax rationis ad agenda queque
non fortuitis casibus proruit, causas
rerum iuditio rationis inquirit nec
tantum, quid agatur, sed cur aliquid
agatur, intendit. Cum enim nullus
se imperatorem vel regem creare possit,
ad hoc unum aliquem super se populus
exaltat, ut iusti ratione inperii se
gubernet et regat, cuique sua distribuat, pios foveat, impios perimat,
omnibus videlicet iusticiam im-
pendat."

[3] Berthold of Constance, 'Annales,'
1077 A.D. (p. 297) : " Recte igitur

demands put forward by the Saxons and Thuringians, in the rising of 1073 against Henry IV., represents them as acknowledging that they were indeed bound by their oath of allegiance to Henry, but only if he used his authority for the building up, and not the destruction of the Church of God, if he governed justly and lawfully according to ancestral custom, if he maintained for every man his rank and dignity and law.[1]

Again, in the twelfth century John of Salisbury asserts with great emphasis that the Prince is entrusted with his great authority, is even said to be " legis nexibus absolutus," not because he may do unjust things, but because it is his essential character to do justice and equity not out of fear but from love of justice. Who would speak of the mere will of the prince in regard to public matters, when he may not will anything but that which law and equity and the public interest requires ? The prince is the minister of the public utility and the servant of equity, and is the representative of the commonwealth, because he punishes all injuries and crimes with equity.[2]

We have been compelled to give some space to the consideration of the questions discussed in these two chapters

faciendo nomen regis tenetur, alioquin amittitur, unde est hoc vetus elogium : ' Rex eris, si recte facis ; si non facis, non eris ' . . . cur non magis proprie tyranni in huiusmodi fortissimi, quam abusive et absque rei veritatis reges sint nuncupandi."

[1] Lambert of Hersfeld, 'Annales,' 1073 A.D. (p. 197) : " Sacramento se ei fidem dixisse ; sed si ad ædificationem, non ad destructionem ecclesiæ Dei, rex esse vellet, si iuste, si legitime, si more maiorum rebus moderaretur, si suum cuique ordinem, suam dignitatem, suas leges tutas inviolatasque manere pateretur."

[2] John of Salisbury, 'Policraticus,' iv. 2 : " Princeps tamen legis nexibus dicitur absolutus, non quia ei iniqua liceat, sed quia is esse debet, qui non timore pœnæ sed amore iustitiæ æquitatem colat, rei publicæ procuret utilitatem, et in omnibus aliorum commoda privatæ præferat voluntati. Sed quis in negotiis publicis loquitur de principis voluntate, cum in eis nil sibi velle liceat, nisi quod lex aut æquitas persuadet aut ratio communis inducit ? Eius namque voluntas in his vim debet habere iudicii ; et rectissime quod ei placet in talibus legis habet vigorem, eo quod ab æquitatis mente eius sententia non discordet. De vultu tuo, inquit, iudicium meum prodeat, oculi tui videant æquitatem ; iudex etenim incorruptus est cuius sententia ex contemplatione assidua imago est æquitatis. Publicæ ergo utilitatis minister et æquitatis servus est princeps, et in eo personam publicam gerit, quod omnium iniurias et dampna sed et crimina omnia æquitate media punit."

H

only because there has been some uncertainty as to the position of the political theorists of the eleventh and twelfth centuries, and this uncertainty has arisen owing to the supposed influence of some aspects of St Augustine's theories of Church and State.   We shall have to consider the nature of this influence more closely when, in our next volume, we deal with the theory of the relations of the spiritual and temporal powers, and we hope that we shall then be able to see more precisely what influence St Augustine may have exercised.   In the meanwhile it is, we hope, quite evident that the conception that the political theorists of the eleventh and twelfth centuries doubted or denied either the divine origin of the State, or the principle that its end and purpose was an ethical one, namely, the maintenance of justice, is a complete mistake.   No such doubt was seriously entertained, and the theorists were all convinced that as temporal authority came from God, so also its purpose or function was to maintain the divine justice in the world.

CHAPTER IV.

THE THEORY OF THE " DIVINE RIGHT."

IT is we hope now sufficiently clear that substantially there was
no doubt in the great formative period of the Middle Ages
which we are now considering—that is, in the eleventh and
twelfth centuries—that the State was a divine institution, that
political as well as ecclesiastical authority was derived from
God, and had an ethical or moral, as well as a material function.
We hope to consider the systematic theories of the thirteenth
century in a later volume, and cannot here anticipate our
discussion of them.

This conception, which, as we have shown, was fully admitted
even by the most determined papalists, found its most emphatic
expression when the king was called the Vicar of God. The
title was not so far as we have seen used by any of the more
strictly papalist writers during this period, though it had been
frequently used by the Churchmen of the ninth century,[1] but
if the phrase was not actually used by them, the conception
which it expressed, that the authority of the king is derived
from God, was unreservedly admitted.

We have now to consider how far this principle may have
been interpreted, in the period which we are now considering,
as implying that the authority of the king or ruler was in such
a sense divine that resistance to him was under any and all
circumstances unlawful. We have endeavoured to set out the
origin of this conception in our first volume ;[2] as far as we can
judge, it seems to us clear that the conception was substantially

---

[1] Cf. vol. i. pp. 149, 215, 216.   [2] Cf. vol. i. pp. 30, 31, and chaps. 13 and 17.

an oriental one, which came into the West in the main through certain of the Fathers, and that it was derived by them, immediately, from a one-sided study of certain passages in the historical books of the Old Testament. It was St Gregory the Great who formulated it, and as we shall presently see, it is to his influence that we can generally trace the appearance of the conception in the Middle Ages. We have also showed that while St Gregory the Great drew out the conception with great clearness, and while certain other Fathers may have inclined towards it, yet others, and especially St Ambrose and St Isidore, set out a fundamentally different principle, and that St Isidore especially drew a very sharp distinction between the king and the tyrant.[1]

The writers of the ninth century inherited both traditions, and they cited the phrases which belong to both, but it is clear that while they might use the phrases of St Gregory, they were governed rather by the tradition of St Ambrose and St Isidore, and that while they looked upon the secular authority as a divine institution, it was to them divine only so far as it represented the principles of justice and the authority of law.[2]

These two principles were inherited by the men of the Middle Ages. What did they make of them? How did they relate them to each other? We have seen that both parties, in the great conflict of the temporal and spiritual powers, maintained that all authority, whether ecclesiastical or secular, came from God, and that they were at one in maintaining that the function of authority was to uphold justice and righteousness. But there were some who maintained that while this was true, yet the king was answerable only to God, that there was no authority which could judge him, and that the subject must therefore submit even to injustice and oppression, looking only to the just judgment of God to punish the oppressor and to defend the innocent. As we shall presently see, there are traces of this view even before the outbreak of the great conflict between the Papacy and the Empire, but, not unnaturally, in the great conflict, some imperialists, in their anxiety to lay hold of every

[1] Cf. vol. i. chap. 14.   [2] Cf. vol. i. chaps. 18 and 19.

instrument of defence against the Popes, tended to assert this
view with much greater emphasis.

In the tenth century Atto of Vercelli, in one of his letters,
maintains very dogmatically that it is an impious thing to
resist the king, even though he is unjust and wicked. As St
Gregory the Great had done, he cites the example of David, his
veneration for the Lord's anointed, and his refusal to lift his
hand against him, and he alleges the example of the submis-
sive tone of St Gregory in writing to the Emperor Maurice. He
also quotes a passage, which he thinks comes from the writings
of St Chrysostom, in which it is said that while it is true that
the people elect the king, when he is once elected they cannot
depose him, and some canons of a Council of Toledo which
condemn revolt against the king, under penalty of excommunication.[1] And, in a passage from another treatise of which we
have already cited some words, he explains away a passage of
Hosea which seems to imply that there might be kings who had
not derived their authority from God, and maintains that even
in matters of religion a good man must not resist the king, but
must submit patiently to persecution however unjust.[2]

[1] Atto of Vercelli, Epistle I. : " Non
leve est regalem impugnare maies-
tatem, etsi iniusta in aliquo videatur.
Dei enim ordinatio est ; Dei est dispensatio. Profanum est enim violare
quod Deus ordinat. . . . Sane
sciendum, quia cum Deus omnipotens
utilem populo principem donare
dignatur, iustum est ut eius hoc
pietati ascribant, et grates exinde
dignas persolvant, si autem adversus
fuerit, suis hoc imputent peccatis,
ipsumque flagitare non desinant, ut
hoc secundem multitudinem misericordiæ suæ propitius disponat. Nam
deiiciendus vel impugnandus nullo
modo est a populo, qui iam ordinatus
est a Deo. . . . Venerabilis etiam
Ioannes Chrysostomus in quadam
homilia sua ait. ' Sicut enim videmus
in istis mundialibus regnis quomodo in
primis quidem nemo potest facere
se ipsum regem, sed populus eligit
sibi regem, quem vult : sed cum rex
ille fuerit factus et confirmatus in
regno, iam habet potestatem in hominibus, et non potest populus iugum de
cervice sua repellere. Nam primum
quidem in potestate populi est facere
sibi regem quem vult ; factum autem
de regno repellere, iam non est in
potestate eius, et sic voluntas populi
postea in necessitatem convertitur.' "
The passage attributed to St
Chrysostom does not come from his
writings, but from a " Privilegium " of
Pope Leo VIII. Cf. M. G. H., ' Libelli
de Lite,' vol. ii. p. 422, note 2.
[2] Id., ' Exp. in Ep. Pauli ad Romanos,' xiii. 1 : " Cur autem subditi
esse debeamus ostendit, subiungens ;
' Non est enim potestas nisi a Deo.'

In a commentary on the Psalms by St Bruno, who was
Bishop of Würzburg from 1034 to 1048, the words, " Against
Thee only have I sinned " (Ps. li. 4), are interpreted as meaning that while a private person who commits an offence
transgresses against God and the king, the king transgresses
only against God, for there is no man who can judge his
actions.[1]

The excommunication and deposition of Henry IV. by
Gregory VII. raised in its most acute form the question which
had already arisen with the great Saxon revolt of 1073, the
question how far revolt against the royal authority was a thing
legitimate, and more especially the question how far such a
revolt was consistent with the Christian conception of the

Sed cum in libro cuiusdam sapientis
scriptum sit : ' Reges regnaverunt, sed
non per me ; principes exstiterunt, et
non cognovi ' (Hosea viii. 4) quomodo
non est potestas, nisi a Deo ? Sciendum
est ergo, quia sunt quæ Deus propitius
ordinat, et disponit ; sunt quæ iratus
fieri permittit. . . . . .
' Quæ autem sunt a Deo ordinatæ
sunt ; ' a bono quippe ordinatore nihil
inordinatum relinquitur.   Ostendit
ergo his verbis Apostolus manifeste,
quoniam omnis potestas, tam apud
paganos quam apud Christianos, a Deo
ordinata est, sive propitio sive irato.
Deerat enim timor Dei hominibus ;
ideoque ne more piscium ab invicem
consumerentur, datæ sunt potestates
etiam malis, ut boni patientiæ virtute
probarentur, et mali legibus mundanis
cœrcerentur, et punirentur. . . .
Verum, quia erant nonnulli dicentes :
' In secularibus negotiis nos subditos
esse oportet ; in fide autem, et in his,
quæ ad Deum pertinent, nullo modo ; '
idcirco volens apostolus ostendere,
quia in omnibus subditos esse oportet
propter Deum, adjecit : ' Qui autem
resistunt, ipsi sibi damnationem ac-
quirant.' Ac si aperte dicerit : Dum
ipsi persequendi occasionem tribuunt,
suos persecutores excusabiles, et se
improbabiles reddunt ; ideoque dig-

nam causam mortis habeant, sed
dignum mortis præmium accipiunt.
Cur autem principes dati sint mani-
festat, subiungens ; ' Nam principes
non sunt timori boni operis, sed
mali ; ' non enim ideo principes dati
sunt, ut eos terreant qui bona operan-
tur, sed qui mala.
Igitur, ut ostenderit vim potestatis,
et quare potestas data sit, adjunxit :
' Vis ergo non timere potestatem ?
bonum fac, et habebis laudem ex illa.'
Sed forte aliquis dicet : ' Nunquid
sancti apostoli potestatibus subditi
fuerunt, qui principibus usque ad
mortem restiterunt, ne Christi fidem
amitterent ? ' Vere subditi fuerunt,
quoniam non propter mala opera, sed
propter bona persequendi occasionem
dederunt."

[1] Bruno of Würzburg, ' Expositio
Psalmorum,' l. 5 (li. 4) : " ' Tibi soli
peccavi.' . . . Si quis enim de populo
erraverit, et Deo peccat et regi.
Nam quando rex delinquit, soli Deo
reus est. Iste igitur rex soli Deo
peccare se dicit, quia hominem non
habet qui eius facta diiuidicet."

This passage, which is also cited
by Atto of Vercelli in the letter we
have just considered, is taken from
Cassiodorus's Commentary on the
Psalms.

divine nature of secular authority. We do not yet discuss the question of the relation of the spiritual authority to the temporal, though it must be remembered that this was always present to men's minds.

The imperialist party did not necessarily or always take up the position that the temporal power was in such a sense sacred, that it could never under any circumstances be justifiable to revolt against it, but it was natural enough that some of them should have recourse to that tradition of the Church. In Henry IV.'s reply to the bull of deposition of 1076, he denounces Gregory VII.'s arrogance and audacity in venturing to raise his hand against him who had been anointed to the kingdom, while the tradition of the holy Fathers taught that he could be judged by God alone, and could be deposed for no crime, except for that of departing from the faith ; the Fathers indeed had not judged or deposed even the apostate Julian, but had left him to the judgment of God.[1] Berthold of Constance, in his Annals for the year 1077, relates how some of the clergy were continually proclaiming that neither the Pope nor any other authority could judge kings, whatever might be the crimes of which they were guilty, even if they were heretics.[2] Berthold himself holds this conception to be absurd, but his evidence is only the more important.

The source of this opinion is obviously in the main the tradition of some of the Christian Fathers, and especially of St Gregory the Great. There is a very good example of this in a treatise written about 1080 by Wenrich, the head of the educational school at Trier, afterwards Bishop of Vercelli, in the name of Theodoric, the Bishop of Verdun, who was at

---

[1] M. G. H., Legum, Sect. IV. Const., vol. i. 62 (1076): "Me quoque, qui licet indignus inter christos ad regnum sum unctus, tetigisti, quem sanctorum patrum traditio soli Deo iudicandum docuit, nec pro aliquo crimine, nisi a fide quod absit exorbitaverim, deponendum asseruit ; cum etian Iulianum apostatam prudentia sanctorum patrum non sibi sed soli Deo iudicandum deponendumque commiserit."

[2] Berthold of Constance, 'Annales,' 1077 A.D. (p. 296): "Tunc vero quæ hæresis et seminarium erat clericorum, pertinaces nonnulli passim concionati sunt, in reges quamquam hereticos et cunctis flagitiorum facinorumque reatibus exoletos, sanguinarios nefandissimos, nec non omnifariam profanos et sacrilegos, nec ipsius papæ nec alicuius magistratuum iudicium et sententiam cadere non debere."

that time one of the supporters of Henry IV. It is a protest against Gregory VII.'s action in deposing Henry IV. and encouraging the German princes to revolt against him. He maintains that such conduct was contrary to the law of God,[1] and urges the example of the humility and courtesy of Gregory the Great, who even when he reproved the authorities of the State was careful to address them in terms befitting their dignity, and protested that he recognised that he owed obedience to kings, and acted in this spirit even in regard to actions of which he disapproved. When the emperor required him to promulgate a law forbidding the reception of soldiers into monasteries, he protested against it as contrary to the law of God, but he carried out the imperial order for its promulgation.[2]

Another example will be found in the treatise ' De unitate ecclesiæ conservanda.' The author was a determined partisan of the cause of Henry IV. against the Hildebrandine party, and contrasts Hildebrand's conduct with that of Gregory the Great. Hildebrand claimed to have authority over kings and kingdoms,

[1] Wenricus, Scolasticus Treverensis, Epistola, 1-3.

[2] Id. id., 4 : " Hoc plane lacte nutritus beatus papa Gregorius in verbis, in moribus, in ipsis denique suis increpationibus humilitatem et mansuetudinem ubique redolet. Hinc est quod in sublimi loco positas personas, quacunque inutiles vel etiam infames, dignitatum tamen vocabulis, appellat, reverendis allocutionibus honorat, potestatem eorum qualibus potest verbis attollere et exaltare non dissimulat. Summus pontifex obœdientiam se regibus debere protestatur et asserit, ea debiti necessitate ad ea, quæ mentis iudicio ipse reprobat, pro tempore toleranda aliquando descendit, quæ tamen ipsa quantum sibi displiceant, adopta oportunitate, salva in omnibus principis reverentia, aperte innotescit. Unde cum legem de militibus ad conversionem minime recipiendis imperator promulgari iussisset, legem quidem latam, quam Deo adversari videbat, statim exhorruit, sed tamen illam ex iussione principis ad omnium notitiam ipse, qui eam inprobabat, insinuare non distulit.   Expleta humiliter, obœdientia ad eundem imperatorem : ' Ego,' inquit, ' iussioni subditus eamdem legem per diversas terrarum partes feci transmitti ; et quia lex ipsi omnipotenti Deo minime concordet, ecce per suggestionis meæ paginam serenissimis dominis nuntiavi. Utrobique ergo quæ debui exsolvi, qui et imperatori obœdientiam præbui et pro Deo quod sensi non tacui.' "

We have drawn attention to the importance of these words of Gregory the Great in vol. i. p. 155. The influence of these words of Gregory are again illustrated by the use made of them by the author of the ' Tractatus Eboracenses,' iv. (M. G. H., ' Libelli de Lite,' vol. iii. p. 671).

while Gregory the Great, with true humility, called himself the
servant of servants, and in his book on "Pastoral Care" he set
out the conduct of David as an example to all good subjects
who have bad rulers. David would not take advantage of the
opportunity to slay his persecutor, but repented that he had even
cut off the skirt of his cloak ; and the author cites the words of
Gregory the Great, in which he condemns even criticism of the
conduct of the ruler, lest men should transgress against God
who gave them their authority.[1] He looks upon the successive
deaths of Rudolph of Suabia and of Hermann of Luxemburg,
who had been set up against Henry IV., as examples of the
judgment of God upon those who revolted against their lawful
king, who had received his authority from God, for neither the
princes nor the people of that party could destroy that authority.[2]

The same principles were maintained by others of the imperialist party. In the work known as the 'Liber Canonum
contra Henricum quartum,' which, as it is thought, was com-
piled in the year 1085, the supporters of Henry IV. are represented as bringing forward the authority of St Augustine and

[1] 'De Unitate Ecclesiæ Conservanda,' ii. 1 : "Unde et Gregorius papa
cum esset summus pontifex et virtutum artifex, in tantum se infra omnes
humiliavit, ut primus ipse in epistolis
suis servum servorum Dei se appel-
averit et hoc humilitatis nomen ad
posteros quoque transmiserit. Qui in
libro pastoralis curæ proposuit de
bonis subditis et malis rectoribus exemplum Saulis et David, qui certe,
dum eum posset eundemque persecu-
torem suum occidere, noluit occidere,
eo quod esset christus Domini, insuper et viros suos, ne consurgerent
in eum legitur sermonibus confregisse
et, quia vel oram chlamydis suæ ipse
præcidisset, pœnituisse. 'Si quando,'
inquit, 'contra rectores vel in minimis
lingua labatur, per afflictionem pœni-
tentiæ cor prematur, et cum præ-
positæ potestati aliquis prælata est,
eius iudicium, a quo sibi prælata est,
perhorrescat ; quia, cum in præposi-
tos,' ait, 'delinquimus, eius ordina-

tioni, qui eos nobis prætulit, obvi-
amus.'"
   Cf. id., ii. 15 ; cf. vol. i. p 152,
153.
   [2] Id., i. 13 : "Duo enim reges, unus
post unum, substituti sunt nostris
temporibus a parte principum, et partem regni tenuerunt, et non totum ;
quod scilicet 'totum' habet magnum
pietatis mysterium in unitate fidelium.
Sed quia hoc consilium et hoc opus
ex hominibus erat, dissolutum est,
quod ex Deo non erat, quoniam post
breve temporis spatium ipsam quoque
partem regni utrique amiserunt, et
unus in prælio, alter in expugnatione
unius castelli miserabiliter perierunt,
superstite eo cui potestas data est a
Deo, quam scilicet potestatem nec
principes nec populus partis illius
dissolvere potuerunt ullo modo, quando
quidem ipsi quoque regi possint iam
donante Deo filii succedere in regnum,
sicut ipse patribus suis successit in
regnum."

St John Chrysostom to prove the impropriety of the action of
Hildebrand in excommunicating Henry IV. The passage cited
from St Augustine affirms the divine origin of the temporal
authority, and the duty of obedience by Christian men even
to an unbelieving emperor such as Julian. The passage attributed to St John Chrysostom is the same as that quoted by
Atto of Vercelli, and sets out the principle that, while no man
can make himself king but only the people, when the king has
once been elected and confirmed the people cannot depose
him.[1] These words are again substantially reproduced in the
collection of Epistles, &c., of the Cardinals who were in opposition to Hildebrand and Urban II.[2]

Again, Sigebert of Gembloux, in a letter written in the name
of the clergy of Liège about the year 1103 against Pope
Paschal II., urges that even if the emperor were such as the
papal party represented him to be, his subjects must submit,
for it is their sins which merited such a ruler.[3]

The most complete statement, perhaps, of the doctrine of
non-resistance, and of the conception that the king is responsible only to God for his conduct, which is to be found in the
literature of this period, is contained in the treatise written by
Gregory of Catino in the name of the monks of Farfa, probably in the year 1111. He maintains very emphatically that
the royal or imperial authority could not be condemned or
overthrown by any man. The authority of the saints both of
the Old and New Testaments showed that rulers must be
endured rather than condemned ; no one of the saints and
prophets and other orthodox Christians had ever ventured to
condemn or depose a king or emperor, even though he had
been unjust or impious or heretical. That wisdom which is
Christ said, " By Me kings reign," and by Him therefore alone
can they be condemned. Saul and David sinned, but neither

---

[1] M. G. H., 'Libelli de Lite,' vol. i.
p. 491, 2 ; cf. p. 117.

[2] Id. id., vol. ii. p. 422.

[3] 'Leodicensium Epistola Adversus
Paschalem Papam,' 9 : " Nihil modo
pro imperatore nostro dicimus. Sed
hoc dicimus, quod, etiamsi talis esset,
tamen eum principari nobis pateremur ;
quia, ut talis nobis principetur, pec-
cando meremur. Esto, concedimus
vobis inviti eum talem esse, qualem
dicitis. Nec talis a nobis repellendus
esset armis contra eum sumptis, sed
precibus ad Deum fusis."

Samuel nor Nathan ventured to condemn them. Many kings and emperors both before and after the coming of Christ were wicked and heretical, but none of the prophets, or apostles, or saints condemned them or attempted to take from them the obedience and dignity which was their due, but left this to God, and endured their persecutions for Christ's sake ; even Christ Himself, while He lived in the flesh, condemned no man. Gregory then relates a number of examples of the conduct of the Christian Fathers, as illustrating this principle, and it is noteworthy that he points out quite correctly that Pope Gregory II. restrained the Italians when they wished to revolt against Leo the Iconoclast and to set up another emperor. Finally, summing up the whole matter, he urges that it is God only, the Almighty creator of kingdoms and empires, who can grant them or take them away, and that he who resists the powers that have been ordained by God resists the ordinance of God.[1]

[1] Gregorii Catinensis, ' Orthodoxa defensio imperialis.' 7. " Sublimiores vero potestates, id est regia vel imperialis magnitudo, a Deo aut permissa aut constituta, aut a nullo contemnatur aut condemnetur sive destruatur. Sanctorum habemus auctoritates plurimorum et in testamento veteri et in nova gratia evangelii, qui magis huiusmodi sufferentes portarunt quam condemnare presumpserunt. . . . Quod si ita habetur, certissime in omnium auctoritatibus sanctorum, prophetarum, apostolorum ac reliquorum orthodoxorum, quorum nullus potestatem regiam vel imperialem, licet iniquam, licet impiam, licet hereticam condemnare vel deponere ausus est nec aliquo modo presumpsit ; . . .

8. Veteris enim et novi actus historias relegentes et bonos principes invenimus et malos, sed nunquam repperimus conscripto iudicio ab aliquo sanctorum fuisse condempnatos. De ipsis enim sapientia, quæ Christus est, dicit : ' Per me reges regnant.' Per ipsum ergo solum condemnandi sunt, per

quem solum regnare noscuntur. Si quis vero id, quod soli Deo reservandum est, voluerit condemnare, nunquam evadit punitionem. Denique Saul peccavit et a Deo recessit et Deus ab eo, et tamen propheta Samuel non illum condemnare a se ausus est. David quoque regem tribus pessimis criminibus delinquentem propheta Natan non condemnavit, sed magis penitentem recepit. . . . Itaque si omnes discuciantur historiæ vel leges, contra hoc notissimum dictum non invenies proposicionem. Nam multi regum vel imperatorum et ante et post adventum Christi pessimi vel heretici fuerunt, quos prophetæ vel apostoli sanctique patres et reliqui doctores ecclesiæ ad mortem non condemnarunt nec debitum obsequium vel decus ipsis proprium abstulerunt, sed soli hoc Deo reliquerunt et eorum nephandas malicias vel persecuciones ad tempus Christi amore substinuerunt, quia eius omnimodis membra extiterunt. De quo dicit apostolus Johannes : ' Qui dicit se in Christo manere, sicut ipse ambulavit, debet

ambulare.' Christum enim, qui legem
non venit solvere, sed adimplere, neminem legimus condemnasse adhuc in
carne vivens. . . . Gregorius eciam
papa secundus Romanos omnesque
Italicos   Constantinopoli   pergere
atque Leonem augustum volentes in-
terficere et aliam imperatorem eligere
compescuit. Iusserat enim idem imperator sacras imagines deponi et impie
concremari et prefatum pontificem sibi
in hoc non obedientem crudeliter
occidi. . . .

10. Hæc idcirco omnia prænotavim-
us, ut Deum solummodo omnipotentem
regnorum et imperii omniumque potestatum ordinatorem, concessorem trans-
latoremque evidentissimis sanctorum
catholicorum documentis ostenderemus.
Ordinatas autem a Deo potestates qui
condemnare vel secundum apostolum eis
resistere presumit, Deo eiusque ordinationi resistit, quia non est potestas
nisi a Deo, et licet mala sit potestas,
sicut Saul vel sicut Nabuchodonosor et

multi alii ante adventum Domini in
diebus prophetarum, et post adventum
Domini temporibus apostolorum eorum-
que successorum orthodoxorum fuerunt,
nullus tamen eam condemnare vel ei
vectigal vel censum sive debitum honorem contemnere debet, maxime cum
dominus Christus et magister noster pro
se tributum reddere est dignatus. Si
enim ipse reddidit, qui pro nobis pauper
extitit nihilque in hoc seculo possedit,
quis demens, quis vecors, quis stultus
Christo religiosior aut sublimior vel esse
temptet sanctior ? Et quis præpotens
sine gravi offensione in Deum condemnare potest eum, quem Deus omnipotens, qui celestia simul et terrena mode-
ratur, inextimabili providentia suffert ?
Denique ipse solus ordinator et sibi
tempore placito cuiuscunque potestatis
interemptor est et translator, quia in
manu eius sunt omnes fines terræ
et ipse omnium flatum viventium
continet.''

CHAPTER V.

JUSTICE AND LAW.

WE have so far endeavoured to make it clear that the political theory of the eleventh and twelfth centuries held firmly to the principle of the divine origin and authority of government, and the conviction that its function was to maintain righteousness and justice. In the last chapter we have seen that with some writers, and especially among those who were engaged in defending the imperial position in the great conflict with the papacy, the principle of the divine nature of government sometimes passes into the conception that the authority of the ruler was in such a sense divine that it could never be resisted, whether it was used justly and wisely, or foolishly and unrighteously, and that the king was responsible for his actions to God only.

This conception was not unimportant, and indeed in later times, and especially in the seventeenth century, assumed a considerable significance. But it was not the normal theory of the Middle Ages, and we must now consider aspects of the political ideas and principles of those times which were both more completely developed in theory, and also much more closely related to the actual political and constitutional movements of these centuries.

As we have already seen, there were two traditions which had come down from the Fathers—the one, with which we have just dealt, that the authority of the king was always sacred, whether it was used justly or unjustly, the other, that as the function of kingship lay in maintaining justice and righteousness, he was no true king who did not behave justly, who did not govern himself and his people under the terms of righteousness and equity. In the first volume of this work it has been pointed out how fully this conception was developed, and how firmly it was held in the ninth century,[1] and as we shall presently see it was equally firmly maintained in the eleventh and twelfth centuries.

There was a related principle which had governed men's minds and controlled their actions in the earlier Middle Ages, which has also been fully dealt with in the first volume, and that is the principle that the just order of the State is embodied in its law, that to govern justly is to govern according to the law.[2] We have in the first part of this volume considered the high development of this conception in the feudal organisation of society, and in the principles of the feudal lawyers ; we have now to consider its place in the political circumstances and in the general political theory of this period.

And finally, we have in the first volume considered the early stages of the conception of the authority of the ruler as representing the authority of the community, and as being dependent upon the faithful discharge of the obligations which he had undertaken,[3] we must now consider the rapid development and the great importance of this principle in the Middle Ages.

We have already pointed out that the writers of the period with which we are dealing are united in maintaining that the purpose and function of all authority is to maintain righteousness and justice, that the ambiguities of St Augustine had no effect upon them. We must now observe that this principle was constantly drawn out to the very important conclusion that where there was no justice there was no King, but only a Tyrant. This distinction between the King and the Tyrant was indeed one of the most important of the political conceptions of the Middle Ages. The distinction is the same in principle as that of Aristotle, but it was not from him that it was drawn, at least directly. Directly it came to them from St Isidore of Seville [4] and the writers of the ninth century, and it is probable that it is Cicero from whom St Isidore derived it.

The most complete statement of the conception is to be found

---

[1] Cf. vol. i. chap. 18.　　　[3] Cf. vol. i. chap. 20.
[2] Cf. vol. i. chap. 19.　　　[4] Cf. vol. i. pp. 172-73 ; 221-28.

in the ' Policraticus ' of John of Salisbury. We shall have to discuss his political theory in detail presently, but we may begin by noticing some words in which he expresses this principle. This, he says, is the only or the supreme difference between the tyrant and the prince, that the prince governs the people according to law and obeys the law himself,[1] the tyrant is one who oppresses the people by violence, and is never satisfied unless he makes the law void and reduces the people to slavery.[2] The essence of kingship is respect for law and the just rights and liberties of the people, without them a man may have the name, but not the reality of authority. We can trace the significance of this conception through the whole political literature of the Middle Ages.

We have seen its great importance in the ninth century, and even in the scanty literature of political theory in the tenth and early eleventh centuries we find the essential principle firmly maintained. We have already referred to a passage in the ' Præloquiorum ' of Ratherius of Verona which has this meaning, but it is worth while to look at it again. There are certain qualities without which a man may indeed have the name but not the reality of kingship ; the king must be prudent, just, brave, and self-restrained ; the man who possesses these qualities, though he were a peasant, may not improperly be called a king—without them, even if a man held the dominion of the whole world, he could not justly be called a king, for when a man governs ill he loses his authority.[3] We

---

[1] John of Salisbury, ' Policraticus,' iv. 1 : " Est ergo tiranni et principis hæc differentia sola vel maxima, quod hic legi obtemperat, et eius arbitrio populum regit, cuius se credit ministrum."

[2] Id id., viii. 17 : " Est ergo tirannus, ut eum philosophi depinxerunt, qui violenta dominatione populum premit, sicut qui legibus regit princeps est. . . . Princeps pugnat pro legibus et populi libertate ; tirannus nil actum putat nisi leges evacuet et populum devocet in servitutem."

[3] Ratherius of Verona, ' Præloquiorum,' iii. 1. : " ' Rex es ' ? Dignitas, rogo, ipsa te dum delectat, instruat. Sunt quædam regalis ordinis insignia, quibus sine, etsi nomen utcumque, re tamen vera certe non potest consistere dignitas tanta. His ergo utere, his exercere, his exornare. Esto prudens, justus fortis et temperatus. . . . Hæ quatuor regales proprie noscuntur esse virtutes, ut cum his quilibet etiam rusticus, rex non incongrue dici ; sine his, nec ipse universam pene monarchiam obtinens mundi, quamquam abusive, rex valeat iuste vocari : male enim imperando, ut ait qui supra, summum imperium amittitur."

may put beside this a phrase from the " Proverbs " attributed
to that Wippo, from whose life of Conrad the Salic we have
already quoted. The king, he says, must learn and hearken
to the law, for to keep the law is to reign.[1]

We have begun by citing these phrases, not because they are
in themselves specially important, but only in order that we
may be clear that these principles were not merely thrown out
in the great conflicts of the eleventh and twelfth centuries, but
that they represent the normal convictions of mediæval society,
which were continuous with those of the ninth century. It is
true that these great conflicts forced men to consider over again
their principles, and to determine what practical action they
were prepared to take in order to enforce them ; the political
development of European civilisation from the middle of the
tenth century to the end of the thirteenth was indeed almost
incredibly rapid, and it would be absurd to imagine that the
ideas or principles embodied in these constitutional developments were not themselves greatly modified, or enlarged, in the
process ; but at least, as we understand it, the movement of
ideas was continuous and organic.

The principle that unless the king is just and rules according
to law he is no true king is the first principle of the mediæval
theory of government, and was firmly held even before the
great political agitations of the eleventh and twelfth centuries
compelled men to think out the real nature of their political
convictions. While, however, this is true, it is also true that
these great disturbances had in a very high degree the effect
of stimulating political reflection, and it is no doubt to this that
we owe it that, after the comparative silence of the tenth
century, we suddenly find ourselves, in the latter part of the
eleventh century, and in the twelfth, in face of a great pro-
duction of political pamphlets and treatises.

It is not our part here to trace the political and constitutional
movements of the several European countries, but the history

[1] Wippo, ' Proverbia '—

" Decet regem discere legem,
Audiat rex, quod præcipit lex,
Legem servare, hoc est regnare."

of political ideas would be unintelligible if we were not to bear
in mind something of the general nature of these movements.
We must not make the mistake of imagining that the interests
and energies of the European people were concentrated upon
the struggle between the Papacy and the Empire, or the related
conflicts of Church and State in the various European countries.
No doubt these were not only of high importance in themselves,
but they had a great influence in stimulating political thought.
And yet it may be doubted whether they had, taken by themselves, any serious effect on the constitutional development of
European civilisation. We hope in the next volume to examine the questions related to these conflicts in detail, and to
consider the nature of the oppositions or difficulties which lay
behind them. But the political or constitutional development
of Europe was not caused by them, or dependent upon them.
All this is familiar to the students of the constitutional history
of the European countries, but it is sometimes forgotten by
those who are not well acquainted with this.

The history of the political theory of the Middle Ages was
organically and continually related to the development of the
political civilisation of Europe ; no doubt, as we have constantly
endeavoured to show, it derives its terms, and much of its substantial tradition from the past, but it was shaped and moulded
in the actual movement of these times.

It was with the political agitations and revolts of Germany
in the latter part of the eleventh century that active political
speculation and controversy began. We cannot here deal with
the real nature of the circumstances which lay behind the
great revolt of the Saxons and Thuringians against Henry IV.
It is enough for our purpose to observe that it raised at once
the fundamental questions as to the nature and conditions of
political authority. We have cited the words of Ratherius and
Wippo as illustrating the commonplaces of literature before
the great movements of the eleventh century ; with the outbreak of the Saxon revolt against Henry IV. in 1073 these
commonplaces assumed another aspect, and became the foundations of a rapidly developing political theory.

We have already [1] referred to the terms of the demands
which Lambert of Hersfeld attributes to the Saxons and Thuringians in the revolt of 1073, but we must now consider these a
little more closely. They demand that he should do justice to
the Saxon princes whose properties he had confiscated without
legal process, and that he should do this in accordance with the
judgment of the princes, that he should put away from his court
the lowborn persons by whose counsels he had administered the
state, and should entrust the care of the great affairs of the
kingdom to the princes to whom this belonged, that he should
dismiss his concubines and restore the queen to her proper
position, and that he should do justice to those who asked for
it. If he would do these things they would with ready minds
obey him, under those terms which became free men born in a
free empire, but if he would not amend his ways, they as
Christian men would not associate with one who was guilty of
the worst crimes. They had indeed sworn obedience to him,
but only as to a king who would uphold the Church of God,
and would rule justly and lawfully according to ancestral
custom, and would maintain the rank and dignity, and hold
inviolate the laws proper to every man. If he violated these
things they would not hold themselves bound by their oath, but
would wage a just war against him as a barbarian enemy, and
an oppressor of the Christian name, and would fight till their
last breath for the Church of God, for the Christian faith, and
for their own liberty. [2]

[1] Cf. pp. 112, 113.

[2] Lambert of Hersfeld, 'Annales,' A.D.
1073 (p. 196): " Ut principibus Saxoniæ
quibus sine legitima discussione bona
sua ademerat, secundum principum
suorum iurisdictionem satisfaceret . . .
ut vilissimos homines, quorum consilio
seque remque publicam praecipiter dedisset, de palatio eiceret, et regni
negocia regni principibus, quibus ea
competerent, curanda atque adminis-
trada permitteret : ut abdicato grege
concubinarum, quibus contra scita
canonum attrito frontis rubore incubabat, reginam, quam sibi secundum

ecclesiasticas traditiones thori sociam
regnique consortem delegisset, coniugali loco haberet et diligeret ; ut cetera
flagitiorum probra, quibus dignitatem
regiam adolescens infamaverat, nunc
saltem maturato sensu et ætate abdicaret. Postremo per Deum rogant,
ut iusta postulantibus sponte annueret,
nec sibi magni cuiusquam et inusitati
facinoris necessitatem impeneret. Si
ita faceret, se promptissimo animo ei
sicut actenus servituros, eo tamen
modo, quo ingenuos homines atque in
libero imperio natos regi servire opor-
teret ; sin autem, christianos se esse,

As we have just said, we are not here concerned with the real nature of the revolt of the Saxons and its ultimate causes and character, it is not difficult to recognise even in this passage something of the complexity of the situation, and we cannot feel any confidence that these particular principles were urged by the leaders of the revolt against Henry IV. in these terms. We must indeed take them rather as representing the ideas and theories and, probably, the literary reminiscences of Lambert. But they are not the less significant on that account. The passage contains some constitutional conceptions with which we shall deal later, but in the meanwhile we can fix our attention on the sharp and definite character of the distinction between the king to whom men swear allegiance, and the unjust ruler who sets at naught the law and rights of his subjects, and to whom therefore men are under no obligations. It is the history of this conception which we must trace farther.

We may put alongside of this passage from Lambert the terms of a speech which Bruno, the author of the ' De Bello Saxonico,' puts into the mouth of Otto, who had been Duke of Bavaria. It is represented as addressed to the Saxons at "Normeslovo " in 1073. He exhorts them to rise against Henry, and urges upon them that the castles which Henry was building were intended to destroy their liberty, and in fiery terms he asks whether, when even slaves would not endure the injustice of their masters, they who were born in liberty were prepared to endure slavery. Perhaps, he says, as Christian men they feared to violate their oath of allegiance to the king ; yes ! but they were made to one who was indeed a king. While Henry was a king, and did those things which were proper to a king, he had kept the faith which he had sworn to him whole and undefiled, but when he ceased to be a king he was no longer such that he

nec velle hominis, qui fidem christi- anam capitalibus flagitiis prodidisset, communione maculari. . . . Sacramento se ei fidem dixisse, sed si ad ædifica- tionem, non ad destructionem ecclesiæ Dei, rex esse vellet, si iuste, si legitime, si more maiorum rebus moderaretur, si suum cuique ordinem, suam dignitatem, suas leges tutas inviolatasque manere pateretur. Sin ista prior ipse temer- asset, se iam sacramenti huius religione non teneri, sed quasi cum barbaro hoste et christiani nominis oppressore iustum deinceps bellem gesturos, et quoad ultima vitalis caloris scintilla superesset, pro ecclesia Dei, pro fide christiana, pro libertate etiam sua dimicaturos."

should keep faith to him. He had taken up arms, and adjured them to take up arms, not against the king, but against the unjust assailant of his liberty, not against his country, but for his country, and for that liberty which no good man would consent to lose except with his life.[1]

Lambert of Hersfeld sets out the same principle, but in more technical terms. He represents Otto as urging at another time that herein lay the difference between the king and the tyrant, that the tyrant compels the obedience of unwilling subjects by violence and cruelty, while the king governs his subjects by laws and ancestral custom.[2]

Berthold of Constance in his Annals for the year 1077 relates, as we have already mentioned,[3] how on Henry's return to Germany after his absolution by Hildebrand at Canossa, many of the clergy maintained that no one could judge or condemn a king however wicked and criminal. Berthold himself holds that this opinion is absurd, and cites, though without mentioning his source, St Isidore of Seville's phrases, that the king holds his title while he does right, if he acts wrongfully he loses it ; and maintains that those who do wickedly and unjustly are really tyrants, and are only improperly called kings.[4] The

[1] Bruno, 'De Bello Saxonico,' 25 : "Servi ære parati iniusta imperia dominorum non perferunt, et vos in libertate nati, æquo animo servitutem tolerabitis ? Fortasse quia Christiani estis, sacramenta regi facta violare timetis. Optime, sed regi. Dum mihi rex erat, et ea quæ sunt regis faciebat, fidelitatem quam ei iuravi, integram et impollutam servavi, postquam vero rex esse desivit, cui fidem servare deberem, non fuit. Itaque non contra regem, sed contra iniustum meæ libertatis ereptorem ; non contra patriam, sed pro patria et pro libertate mea, quam nemo bonus, nisi cum anima simul amittit, arma capio, et ut vos ea mecum capiatis expostulo."

[2] Lambert of Hersfeld, 'Annales,' A.D. 1076 (p. 249): "Hanc regis ac tiranni esse distantiam, quod hic vi atque crudelitate obedientiam extorqueat ab invitis, ille legibus ac more

maiorum moderetur subiectis præcipiatque facienda."

[3] See p. 119.

[4] Berthold of Constance, 'Annales,' 1077 A.D. (p. 297) : "Recte igitur faciendo nomen regis tenetur, alioquin amittitur, unde est hoc vetus elogium : 'Rex eris, si recte facis ; si non facis non eris.' . . . Si autem nec iuste iudicent, nec pie condescendant, neque regulam officii sui vel sola saltem nominationis imagine minimum quid attingant, set potius ultra modum et insanias ethnicorum superlativas, vitæ facinorosæ et luxuriosæ libertatem nefandissimi omnifariam et portentuosi exerceant, crudelissima dominandi maiestate populum supprimant, et miserrime suppressum devorent, et ad interneciem usque consumant, cur non magis proprie tyranni in huiusmodi fortissimi, quam abusive et absque rei veritate reges sint nuncupandi."

same phrases are again quoted by Hugh, Abbot of Flavigny, in defending the deposition of Henry IV.[1]

Herrand, Bishop of Halberstadt, writing in the name of Louis the Count of Thuringia about 1094 or 1095, expresses the same conceptions, but in a more developed form, in his answer to a letter of Waltram the Bishop of Naumburg. Waltram had urged the authority of the words of St Paul : " Let every soul be subject to the higher powers, for there is no power but of God." Herrand replies that Waltram was misinterpreting St Paul, for if every authority was from God how could the prophet (Hosea viii. 4) have spoken of princes who reigned, but not as of God. They were willing to obey an ordered power, but how could such a government as that of Henry IV. be called an order at all ; it is not order to confound right and wrong. Again, in a later passage, answering Waltram's contention that concord was useful to the kingdom, Herrand replies that it was absurd to speak thus of a society which could not be called a kingdom, for a kingdom is something rightful ; could that be called a kingdom where innocence was oppressed, where there was no place for reason, for judgment, or for counsel, where every desire was reckoned to be lawful ? Such a kingdom should rather be called a congregation of the wicked, a council of vanity, the dregs of iniquity ; in such a kingdom concord is unprofitable. Among good men indeed concord is praiseworthy, but among evil men it is blameworthy ; what man in his right mind would speak with approval of a concord of robbers, of thieves, of unclean persons ?[2]

---

[1] Hugo, Abbas Flaviniacensis, Chronicon, ii. fol. 111.

[2] Herrandus, ' Epistola ' : " Ad subiectionem domini Henrici ; quem imperatorem dicunt, nos invitas, et in quantum intelligere datur, ut per omnia subditi simus, quasi apostolico argumento necessitatem imponis, dicens : ' Omnis anima potestatibus superioribus subdita sit ; non est enim potestas nisi a Deo. Qui ergo potestati resistit, Dei ordinationi resistit.' Quam apostoli sententiam te male intelligere, peius interpretari dicimus. Si enim omnis potestas a Deo est, ut tu intelligis, quid est, quod de quibusdam dicit Dominus per prophetam : ' Ipsi regnaverunt, et non ex me, principes extiterut, et non cognovi.' . . . Prævidens per Spiritum sanctum apostolus te tuique similes hereticos in ecclesia emersuros, qui ' bonum malum, malum bonum ' dicerent, qui ' tenebras lucem et lucem tenebras ' ponerent, qui de sententiis veritatis occasionem inducendi erroris captarent, cum præmisisset : ' Non est potestas nisi a Deo ' ut coniecturam reprobi intellectus amputaret : ' Quæ autem sunt,' inquit, ' a Deo ordinata sunt.' Da igitur potestatem

The distinction between the true king and the tyrant,
between just and legal authority, which was the characteristic
of the true commonwealth, and mere violence and unjust
power, was indeed firmly fixed in the minds of all mediæval
thinkers, and we find it clearly set out even in the writings of
those who were the strongest upholders of the imperial or royal
authority.   We have already had occasion to discuss the
opinions of Hugh of Fleury as represented in his treatise on the
royal and sacerdotal powers, addressed to Henry I. of England.
We have seen how stoutly he maintains, against the apparent
meaning of certain phrases of Hildebrand, that the authority of
the king is from God, and that he even repeats those phrases,
which had been used by Ambrosiaster and Cathulfus, in which
the king is described as bearing the image of God, while the
bishop bears that of Christ.[1]   And while, as we have seen, he
holds very clearly that the function of the king is to maintain
justice and equity, he also urges that the honour due to those
in authority must not be measured by their personal qualities,
but by the place which they hold, and that therefore even
heathen rulers must receive the honour due to their position.[2]

ordinatam et non resistimus, immo
dabimus ilico manus. Miror autem, si
in te vel gutta sanguinis est, quod non
erubescis dominum Henricum regem
dicere vel ordinem habere. An ordo
tibi videtur ius dare sceleri, fas ne-
fasque, divina et humana confundere.
.   .   .   .
Quomodo autem concordiam utilem
asseris regno, quod nullum est ? Regnum quippe quasi rectum dicitur.
An regnum recte dicitur, ubi omnis
innocentia laborat, ubi neque rationi,
neque iudicio, neque consilio locus est ;
sed quidquid libitum id licitum putatur?
Tale regnum ecclesiam malignantium,
concilium vanitatis, denique totius iniquitatis sentinam rectius appellaveris.
Tali regno nos concordiam inutilem
dicimus.   Sicut enim inter bonos
laudabilis, ita inter malos repre-
hensibilis concordia est. Quis enim
concordiam latronum, quis furum, quis

immundorum, nisi mente captus, ap-
probat ? ”

[1] See pp. 98, 111.

[2] Hugh of Fleury, ‘Tractatus de regia
potestate et sacerdotali dignitate,’ i. 4 :
“ Honorandi etiam sunt omnes, qui in
potestate sunt positi, ab his quibus
præsunt, etsi non propter se, vel propter ordinem et gradum, quem a Deo
acceperunt. Sic enim iubet apostolus
dicens. ‘ Omnibus,’ inquit, ‘ potestatibus sublimioribus subditi estote.
Non est enim potestas nisi a Deo.
Quæ enim sunt, a Deo ordinatæ sunt.’
Ipse nempe, sicut iam superius osten-
sum est, per pravas malorum hominum
voluntates explere nonnumquam con-
suevit suam æquam ac iustissimam
voluntatem, sicut per Judeos malivolos,
bona voluntate Patris, Christus pro
nobis occisus est. Quod scientes atque
credentes, et præceptum apostoli pariter
observantes, etiam gentiles in potestate

And yet he also warns kings and princes and tyrants that those who refuse to keep the commandments of God are wont to lose their power and authority, and that it frequently happens that the people revolt against such a king.[1]

The author of the controversial pamphlets which have been published as the ' Tractatus Eboracenses ' sets the temporal power higher perhaps than any other writer of the Middle Ages, and in a strange phrase which has some resemblance to that of Hugh of Fleury he speaks of the priest as representing the human nature of Christ, while the king represents the divine nature.[2] But even he recognises that there have been kings who were no true kings but only tyrants.[3] He does not indeed say that they are to be resisted, but he is aware of the distinction between the true and false king. In another passage he makes the distinction very clear between the authority which is always good, and the person of the ruler who may be evil. Our Lord had bidden men give to Cæsar that which was Cæsar's. He did not say, render to Tiberius that which is

positos honoramus, et mala quam nobis ingerunt æquanimiter toleramus, ne Deo iniuriam facere videamur, qui illos ordinis titulo super homines extulit atque sublimavit, licet illi indigni sint ordine quo fruuntur.

[1] Id. id., i. 9 : " Porro ipsi reges et principes atque tyranni, dum Deo subesse et eius præcepta custodire renuunt, dominationis suæ vim et potestatem plerumque solent amittere, sicut primus homo dominationis suæ vigorem et dignitatis prærogativam post suam transgressionem cognoscitur amisisse. Postquam nempe divino noluit esse subiectus imperio, ipsa etiam corporis sui membra sibi rebellare et ignitos aculeos carnalis concupiscentiæ statim contra suam voluntatem in sua carne sevire persensit. Pisces quoque maris et volucres cæli et bestiæ agri, quæ illi ante comissum facinus quasi privata animalia subiacebant, iugum dominationis eius a se ceperunt abigere, et iam ei amplius solito servire nolebant. Quæ tamen omnia vi rationis suæ cæpit

domum paulatim sibi subigere et ad suos usus exquisitis artibus retorquere. Itaque pari modo regi Deo contrario populus sibi subiectus multocies incipit adversus eum insurgere et variis ac multiplicibus insidiis illum appetere et multis adversitatibus fatigare."

[2] Tractatus Eboracenses,' iv. (M. G. H., ' Libelli de Lite,' vol. iii. p. 666) : " Sacerdos quippe aliam præfigurabat in Christo naturam, id est hominis, rex aliam, id est Dei. Ille superiorem qua equalis est Deo patri, iste inferiorem qua minor est patre."

[3] Id. id. id. : " Similiter et de ceteris regibus sentiendum est, qui in spiritu Dei venerunt et virtute, non de illis qui regnaverunt et non ex Deo, quoniam non reges, sed tiranni fuerunt et in spiritu maligno et contraria virtute venerunt. Quorum unus fuit Ozias, qui, quoniam per superbiam usurpavit sacerdotium, lepra percussus est, quoniam non erat Christus Domini, nec cum Domino unus erat spiritus, sed agebatur spiritu huius mundi."

Tiberius'; render to the authority, not to the person, the person may be evil, the authority is just, Tiberius may be wicked, but Cæsar is good. Render, therefore, not to the evil person, to the wicked Tiberius, but to the just authority, to the good Cæsar, that which is his.[1]

If these are the judgments, even of those who defended the temporal authority against what they conceived to be the unreasonable claims of the spiritual power, we need not be surprised that the supporters of the political or ecclesiastical opposition pressed them still more emphatically. We shall have occasion presently to deal with the position of Manegold in detail, but in the meanwhile we may observe how sharply he draws the distinction between kingship and tyranny, and how emphatically he states the conclusion that the ruler who governs tyrannically has no claim whatever upon the obedience of his people. The people, he says, did not exalt the ruler over themselves in order that he should have freedom to tyrannise over them, but in order that he should defend them from the tyranny of others. It is therefore clear that when he who was elected to restrain the wicked and to defend the good, actually becomes evil, oppresses the good, and is guilty of that tyranny which it was his duty to repel, he justly falls from the dignity which was granted to him, and that the people are free from their subjection to him, inasmuch as he has violated that agreement in virtue of which he was appointed.[2]

As we have already said, the conception of the fundamental difference between the king and the tyrant is developed more

---

[1] 'Tractatus Eboracenses,' iv. (M. G. H., 'Libelli de Lite,' vol. iii. p. 671) : "Reddite, inquit, quæ sunt cesaris cesari, non quæ sunt Tyberii Tyberio. Reddite potestati, non persone. Persona enim nequam, sed iusta potestas. Iniquus Tyberius, sed bonus cesar. Reddite ergo non personæ nequam, non iniquo Tyberio, sed iuste potestati et bono cesari que sua sunt."

[2] Manegold, 'Ad Gebehardum,' xxx. : " Necesse est ergo, qui omnium curam gerere, omnes debet gubernare, maiore gratia virtutum super ceteros debeat splendere, traditam sibi potestatem summo equitatis libramine studeat administrare. Neque enim populus ideo eum super se exaltat, ut liberam in se exercendæ tyrannidis facultatem concedat, sed ut a tyrannide ceterorum et improbitate defendat. Atque, cum ille, qui pro coercendis pravis, probis defendendis eligitur, pravitatem in se fovere, bonos conterere, tyrannidem, quam debuit propulsare, in subiectos ceperit ipse crudelissime exercere, nonne clarum est, merito illum a concessa dignitate cadere, populum ab eius

clearly and completely by John of Salisbury than by any other writer of these centuries. We have from time to time cited various passages from his 'Policraticus,' but his position in the history of political theory is so important and so representative that we must consider it briefly as a whole.

We have already cited some of the phrases in which he draws out the distinction between the king and the tyrant; we must look at these more closely. This, he says, is the only or the greatest difference between the prince and the tyrant, that the prince obeys the law, and governs the people, whose servant he reckons himself to be, according to the law; he claims, in the name of the law, the first place in carrying out the public offices, and in submitting to the burdens of the commonwealth; he is superior to other men in this, that while others have their particular obligations, he is bound to bear all the burdens of the State. The prince is endued with the authority of all, in order that he may the better minister to the needs of all. The will of the prince is never contrary to justice. The prince is the public authority, and an image on earth of the divine majesty, and his authority is derived from God. The passage concludes with those famous phrases of the Code in which it is said that the authority of the prince depends upon the law, and that it is a thing greater than empire to submit the princely authority to the laws.[1]

dominio et subiectione liberum existere, cum pactum, pro quo constitutus est, constet illum prius irrupisse ? . . .

Ut enim imperatoribus et regibus ad tuenda regni gubernacula fides et reverentia est adhibenda, sic certe, sic firma ratione, si tyrannidem exercere eruperint, absque omni fidei lesione vel pietatis iactura nulla fidelitas est vel reverentia impendenda."

[1] John of Salisbury, 'Policraticus,' iv. 1: "Est ergo tiranni et principis hæc differentia sola vel maxima, quod hic legi obtemperat, et eius arbitrio populum regit cuius se credit ministrum, et in rei publicæ muneribus exercendis et oneribus subeundis legis beneficio sibi primum vendicat locum, in eoque præfertur ceteris, quod, cum

singuli teneantur ad singula, principi onera imminent universa. Unde merito in eum omnium subditorum potestas confertur, ut in utilitate singulorum et omnium exquirenda et facienda sibi ipse sufficiat, et humanæ rei publicæ status optime disponatur, dum sunt alter alterius membra. In quo quidem optimum vivendi ducem naturam sequimur, quæ macrocosmi sui, id est, mundi minoris, hominis scilicet, sensus universos in capite collocavit, et ei sic universa membra subiecit, ut omnia recte moveantur, dum sani capitis sequuntur arbitrium. Tot ergo et tantis privilegiis apex principalis extollitur et splendescit, quot et quanta sibi ipse necessaria credidit. Recte quidam, quia populo nichil utilius est quam ut principis

For the definition of the tyrant we must turn to a later passage, where we find it said that the philosophers have described him as one who oppresses the people by violent domination, while the prince is one who rules by the laws. The prince strives for the maintenance of the law and the liberty of the people ; the tyrant is never satisfied until he has made void the laws and has reduced the people to slavery. The prince is the image of God, and is to be loved and cherished ; while the tyrant is the image of wickedness, and often it is meet that he should be slain. The origin of tyranny is iniquity, and it is this poison of unrighteousness and injustice which is the source of all the troubles and conflicts of the world.[1]

It is specially important to observe that to John of Salisbury the essence of the distinction between the tyrant and the prince lies in his relation to law. In other places he enforces the principle in very interesting phrases. There are some, he says, who whisper or even publicly proclaim that the prince is not subject to the law, and that whatever pleases him has the force of law ; that is, not merely that which he, as legislator, has established as law in accordance with equity, but whatever he may chance to will. The truth is, that when they thus with-

necessitas expleatur ; quippe cum nec voluntas eius iustitiæ inveniatur adversa. Est ergo, ut eum plerique diffiniunt, princeps potestas publica et in terris quædam divinæ maiestatis imago. . . . Omnis etenim potestas a Domino Deo est, et cum illo fuit semper, et est ante evum. . . . Digna siquidem vox est, ut ait Imperator, maiestate regnantis se legibus alligatum principem profiteri. Quia de iuris auctoritate principis pendet auctoritas ; et revera maius imperio est, summittere legibus principatum (Cod. i. 14. 4) ; ut nichil sibi princeps licere opinetur, quod a iustitiæ æquitate discordet.''

[1] John of Salisbury, ' Policraticus,' viii. 17 : '' Est ergo tirannus, ut eum philosophi depinxerunt, qui violenta dominatione populum premit, sicut qui legibus regit princeps est. . . . Princeps pugnat pro legibus et populi libertate ; tirannus nil actum putat nisi lcges evacuet et populum devocet in servitutem. Imago quædam divinitatis est princeps, et tirannus est adversariæ fortitudinis et Luciferianæ pravitatis imago, siquidem illum imitatur qui affectavit sedem ponere ad aquilonem et similis esse altissimo, bonitate tamen deducta. . . . Imago deitatis, princeps amandus, venerandus est et colendus ; tirannus, pravitatis imago, plerumque etiam occidendus. Origo tiranni iniquitas est et de radice toxicata mala et pestifera germinat et pullulat arbor securi qualibet succidenda. Nisi enim iniquitas et iniustitia caritatis exterminatrix tirannidem procurasset, pax secura et quies perpetua in evum populos possedisset, nemoque cogitaret de finibus producendis.''

draw the king from the bonds of the law they make him an outlaw. John does not indeed desire to destroy the dispensing power of the ruler, but he refuses to submit the permanent commands or prohibitions of the law to his caprice.[1] We may compare with these words those of another passage in which he urges that all men are bound by the law ; the prince is said to be free from the law, not because he may do unjust things, but because his character should be such that he follows equity and serves the commonwealth, not from fear of punishment, but for love of justice, and that he always prefers the convenience of others to his own personal desires. It is indeed meaningless to speak of the prince's desires in respect to public matters, for he may not desire anything but what law and equity and the common good require ; his will has indeed in these matters the force of law, but only because it in no way departs from equity. The prince is the servant of the public good and the slave of equity, and bears the public person, because he punishes all injuries and crimes with equity.[2]

[1] Id. id., iv. 7 : " Procedant nunc dealbatores potentum, susurrent aut, si hoc parum est, publice præconentur principem non esse legi subiectum, et quod ei placet, non modo in iure secundum formam æquitatis condendo, sed qualitercumque, legis habere vigorem. Regem quem legis nexibus subtrahunt, si volunt et audent, exlegem faciant, ego, non modo his renitentibus sed mundo reclamante, ipsos hac lege teneri confirmo. In quo enim, inquit, qui nec fallit nec fallitur, iudicio iudicaveritis, iudicabimini. Et certe iudicium gravissimum in his qui præsunt fiet, eo quod mensura bona conferta coagitata et supereffluens refundetur in sinus eorum. Nec tamen dispensationem legis subtraho manibus potestatum, sed perpetuam præceptionem aut prohibitionem habentia libito eorum nequaquam arbitror subponenda. In his itaque dumtaxat quæ mobilia sunt, dispensatio verborum admittitur ; ita tamen ut compensatione honestatis aut utilitatis mens legis integra conservetur."

[2] Id. id., iv. 2 : " Omnes itaque necessitate legis servandæ tenentur adstricti, nisi forte aliquis sit cui iniquitatis licentia videatur indulta. Princeps tamen legis nexibus dicitur absolutus, non quia ei iniqua liceant, sed quia is esse debet, qui non timore penæ sed amore iustitiæ æquitatem colat, rei publicæ procuret utilitatem, et in omnibus aliorum commoda privatæ præferat voluntati. Sed quis in negotiis publicis loquetur de principis voluntate, cum in eis nil sibi velle liceat, nisi quod lex aut æquitas persudet aut ratio communis utilitatis inducit ? Eius namque voluntas in his vim debet habere iudicii ; et rectissime quod ei placet in talibus legis habet vigorem, eo quod ab æquitatis mente eius sententia non discordet. De vultu tuo, inquit, iudicium meum prodeat, oculi tui videant æquitatem ; iudex etenim incorruptus est cuius sententia ex contemplatione assidua imago est æquitatis. Publicæ ergo utilitatis

It is important to observe, in considering these passages, how much John of Salisbury is affected by the revived study of the Roman law ; his reference to Vacarius, and the progress of the influence of the Roman jurisprudence in England, in spite of the attempts to restrain it, is well known ; [1] and the effects of his own study are very clearly illustrated in the passages we have just discussed. He is evidently gravely concerned to find a just meaning for such phrases, as that the prince is " legibus solutus," or " quod principi placuit legis habet vigorem," for evidently they had, by some, been used to defend the conception that the prince was not subject to the law, and that even his capricious desires might override the law. Such conceptions seem to him monstrous and impossible. The will of the prince which is to have the force of law can only be that which is in accordance with equity and law. He is only free in relation to law in the sense that his true character is that of a man who freely obeys the law of equity. It is specially interesting to notice his phrase about the result of withdrawing the prince from the authority of the law, that the true result of this is to make him an outlaw—that is, a person to whom all legal obligations cease.

To appreciate the significance of these principles of John of Salisbury completely, we must bear in mind not only the traditions which we have considered in this chapter, but also the whole tradition of the feudal lawyers, culminating in the dogmatic affirmation of Bracton that the king is under the law. [2] It is evident that John approaches the discussion of these questions formally through the medium of the Roman law and other literary traditions, but that his actual judgment corresponds with and expresses the effects of the political traditions and the practical circumstances and necessities of his own time.

The legitimate prince or ruler is thus distinguished, in John of Salisbury's mind, by this, that he governs according to law.

---

minister et æquitatis servus est princeps, et in eo personam publicam gerit, quod omnium iniurias et dampna sed et crimina omnia æquitate media punit."

[1] John of Salisbury, 'Policraticus,' viii. 22.

[2] Cf. p. 67.

What is then the law to which he is subject, and which it is his function to administer? It does not represent the arbitrary will of the ruler, nor even of the community. John finds expression for his principles in terms derived partly from the contemporary Civilians and partly from the Digest. The prince, he says, must remember that his justice is subordinate to that of God, whose justice is eternal and whose law is equity. He defines equity in terms used by a number of the Civilians, as "rerum convenientia . . . quæ cuncta coæquiparat ratione et imparibus (in paribus) rebus paria iura desiderat," and as that which gives to every man his own. Law is the interpreter of this equity, and he cites the words of Chrysippus as quoted in the Digest, that it is law which orders all things divine and human, and those of Papinian and Demosthenes, that law is formed and given by God, is taught by wise men, and established by the commonwealth. All, therefore, he concludes, are bound to obey the law, unless perchance some one claims to have licence to commit iniquity.[1]

In another place John of Salisbury takes from the work which he knew as the 'Institutio Traiani,' and attributed to Plutarch, a definition of the commonwealth which represents the conception that all political authority embodies the principles of equity and reason. The commonwealth, he represents the work as saying, is a body which is animated by the benefit of the divine gift, and is conducted at the

[1] Id. id., iv. 2: "Nec in eo sibi principes detrahi arbitrentur, nisi iustitiæ suæ statuta præferenda crediderint iustitiæ Dei, cuius iustitia iustitia in evum est, et lex eius æquitas. Porro æquitas, ut iuris periti asserunt, rerum convenientia est, quæ cuncta coæquiparat ratione et imparibus (in paribus?) rebus paria iura desiderat, in omnes æquabilis, tribuens unicuique quod suum est. Lex vero eius interpres est, utpote cui æquitatis et iustitiæ voluntas innotuit. Unde et eam omnium rerum divinarum et humanarum compotem esse Crisippus asseruit, ideoque præstare omnibus bonis et malis et tam rerum quam hominum principem et ducem esse. Cui Papinianus, vir quidem iuris experientissimus, et Demosthenes, orator præpotens, videntur suffragari et omnium hominum subicere obedientiam, eo quod lex omnis inventio quidem est et donum Dei, dogma sapientum, correctio voluntariorum excessuum, civitatis compositio, et totius criminis fuga; secundum quam decet vivere omnes qui in politicæ rei universitate versantur. Omnes itaque necessitate legis servandæ tenentur adstricti, nisi forte aliquis sit cui iniquitatis licentia videatur indulta."

Cf. vol. ii. pp. 7, 8, and vol. i. p. 56 (Digest, i. 3. 1 and 2).

bidding of the highest equity, and controlled by the rule of reason.[1]

The authority of the law and the State is the authority of justice and reason, and it is impossible therefore for John to conceive of any ruler as being legitimate, or as having any real claim to authority, unless he is obedient to the law, which is the embodiment of justice and reason.

What are then the conclusions which John of Salisbury draws from these principles, in regard to the practical questions of the relations of subjects and rulers ? It is true that he is a little hampered by the recollection of the Augustinian and Gregorian tradition ; that he remembers that in the patristic tradition the evil ruler may be the instrument of God's punishment upon an evil people.[2] And in one passage he

---

[1] John of Salisbury, ' Policraticus,' v. 2 : " Est autem res publica, sicut Plutarco placet, corpus quoddam quod divini muneris beneficio animatur, et summæ æquitatis agitur nutu et regitur quodam moderamine rationis."

For a discussion of this work see C. C. Webb's edition of the ' Policraticus,' vol. i. p. 280, note 15.

[2] Id. id., v. 4 : " Nos autem, quibus de celo veritas illuxit, non deorum, qui nulli sunt, sed veri Dei ministris et amicis magnam reverentiam credimus exhibendam ; sed et inimicis eius interdum, quoniam hoc ipse præcepit qui sæpe maximam ad eruditionem suorum pessimis hominibus contulit potestatem. Unde illud : ' Subiecti estote omni humanæ creaturæ propter Deum, sive regi quasi præcellenti sive ducibus tamquam ab eo missis ad vindictam malefactorum laudem vero bonorum.' Et illud : ' Servi, subditi estote dominis vestris, non tantum bonis et modestis sed etiam discolis.' "

Id. id., viii. 18 : " Ministros Dei tamen tyrannos esse non abnego, qui in utroque primatu, scilicet animarum et corporum, iusto suo iudicio esse voluit per quos punirentur mali et corrigerentur et exercerentur boni. Nam et peccata populi faciunt regnare ypocritam et, sicut Regum testatur historia, defectus sacerdotum in populo Dei tirannos induxit. Siquidem primi patres et patriarchæ vivendi ducem optimam naturam secuti sunt. Successerunt duces a Moyse sequentes legem, et iudices qui legis auctoritate regebant populum ; et eosdem fuisse legimus sacerdotes. Tandem in furore Domini dati sunt reges, alii quidem boni, alii vero mali. Senuerat enim Samuel et, cum filii eius non ambulaverunt in viis suis sed avaritiam et immunditias sectarentur, populus, qui fortasse et ipse meruerat ut ei tales præessent sacerdotes, a Deo, quem contempserat, sibi regem extorsit. Electus est ergo Saul, regis tamen iure prædicto, id est qui filios eorum tolleret ut faceret aurigas, et filias ut panificæ fierent et focariæ, et agros et prædia ut ea pro libito distribueret servis suis, populumque totum servitutis premeret iugo. Idem tamen christus Domini dictus est, et tirannidem exercens regium non amisit honorem. Incussit enim Deus timorem omnibus, ut eum quasi minis-

seems at least doubtful whether it is lawful for a man to seek
the death of him to whom he is bound by fidelity and oath,
and he mentions with approbation the conduct of David who
would not use violence against Saul, and of those who in
oppression pray to God for deliverance.[1]

When, however, we have allowed for certain qualifications, it
remains true that John of Salisbury maintains very emphatically that the tyrant has no rights against the people, and may
justly and rightfully be slain. He deals with the matter first
at the end of the third book, and says that it is not only lawful
to kill the tyrant, but equitable and just, for it is right that he
who takes the sword should perish by the sword. That is, he
who usurps the sword, not he who receives it from the Lord.
He who receives his authority from God, serves the law, and
is the minister of justice and the law, while he who usurps

trum Domini, cuius quodammodo
gestabat imaginem, venerarentur.
Amplius quidem adiciam; etiam
tyranni gentium reprobati ab eterno
ad mortem ministri Dei sunt et christi
Domini appellantur. Unde propheta;
'Ingredientur portas Babilonis duces,'
videlicet Cirus et Darius; 'ego enim
mandavi sanctificatis meis et vocavi
fortes meos in ira mea et exultantes in
gloria mea.' Ecce quia sanctificatos
vocat Medos et Persas, non quod
sancti essent, sed Domini adversus
Babilonem implebant voluntatem.
Alias quoque : 'Ecce ego adducam,'
inquit, 'Nabugodonosor servum meum,
et, quia bene michi servivit apud Tirum,
dabo ei Egiptum.' Omnis autem
potestas bona, quoniam ab eo est a quo
solo omnia et sola sunt bona. Utenti
tamen interdum bona non est aut
patienti sed mala, licet quod ad uni-
versitatem sit bona, illo faciente qui
bene utitur malis nostris. Sicut
enim in pictura fuscus aut niger color
aut aliquis alius per se consideratus
indecens est, et tamen in tota pictura
decet ; sic per se quædam inspecta
indecora et mala, relata ad universi-
tatem bona apparent et pulchra, eo

omnia sibi adaptante cuius omnia opera
valde sunt bona. Ergo et tiranni
potestas bona quidem est, tirannide
tamen nichil peius. Est enim tirannis
a Deo concessæ homini potestatis
abusus. In hoc tamen malo multus
et magnus est bonorum usus. Patet
ergo non in solis principibus esse
tirannidem, sed omnes esse tirannos
qui concessa desuper potestate in
subditis abutuntur."

[1] Id. id., viii. 20 : "Hoc tamen
cavendum docent historiæ, ne quis illius
moliatur interitum cui fidei aut sacramenti religione tenetur astrictus. . . .
Nam et Sedechias ob neglectam fidei
religionem legitur captivatus ; et quod
in alio regum Iudæ non memini, eruti
sunt oculi eius, quia Deum, cui iuratur,
etiam cum ex iusta causa cavetur
tiranno, lapsus in perfidiam non proposuit ante conspectum suum. . . .
(The example of David and Saul.) . . .
Et hic quidem modus delendi tirannos
utilissimus et tutissimus est, si qui
premuntur ad patrocinium clementiæ
Dei humiliati confugiant et puras
manus levantes ad Dominum devotis
precibus flagellum quo affliguntur
avertant."

authority subjects the law to his will.   It is therefore right
that the laws should take arms against him who disarms them.
There are many forms of treason, but there is none graver than
that which attacks the whole system of justice.   If in the case
of treason any one may act as a prosecutor, how much more in
the case of that crime which attacks the laws which should
control even the emperor.   Assuredly no one will avenge the
public enemy, and he who does not attack him is guilty of a
crime against himself and the whole body of the Commonwealth.[1]

These principles are constantly maintained by him.   We
have already seen how, in that passage in which he describes
the character of the tyrant, he says that while the prince, who
bears the divine image, is to be loved and venerated, the
tyrant, who has the image of wickedness, often ought to be
slain.   Again, in the same chapter, where he has urged that
there may be ecclesiastical as well as secular tyrants, he says
that if the secular tyrant may properly, according to divine
and human law, be slain, we cannot think that the tyrant who
bears the priesthood is to be loved and cherished.   And again,
in a later chapter, he says that it is clear from history that it is
just to slay public tyrants, and to set free the people for the
service of God ; the priests of the Lord reckon their slaughter
to be an act of piety.[2]

---

[1] John of Salisbury, ' Policraticus,'
iii. 15 : "Porro tirannum occidere
non modo licitum est sed æquum
et iustum. Qui enim gladium accipit, gladio dignus est interire. Sed
accipere intelligitur qui eum propria temeritate usurpat, non qui
utendi eo accipit a Domino potestatem.
Utique qui a Deo potestatem accipit,
legibus servit et iustitiæ, et iuris
famulus est. Qui vero eam usurpat,
iura deprimit et voluntati suæ leges
summittit. In eum ergo merito ar-
mantur iura qui leges exarmat, et
publica potestas sevit in eum qui
evacuare nititur publicam manum. Et,
cum multa sint crimina maiestatis,
nullum gravius est eo, quod adversus

ipsum corpus iustitiæ exercetur. Tirannis ergo non modo publicum crimen
sed, si fieri posset, plus quam publicum
est. Si enim crimen maiestatis omnes
persecutores admittit, quanto magis
illud quod leges premit, quæ ipsis
debent imperatoribus imperare ? Certe
hostem publicum nemo ulciscitur, et
quisquis eum non persequitur, in
seipsum et in totum rei publicæ mun-
danæ corpus delinquit."

[2] Id. id., viii. 17 : "Imago deitatis,
princeps amandus, venerandus est et
colendus ; tirannus, pravitatis imago,
plerumque etiam occidendus."

Id. id. id. id. : "Si enim tirannus secularis iure divino et humano
perimitur, quis tirannum in sacer-

His judgment is admirably summed up in the chapters in which he illustrates the just end of the tyrant from Roman and from Jewish history. He sets out in eloquent words the greatness and excellence of Julius Cæsar, " Homo perpaucorum et cui nullum expresse similem adhuc edidit natura mortalium," and yet, because he took command of the commonwealth by force of arms, he was deemed to be a tyrant, and, with the consent of a great part of the senate, was slain in the Capitol. Augustus forbad men to call him lord, and living as a citizen avoided both the name and the reality of tyranny. Tiberius was slain by poison, and though poisoning is a detestable thing, yet the world judged the poison by which he was destroyed to be life-giving. Caligula, the third tyrant, was slain by his servants, and with the death of Nero, the most monstrous and wicked of men, the family of the Cæsars came to an end. Lest it should be thought that such deeds against tyranny were permitted by the laws against that family only, John recalls the murder of Vitellius and Domitian. With the cruel tyranny and bloody end of those tyrants he contrasts the justice and felicity of the emperors from Nerva to Marcus Aurelius. Passing then to Jewish history, he describes the end of many tyrants, from Eglon, King of Moab, to Holofernes, " Finis enim tirannorum confusio est ; ad interitum quidem, si in malitia perseverant ; si revocantur, ad veniam." [1]

John of Salisbury sums up, no doubt in extreme and somewhat harsh terms, the normal doctrine of these centuries, that there can be no legitimate government which does not represent

NB

dotio diligendum censeat aut colendum ? "

Id. id., viii. 20 : " Ut autem et ab alia constet historia iustum esse publicos occidi tirannos et populum ad Dei obsequium liberari, ipsi quoque sacerdotes Domini necem eorum reputant pietatem et, si quid doli videtur habere imaginem, religione misterii dicunt Domino consecratum."

Cf. also id. id. id. 18 : " Ex quibus facile liquebit quia semper tiranno

licuit adulari, licuit eum decipere et honestum fuit occidere, si tamen aliter coherceri non poterat. Non enim de privatis tirannis agitur sed de his qui rem publicam premunt."

Id. id. id. 20 : " Sed nec veneni, licet videam ab infidelibus aliquando usurpatam, ullo umquam iure indultam lego licentiam. Non quod tirannos de medio tollendos esse non credam sed sine religionis honestatisque dispendio."

[1] Cf. id. id., viii. 19, 20, 21.

the principle of justice, and that this justice is embodied in the law. The ruler who is unjust, and who violates the laws and customs of his country, has ceased to have any claim to the obedience of his subjects, and may justly be resisted, and if necessary deposed and killed. It is probable that the somewhat harsh terms of his doctrine of tyrannicide are due to the influence of his study of classical literature and history, and it is interesting to observe the first effects of the direct study of the ancient world. But though the form of his principle of the right of resistance to unjust and illegal authority is probably literary in its origin, and might not have met with general approbation, yet the essential principle which he maintains is the normal view of the Middle Ages.

CHAPTER VI.

CONSTITUTIONAL THEORY AND CONTRACT.

WE have so far endeavoured to trace the development of the conception that political authority is controlled and limited by the principle of justice, and by the law as the embodiment of this. There is no doubt that in this conception we have one of the most important apprehensions of political theory in the Middle Ages. In modern times it may seem that the principle does not take us very far, for we always tend to ask what is justice, and whether the law is just, and this is the natural tendency of a time when men are conscious of movement and change. In the Middle Ages the conditions of civilisation were actually changing probably as rapidly as they are to-day, but men were hardly conscious of change, and the appeal to precedent, to tradition, was probably almost wholly sincere.

While, however, the belief in the supremacy of law and justice is of the first importance, yet it is also true that a society which is civilised and moving towards greater civilisation must not only be possessed of some ideal or ethical principles, but must also develop some method or form for securing the effective authority of its principles. In the Middle Ages this was represented by the development of the conception that the ruler received his authority, sometimes by the principle of hereditary succession in some one family, but never without the election or recognition of the great men, or the community as a whole—and these two cannot be separated in the mediæval apprehension. And the authority which the mediæval ruler thus held by the authority of the community, he exercised and could only exercise normally with the counsel of the great men of the community.

We have considered the earlier stages in the development of these principles in our first volume, and they were too firmly rooted in the structure of mediæval society to die out even in the chaos of the tenth century ; but it is no doubt true that in this respect, as with regard to the other principles of political authority, it was the great civil and religious conflicts of the eleventh and twelfth centuries which made men clearly conscious of ideas and convictions which had always been implicit, but had only occasionally been expressed. It is, however, important to observe that, even before these violent conflicts compelled men to make real to themselves their political principles, we can find occasional but very clear expressions of what we may call the constitutional conception of authority.

Here is, for instance, a very characteristic expression of the principle that the king governs only with the counsel of his faithful men. This is contained in a letter written by Gerbert (afterwards Pope Sylvester II.) in the name of Hugh, King of France, to the Archbishop of Sens. The king was evidently somewhat doubtful of the loyalty of the archbishop, who had probably not been present at his consecration in Rheims in July 987, and admonishes him with some asperity to make his allegiance before November, and, evidently in order to reassure him, declares that he has no intention of abusing the royal power, but intends to administer the affairs of the state with the advice and judgment of his faithful men, among whom he reckons the archbishop as one of the most honourable.[1]

We find the same principle expressed in a contemporary

[1] Gerbert, 'Epistolæ,' 107 : " Regali potentia in nullo modo abuti volentes, omnia negotia reipublicæ in consultatione et sententia fidelium nostrorum disponimus, vosque eorum participes fore dignissimos judicamus. Itaque honeste ac benigno affectu vos monemus uti ante Kl. novemb. eam fidem quam cæteri nobis firmaverunt confirmetis ob pacem et concordiam sanctæ Dei ecclesiæ, tociusque populi christiani. Ne si forte, quod non optamus, persuasione quorumdam pravorum diligenter vobis exequenda minus audiatis, sententiam domni papæ, comprovincialiumque episcoporum duriorem perferatis, nostraque omnibus nota mansuetudo iustissimum correctionis assumat zelum regali potentia."

Cf. the notes to the letter in the edition of J. Havet.

work of Abbo, the Abbot of Fleury. How can the king, he
says, deal with the affairs of the kingdom and drive out injustice except with the advice of the bishops and chief men
of the kingdom ? how can he discharge his functions if they do
not by their help and counsel show him that honour and
reverence which is due ?—the king alone is not equal to all
that the needs of the kingdom require. And he appeals to
the obligations which they had taken upon themselves in
electing him to the kingdom, for it were better not to have
assented to his election than to contemn him whom they had
elected. There are three important elections, he says—that of
the king or emperor, which is made by the agreement of the
whole kingdom ; that of the bishop, which represents the
unanimous agreement of the clergy and people ; and that of
the abbot, which is made by the wiser judgment of the community.[1]

This conception corresponds precisely with the contemporary
forms of legislative or quasi-legislative action. The Capitula
issued by the Emperor Otto I. at Verona in 967 are said to be
established by the emperor and his son Otto the king, with the
chief princes—that is, the bishop, abbots, and judges, along
with the whole people.[2] And again, the Emperor Henry II.

[1] Abbo, Abbas Floriacensis, ' Collectio Canonum,' iv. : " Cum regis
ministerium sit totius regni penitus
negotia discutere, ne quid in eis lateat
iniustitiæ, quomodo ad tanta poterit
subsistere, nisi annuentibus episcopis
et primoribus regni ? Et cum apostolus dicat ' Deum timete, regem
honorificate,' qua ratione sui ministerii vices exercebit in contumacium
perfidia, si ei primores regni auxilio
et consilio non exhibeant debitum honorem cum omni reverentia. Ipse enim
solus non sufficit ad omnia regni utilia.
Idcirco partito in aliis onere, quos
dignos credit honore, honorandus est
et ipse sincera devotione, ne quis ei
contradicat quomodocunque, quia ' qui
potestati resistit, Dei ordinationi resistit.' Siquidem ut melius est non
vovere quam post votum non reddere,

ita melius est electioni principis non
subscribere quam post subscriptionem
electum contemnere vel proscribere,
quandoquidem in altero libertatis amor
laudatur, in altero servilis contumacia
probo datur. Tres namque electiones
generales novimus, quarum una est
regis vel imperatoris, altera pontificis,
tertia abbatis. Et primam quidem
facit concordia totius regni ; secundam
vero unanimitas civium et cleri ; tertiam sanius consilium cœnobialis con-
gregationis. Et unaquæque non pro
sæcularis amicitiæ gratia vel pretio,
sed ad suam professionem pro sapientia
vel vitæ merito. Porro ordinatus rex
ab omnibus subditis fidem sibi sacramento exigit, ne in aliquibus regni sui
finibus discordia generari possit."

[2] M. G. H., Legum, Sect. IV., Constitutiones, vol. i. 13 : " Incipit kapitula

issued in 1022 the Constitution confirming and approving certain synodical legislation of Pope Benedict VIII., along with the senators, the officers of the palace, and the friends of the commonwealth.[1]

It is not within the scope of our work to deal with the development of the constitutions of the European states, but it is impossible to separate the history of political theory from the history of the growth of institutions. This is always true, but especially in the earlier Middle Ages, when there was very little merely abstract political speculation. In the thirteenth and fourteenth centuries this was somewhat different, but we hope to deal with this later. In the eleventh and twelfth centuries it is obvious that political theory arises very largely out of the conflicts of the time, and reflects in the main the constitutional principles of the European societies, as men conceived them. While therefore we must keep clear of any attempt to give an account of the constitutional organisation of Western Europe, we must endeavour by means of a few illustrations to indicate what seem to us to be some of its most important principles.

There is no doubt that in the Middle Ages the authority of the ruler was conceived of as normally depending upon the election, or at least the recognition, of the community. The conception of a strictly hereditary right to monarchy is not a mediæval conception. In France and England no doubt the principle of succession within one family established itself early. But students of English history do not need to be reminded that some form of election or recognition was always

quæ instituit domnus Otto gloriosissi- mus imperator et item Otto filius eius gloriosus rex, una cum summis prin- cipibus, id sunt episcopis, abbatibus, iudicibus, seu cum omni populo."

[1] M. G. H., Legum, Sect. IV., Consti- tutiones, vol. i. 34 : " Omnia quidem quæ pro ecclesiæ necessaria reparatione synodaliter instituit et reformavit pa- ternitas tua, ut filius laudo, confirmo et approbo ; et ut omnes sint paratiores, ea me inviolabiliter servaturum adjuvante Deo promitto. Et in æternum man- sura et inter publica iura semper recipienda et humanis legibus solem- niter inscribenda hac nostra auctori- tate, vivente ecclesia per Dei gratiam victura, cum senatoribus terræ, cum domesticis palatii, et amicis reipublicæ coram Deo et ecclesia ita corrobor- amus."

a regular part of the constitutional process of succession to the throne. And in France it was not really otherwise, though the strictly hereditary principle may be thought of as having established itself there more rapidly. In the Empire the succession was elective, and if at any time during the eleventh century it might have tended to become hereditary, this tendency was abruptly checked in the great civil wars of Henry IV.'s reign, and in the troubles of the thirteenth century.

It is worth while to notice some of the phrases in which this is expressed. Hermann of Reichenau relates how the Emperor Henry III. procured the election of his infant son as king at Tribur in 1053, but mentions that the election was made subject to the condition that he should prove a just ruler.[1] Bruno relates how at the council of Forchheim, in 1077, it was determined by the common consent, and approved by the authority of the Roman pontiff, that no one should receive the royal authority by hereditary succession as had been the custom, but that the son of the king, even though he were wholly worthy, should succeed to the kingdom by free election rather than by hereditary right ; while if he were not worthy, or if the people did not desire him, they should have it in their power to make him king whom they would.[2]

This principle is again expressed, and something more of its significance indicated, in the circular letter issued by the Archbishops of Cologne and Mainz and other bishops and princes on the occasion of the death of Henry V. in 1125. They announce the Emperor's death, and say that they have celebrated his funeral, and that they now propose to hold an assembly to consider the condition of the kingdom and to arrange for a

[1] Herimannus Augiensis, 'Chronicon,' A.D. 1053 : " Imperator Heinricus magno aput Triburiam conventu habito, filium æquivocum regem a cunctis eligi, eique post obitum suum, si rector iustus futurus esset, subiectionem promitti fecit."

[2] Bruno, ' De Bello Saxonico,' 91 : " Hoc etiam ibi consensu communi comprobatum, Romani pontificis auctoritate est corroboratum, ut regia potestas nulli per hæreditatem, sicut ante fuit consuetudo, cederet, sed filius regis, etiam si valde dignus esset, potius per electionem spontaneam quam per successionis lineam rex proveniret ; si vero non esset dignus regis filius, vel si nollet eum populus, quem regem facere vellet haberet in potestate populus."

successor. They disclaim all intention of prejudicing the decision of those to whom they write, but they express the hope
that they will be mindful of the oppression of the Church and
kingdom, and will invoke the help of God that He would so
guide the election of a successor that the Church and kingdom
might be free from the slavery in which they had been held,
and might live under their own laws, and that the princes and
the people might have peace.[1] The writers of the letter not
only claim the right of determining the succession, but also
clearly consider that this right should be used to provide
security for good government and the due observance of the
laws.

We can find another illustration of the recognition of the
elective principle, and of the conception that it involved definite
obligations on the part of the chosen ruler, in the letter sent to
Pope Eugenius III. in the name of Frederick I. (Barbarossa) on
his election to the kingdom in 1152. He speaks of himself as
having been clothed with the royal dignity, partly by the
homage of the lay princes, partly by the benediction of the
bishops, and as having put on the royal mind, and that therefore he purposes, according to the terms of that promise which
he made when he was enthroned and consecrated, to give all
honour and love to the Pope and the Roman Church, to all
ecclesiastical persons the ready justice and defence which was
their due, and to widows and orphans and the whole people
entrusted to him law and peace.[2]

---

[1] M. G. H., Legum, Sect. IV., Constitutiones, vol. i. 112 : " Nullum tamen
præiudicium deliberationi et voluntati
vestræ facientes, nichil nobis singulare
ac privatum in hac re usurpamus.
Quin pocius discretioni vestræ hoc
adprime intimatum esse cupimus,
quatinus memor oppressionis, qua
ecclesia cum universo regno usque
modo laboravit, dispositionis divinæ
providentiam invocetis, ut in sub-
stitutione alterius personæ sic ecclesiæ
suæ et regno provideat, quod tanto
servitutis iugo amodo careat et suis
legibus uti liceat, nosque omnes cum

subiecta plebe temporali perfruamur
tranquillitate."

[2] M. G. H., Legum, Sect. IV., Constitutiones, vol. i. 137 : " Nos vero in
multiplicibus regiæ dignitatis orna-
mentis, quibus partim per laicorum
principum obsequio, partim per re-
verendas pontificum benedictiones ves-
titi sumus, regium animum induimus,
tota mentis virtute intendentes, ut
iuxta professionis nostræ formulam,
quam ab orthodoxis præesulibus in
ipso regni throno et unctione sacra
accepimus, honorem vobis et dilectionem, et sacrosanctæ matri nostræ

We have already dealt with the treatment of this question in
the feudal law books, but it is worth while to notice again the
emphatic terms in which the principle of election is set out in
the ' Sachsenspiegel.' The Germans, according to the law, are
to elect the king, when the king is elected he is to swear that
he will maintain the law, and put down all that is against it.[1]
And in another place the author lays down the principle of
election in the broadest terms when he says that all authority
is founded upon election.[2] What the exact significance of the
latter phrase may be is difficult to say, but at least it seems to
illustrate the breadth and importance of the elective principle.

The fact that in mediæval theory the authority of the king
is founded upon the election or at least the recognition of the
community does not in truth require any serious demonstration.
It is very important, however, to notice that it is not only in
the election or succession of the ruler that the authority of
the community was recognised, but that in some sense or
another the legislative action of the ruler was limited and
conditioned by the counsel and assent of the great men of the
community. This is clear in the first place from the formulæ
which are used in all legislative or quasi-legislative actions.
We may take a few examples from the twelfth century.

The great settlement of Worms in 1122 was embodied in the
' Privilegium Imperatoris,' in which Henry V. agreed to resign
the imperial claim to the right of investiture of bishops with
the ring and staff. This is expressly said to be done with the
counsel and consent of the princes whose names are subscribed.[3]

Romanæ æcclesiæ et omnibus ecclesiasticis personis promptam et debitam
iusticiam ac defensionem exhibeamus,
viduis ac pupillis et universo populo
nobis commisso legem et pacem faci-
amus et conservemus."
    [1] ' Sachsenspiegel,' iii. 52. 1 : " Die
düdeschen solen durch recht den
koning kiesen."
    iii. 54. 2 : " Als man den koning
küset, so sal he dem rike hulde dun,
unde sveren dat he recht sterke unde
unrecht krenke unde it rike voresta

an sime rechte, als he künne und
moge."
    [2] Id., i. 55. 1 : " Al werlik gerichte
hevet begin von kore ; dar umme ne
mach nen sat man richtere sin noch
neman, he ne si gekoren oder belent
richtere."
    Cf. i. 56 and 58. Cf. ' Schwaben-
spiegel,' 71. 1.
    [3] M. G. H., Legum, Sect. IV., Consti-
tutiones, vol. i. 107 : " Hæc omnia acta
sunt consensu et consilio principum
quorum nomine subscripta sunt."

Lothar III.'s Constitution, 'De Feudorum Distractione,' of 1136, was made on the exhortation and counsel of the archbishops, bishops, dukes, and other nobles and judges.[1] Frederick I. issued the feudal constitutions of Roncaglia after taking counsel with the bishops, dukes, marquesses, counts, judges of the palace, and other chief persons.[2]

It is not, however, only in the formal preambles of legislation that we find this principle recognised. It was expressly asserted as a principle of government by so great and masterful an emperor as Frederick Barbarossa. In replying to certain demands of Pope Hadrian IV. in relation to the papal and imperial position in the city of Rome, and to certain claims of the imperial authority on ecclesiastical persons in Italy, Frederick, while giving a provisional answer, says that he cannot give a complete answer until he has consulted the princes.[3]

There is really no doubt whatever that in the normal tradition of the Middle Ages the position of the ruler was conceived of as that of one who ruled with the advice and consent of the chief persons of the community.[4] The relation of this to the feudal conceptions, as we have endeavoured to set them out, is obvious, but the tradition was older than the feudal system.[5] The authority of the mediæval ruler rested upon the election or consent of the community, and was exercised normally and constitutionally with the advice of persons

[1] M. G. H., Legum, Sect. IV., Constitutiones, vol. i. 120 : "Hortatu itaque et consilio archiepiscoporum, episcoporum, ducum . . . ceterumque nobilium, simul etiam judicum, hac edictali lege in omne evum Deo propitio valitura decernimus."

[2] M. G. H., Legum, Sect. IV., Constitutiones, vol. i. 148 : "Habito igitur consilio episcoporum, ducum, marchionum, comitum simul et palatinorum judicum et aliorum procerum, hac edictali lege Deo propitio perpetuo valitura sancimus : ut nulli liceat feudum totum vel partem aliquem vendere, vel impignorare, vel quoquo modo alienare, sine permissione illius domini ad quem feudum spectare dinoscitur."

[3] M. G. H., Legum, Sect. IV., Constitutiones, vol. i. 179 : "Quamvis non ignorem, ad tanta negotia non ex animi mei sententia, sed ex consilio principum me respondere debere, sine prejudicio tamen sapientium hoc absque consultatione respondeo."

[4] The examples we have given are taken from the Empire, but they could as easily be taken from France. Cf. 'Recueil Général des Anciennes Lois Francaises,' ed. Jourdan, Decrusz, and Isambert ; 'Etablissemens des Capétiens,' Nos. 47, 49, 75, 104, 108.

[5] Cf. vol. i. chaps. 19 and 20.

who were not merely his dependents or creatures, but were in some sense, however vague and undetermined, the representatives of the community.

It was the great civil conflicts of the eleventh century which compelled men in the Empire to consider how far the conditions and assumptions of constitutional order gave the community or its chief men the right to take such action as might secure the purposes for which the ruler had been elected or recognised. It is from this standpoint that we must again consider the principles of government which are presented by the historians of the great revolt against Henry IV. We have already dealt with some passages from their writings in considering the theory of the relation of authority to justice, but we must look again at some of these, and consider them from the standpoint of their constitutional theory.

According to the account of Lambert of Hersfeld, the demands of the Saxons and Thuringians in 1073 were, first, that Henry IV. should do justice to the Saxon princes, whose possessions, as they said, he had seized without judicial process, in accordance with the judgment of the princes of the kingdom ; secondly, that he should dismiss from his court the low-born persons by whose advice he had been governing, and should entrust the administration of the affairs of the kingdom to the princes of the kingdom, to whom the charge properly belonged ; and thirdly, that he should put away his concubines and abandon the vicious habits which had disgraced the royal dignity. If he would do these things they were prepared to serve him, but only as became free men in a free empire.[1]

[1] Lambert of Hersfeld, ' Annales,' 1073 (p. 196): "Ut principibus Saxoniæ, quibus sine legitima discussione bona sua ademerat, secundum principum suorum iurisdictionem satisfaceret. . . . Ut vilissimos homines, quorum consilio seque remque publicam præcipitem dedisset, de palatio eiceret, et regni negocia regni principibus, quibus ea competerent, curanda atque administranda permitteret : ut abdicato grege concubinarum, quibus contra scita canorum attrito frontis rubore incubabat,

reginam, quam sibi secundum ecclesiasticas traditiones thori sociam regnique consortem delegisset, coniugali loco haberet et diligeret ; ut cetera flagitiorum probra, quibus dignitatem regiam adolescens infamaverat, nunc saltem maturato sensu et aetate abdicaret. Postremo per Deum rogant ut iusta postulantibus sponte annueret, nec sibi magni cuiusdam atque inusitati facinoris necessitatem imponeret. Si ita faceret, se promptissimo animo ei sicut actenus servituros, eo tamen

As we have already said, we are not discussing the question
of the real nature of the causes which lay behind the revolt of
the Saxons, and we think that the sentiments or motives attributed by Lambert and the other historians to the revolters must
often be taken rather as those of the writers than of those into
whose mouths they are put. We are concerned with the theory
which the great conflicts brought out rather than with the
conflicts themselves, and the passage just cited represents two
constitutional principles of great importance. First, that the
king has no arbitrary power, but that there is a legal authority
in the State to which he and all others must submit ; and
secondly, that the great affairs of the State are not to be
administered by him at his capricious pleasure, but only
through those who have a constitutional right to be consulted.

The principles which are thus expressed in relation to the
beginning of the great revolt are constantly repeated during
the conflicts which followed. Lambert represents even those
who belonged in a measure to the royal party as admitting
their validity. In the speech which he attributes to Berthold,
formerly Duke of Carinthia, Berthold admits the justice of
the complaints of the revolters, but begs them to consider the
reverence which is due to the royal majesty, and urges that
they should lay aside their arms and agree upon a meeting to
which the king should summon the princes of the whole
kingdom, at which he might clear himself, before the common
judgment, of the charges made against him, and might set
right whatever should need correction.[1]

modo, quo ingenuos homines atque in
libero imperio natos regi servire oper-
teret ; sin autem, christianos se esse,
nec velle hominis, qui fidem christi-
anam capitalibus flagitiis prodidisset,
communione maculari. . . . Sacramento se ei fidem dixisse, sed si ad
ædificationem, non ad destructionem
ecclesiæ Dei, rex esse vellet, si iuste,
si legitime, si more maiorum rebus
moderaretur, si suum cuique ordinem,
suam dignitatem, suas leges tutas inviolatasque manere pateretur. Sin ista
prior ipse temeraesset se iam sacra-

menti huius religione non teneri, sed
quasi cum barbaro hoste et christiani
nominis oppressore iustum deinceps
bellum gesturos, et quoad ultima
vitalis caloris scintilla superesset, pro
ecclesia Dei, pro fide christiana, pro
libertate etiam sua dimicaturos."

[1] Lambert of Hersfeld, ' Annales,'
1073 (p. 197) : " Iustam eorum esse
causam, quos summis sæpe iniuriis regis
inclementia ad hæc extrema experienda
cœgisset, honori tamen suo magis
consulendum quam iracundiæ, et deferendum regiæ maiestati, quæ apud

It was indeed this constitutional conception, that the king was in the end responsible to the judgment of the princes of the kingdom, which was maintained throughout the long struggle between Henry IV. and those who revolted against his authority. They maintained steadily that it was for the council of the princes of the kingdom to decide upon the justice or injustice of the charges brought against Henry, and that it was in their power, for sufficient reasons, to declare the throne vacant. Lambert represents Rudolf of Suabia as refusing in 1073, at the meeting between the Saxon princes and those of the royal party at Gerstengen, to be made king, until the matter had been considered by a council of all the princes, and it had been decided that this could be done without involving them in the guilt of perjury.[1]

It is true that when once the great dispute between Henry IV. and Gregory VII. had developed, and when in 1076 Gregory had formally excommunicated Henry, the revolters, as reported by Lambert, eagerly seized upon this new circumstance, and proposed to refer the charges against Henry to the Pope, who was to be invited to attend a council of all the princes at Augsburg, and, when all parties had been heard, to pronounce judgment upon them. They also decided that if Henry was not released from his excommunication within a year, they would no longer recognise him as king.[2]

barbaros etiam nationes tuta inviolataque fuisset; proinde remisso armorum strepitu, pacatis animis, sopitis simultatibus, tempus locumque constituerent, quo rex tocius regni principes evocaret, et iuxta communem sententiam et obiecta purgaret et quæ correctionis egere viderentur corrigeret."

[1] Lambert of Hersfeld, 'Annales,' 1073 (p. 203): "Cumque toto triduo consilia contulissent, et quid facto opus esset communi sollicitudine perquirerent, hæc postremo cunctis sententia convenit, ut, reprobato rege, alium qui gubernando idoneus esset eligerent. . . . Et profecto Ruodolfum ducem ibidem absque dilatatione regem constituissent,

nisi ille pertinaciter resistendo iuraret, numquam se in hoc consensurum, nisi a cunctis principibus conventu habito, sine nota periurii, integra existimatione sua, id facere posse decerneretur."

[2] Lambert of Hersfeld, 'Annales,' 1076 (p. 254): "se tamen rem integram Romni pontificis cognitione reservare; acturos se cum eo, ut in purificatione sanctæ Mariæ Augustam occurrat, ibique celeberrimo conventu habito principum tocius regni, discussis utrarumque partium allegationibus, ipse suo iudicio vel addicat vel absolvat accusatum; quod si ante diem anniversarium excommunicationis suæ, suo præsertim vicio, excommunicatione non absolvatur, absque retractatione in

In our next volume we shall have to examine the whole question of the principles of the papal intervention, here we need only observe that it greatly strengthened the hands of those who were already in revolt against Henry. The revolters would evidently have been glad to put the whole responsibility of Henry's deposition upon the Pope, and indeed at the council of Forchheim in 1077, as Berthold of Constance reports it, they at first assumed that the Pope had finally deposed him, but the Pope's legates seem to have made it clear that this was not so— presumably on account of Henry's absolution at Canossa early in the same year—and intimated that it was for the council to judge and to determine upon their action. It was the princes therefore who declared him to be deposed, and elected Rudolf of Suabia.[1] It soon, however, became clear that there was still a strong party which supported Henry, and Berthold represents the chief men of both parties as agreeing later in the same year that the principal men of the kingdom should meet, and along with the legates of the Pope should consider what should be done, and as determining that they would by common consent repudiate whichever of the kings should refuse to accept their judgment, and would acknowledge and obey the other.[2]

perpetuum causa ceciderit, nec legibus deinceps regnum repetere possit, quod legibus ultra administrare, annuam passus excommunicationem, non possit."

[1] Berthold of Constance, ' Annales,' 1077 (p. 291): " Denique in Idibus prædictis, ut deliberatum est, ex magna parte optimates regni convenerunt. Ibique habito colloquio, perquam multis iniustitiarum et iniuriarum calamito- sissimis proclamationibus et queri- moniis, quas sibi et totius regni pri- matibus et ecclesiis inlatas haberet, regem accusabant ; et quia papa, ne ut regi obœdirent aut servirent, ipsis tam interdixerit ; regni dignitate privabant, neque regis saltem nomine dignum ob inaudita ipsius millefaria flagitia adiudi- cabant ; set alium sibi pro illo eligere et constituere unanimiter destinabant. Legati autem sedis apostolicæ audito

illic tam sacrilego homine, non parum quidem mirati sunt, quod tamdiu illum super se sustinuerunt. Verum tamen id quod iniunctum erat eis, non reticebant, quin potius in audientia cunctorum propalabant suæ legationis communitorium, ut si quolibet suæ cautionis artificio posset fieri, isto adhuc aliquamdiu qualitercumque sustentato, alium sibi regem nequa- quam constituerent ; alioquin ipsi, quia multo melius suæ necessitatis expertum non ignorarent periculum, quodcumque sibi optimum præ cæteris iudicarent, apostolico non contradicente peragerent."

[2] Berthold of Constance, ' Annales,' 1077 (p. 300): " Quatinus maiores totius regni omnes post paululum præter ambos reges ad colloquium iuxta Renum convenirent, et ibidem cum legatis simul apostolicis iustis-

We find another very significant assertion of this principle, that there was in the community an authority which could sit in judgment even upon the supreme ruler and upon his actions, in the last stages of Henry IV.'s tragic reign. In his despair, when he had been overwhelmed by the union of his son Henry V. with his opponents, he wrote, as is reported by Ekkehard, to the bishops and princes of Germany appealing to them against his son's conduct towards him. They replied inviting him to lay his case before the princes and the people, that he might receive and render justice, and that by the due consideration and just settlement of all the causes of discord, the Church and the kingdom might be restored to security.[1]

The claim was indeed far-reaching, and if it stood alone might hardly deserve serious consideration, but as a matter of fact it is only a clear statement of the theory which was represented throughout the reign of Henry IV. And it did not disappear with his death. We find a close parallel to it some years later in a document which belongs to the last stages of the investiture controversy, to the year before the settlement of Worms. This is a statement of the conclusions arrived at in a council of the princes held at Würzburg in 1121. The emperor is to render obedience to the apostolic see, and to make peace with the Pope by the advice and help of the princes, under such conditions that the emperor shall have that which belongs to him, and the churches also shall possess their own in peace and quiet. The princes propose to devise a settlement of the dispute concerning investitures. If the emperor

simo rationis iudiciariæ examine, quid optimum, quidve iustissimum super tam grandi causa foret, diiudicandum deliberarent ; et alterutri regum qui diffinitionibus illorum non consentiret despecto, communi voto contrairent ; alteri tandem consentaneo tota fidelitate et subiectione, ut regi oportet obœdientissime servirent."

[1] Ekkehard Uraugiensis, ' Chronicon Universale,' A.D. 1106 : " Quapropter placet tam regi quam universis regni principibus, immo cuncto exercitui orthodoxo, quo senior idem, ne ulla sibi pateat adversus nos iusta querela, quacunque elegerit securitate, quacunque maluerit statione, coram præsenti senatu simul et populo, causam suam agat, iusticiam suscipiat, iusticiam et reddat, quatinus ab ortu scismatis omnibus seditionis causis, acsi nil inde fuerit diffinitum, undique discussis, tam filio quam patri sua iusticia respondeat, æcclesiæ vero regnique status, non ut ipse more suo proponit post longas inducias, sed inpresentiarum, his controversiis diremptis vacillare desinat."

under any advice or influence should take hostile measures against any one on account of this, the princes, acting under his own authority and consent, determine that they will act together and admonish him not to do this, and, if he should neglect their advice, the princes will abide by the faith which they have pledged to each other.[1]

It is no doubt difficult to measure precisely the reality and value of principles which are put forward in periods of violent controversy and civil war. But in this case we can recognise with confidence that the principle that the ruler is not an arbitrary or irresponsible master of the State, but must govern in accordance with the counsel and judgment of others whose duty it is to see that justice is done to the whole community, was firmly held apart from the mere passion of revolt, and that the stress and pressure of civil conflict only brought out into clearer view conceptions which had always been present and powerful.

It is then from this standpoint that we can profitably examine the political theory of Manegold of Lautenbach, by whom the conception of the limitations and conditions of the royal authority was most clearly and sharply set out. In order to deal adequately with his position we must not consider only a few isolated phrases, but must endeavour to make clear to ourselves the logical structure of his theory.

---

[1] M. G. H., Leg., Sect. IV., Const., vol. i. 106 : " Hoc est consilium in quod convenerunt principes de controversia inter domnum inperatorem et regnum. Domnus inperator apostolicæ sedi obediat. Et de calumpnia quam adversus eum habet ecclesia, ex concilio et auxilio principum inter ipsum et domnum papam componatur, et sit firma et stabilis pax, ita quod domnus inperator que sua et que regni sunt habeat, ecclesie et unusquisque sua quiete et pacifice possideant. . . . Hoc etiam, quod ecclesia adversus inperatorem et regnum de investituris causatur, principes sine dolo et sine simulatione elaborare intendunt, ut in hoc regnum honorem suum retineat. . . . Et si in posterum domnus imperator consilio vel suggestione alicuius ullam in quemquam vindictam pro hac inimicitia exsuscitaverit, consensu et licentia ipsius hoc inter se principes confirment ut ipsi insimul permaneant et cum omni caritate et reverentia, ne aliquid horum facere velit, eum commoneant. Si autem domnus imperator hoc consilium preterierit, principes sicut ad invicem fidem dederunt, ita eam observent."
  Cf. p. 56.

It would be to fall into a complete and deplorable confusion if we were to think that Manegold denied or doubted the sanctity and the divine authority of secular government. On the contrary, as we have already pointed out,[1] if he attacks its abuse, it is in the name of the greatness and the august nature of the office of the king. The royal office, he says, excels all other earthly authorities, and therefore the man who is to administer it should excel all other men in wisdom, justice, and piety, for he who is to have the care of all, to govern all, should be adorned with greater virtue than others, that he may be able to exercise the powers entrusted to him with the highest equity.[2] Again, in defending the right of the opponents of Henry IV. to use violence in resisting him, he urges with great force that the authority of the State in punishing transgressors is a part of the divine order.[3] He does not doubt the truth of the words of St Peter, "Be subject to the king as supreme," and "Fear God, and honour the king," but only argues that they have been misapplied, for the title of king is a description not of a personal quality, but of an office, and obedience is due to the office, not to a man who has been deposed from it.[4] Wenrich

[1] See p. 103, 111.

[2] Manegold, ' Ad Gebehardum,' xxx.: " Regalis ergo dignitas et potentia sicut omnes mundanas excellit potestates, sic ad eam ministrandam non flagitiosissimus quisque vel turpissimus est constituendus, sed qui sicut loco et dignitate, ita nichilonimus ceteros sapientia, iusticia superet et pietate. Necesse est ergo, qui omnium curam gerere, omnes debet gubernare, maiore gratiavirtutum super ceteros debeat splendere, traditam sibi potestatem summo equitatis libramine studeat administrare."

[3] Id., xxxviii. : " Unde martyr sanctissimus et egregius pontifex Cyprianus in nono abusionum gradu inter multa districtionis et disciplinæ ministeria iusticiam regis asserit esse impios de terra eradere, parricidas et periurantes non sinere vivere. . . .

Id., xxxix. : " Unde sanctissimus papa Innocentius in decretis suis cap.

xxii. hos, per quorum ministerium catholici principes et pravos puniunt et pios defendunt, a reatu immunes ostendit dicens : ' Quesitum est super his etiam qui post baptismum administraverunt aut tormenta sola exercuerunt aut etiam capitalem protulerint sententiam. De his nichil legimus a maioribus difinitum. Meminerant enim a Deo potestates has esse concessas et propter vindictam noxiorum gladium fuisse permissum et Dei ministerium esse in huiusmodi datum vindicem. Quemadmodum igitur reprenderent factum, quod auctore Deo viderent esse concessum ? ' "

[4] Id., xliii. : " In eo namque quod dicitur : ' Subditi estote regi quasi præcellenti ' et : ' Deum timete, regem honorificate ' et : ' Subditi estote dominis non tantum bonis et modestis,' multum sibi aplaudunt sibique titulos victoriæ ascribunt, non intelle-

of Trier had urged against Hildebrand that Ebbo the Archbishop of Rheims had been deprived of his see for taking part
in the deposition of Louis the Pious, in the ninth century, and
Manegold admits that this was just, because it was done
without due process and for unjust reasons.[1]

Manegold, that is, recognises fully and explicitly the august
and sacred nature of political authority and its function in
maintaining justice and equity. But, on the other hand, he
refuses to admit that this means that the authority of the ruler
is absolute, or that he is irresponsible and irremovable, and
with characteristic boldness he attacks the tradition of the
absolute divine right of the ruler in its most august source.
Wenrich of Trier had, as we have already seen,[2] urged the
words and the example of Gregory the Great as showing that
even the popes, and even in matters which concerned religion,
had felt themselves bound to obey the commands of the emperor even when they thought them wrong. Manegold meets
this first by suggesting that the words of Gregory are susceptible
of another interpretation ; but he does not hesitate to maintain
that if indeed Gregory meant what was thought, and acted as
he was understood to have done, his words and actions were
wrong and must be repudiated.[3] Manegold was clearly pre-

gentes neque que locuntur neque de
quibus affirmant. Rex enim non nomen
est naturæ, sed officii, sicut episcopus,
presbyter, diaconus. Et cum quilibet
horum certis ex causis de commisso
sibi officio deponitur, non est quod erat,
nec honor officio debitus postea est
inpendendus. Quisquis ergo amissæ
dignitatis postmodum sibi reverentiam
inpendit, potius prevaricator quam
legum servator existit ; quamquam et
si in ipso inperio quod sit contra
Dominum inperant, nullatenus sit
obediendum, sed omni libertate resistendum. Ergo nequaquam contra
apostoli preceptum faciunt qui vestro
Heinrico a regali dignitate deposito
nunc resistunt."

[1] Id., xliv. : " Non enim negamus
Ebonem iuste depositum, qui contra

imperatorem catholicum conspiravit
eumque nullo iudiciario cɔnventu
discussum, nulla vocatione expectatum,
non confessum, non convictum premiis
corruptus deiecit et Lotharium filium
eius regno sublimare contendit."

Cf. Wenrici, Scolastici Treverensis
Epistola, 4.

[2] See pp. 119, 120.

[3] Id., xlv. : " Proferunt namque
beati Gregorii exemplum, si tamen est
verum, quo videlicet astruere conantur,
non modo quoslibet episcopos, sed
ipsum summum pontificem regibus
obedientiæ debito ac necessitate esse
obstrictum, et ex huius debiti necessitate ad ea constringi agenda quæ ipse
non ambigeret Deo contraria et ideo ex
mentis iuditio reprobanda. Quid igitur
huic assertioni nefandius, quid potest

pared to refuse to accept any authority however august which would impose the yoke of an unlimited obedience upon the subject.

It is with the same courage that he deals with the question of the binding nature of the oath of allegiance. Wenrich had made a vigorous attack upon the action of Hildebrand in absolving the subjects of Henry IV. from their oath of allegiance.[1] Manegold answers him not so much by urging the papal authority in this matter as by examining the nature of such an oath and the conditions of its obligation. This, he says, is the superiority of human nature to that of the animal, that in virtue of the power of reason it examines the causes of things, and considers not merely what should be done, but why it should be done. No man can make himself king or emperor, and the people elect a man to this position in order that he may protect the good and destroy the wicked, and administer justice to every man. If he

esse scelestius, contra voluntatem videlicet dominicam cuiquam hominum obedientiam ex debiti necessitate inpendendam ? Hinc ipse princeps apostolorum nos instruit dicens : ' Obedire oportet Deo magis quam hominibus.' Et supra : ' Si iustum est in conspectu Dei vos potius audire quam Deum, iudicate.' Proponunt enim : ' Ego,' inquid Gregorius, ' iussioni subditus eandem legem per diversas terrarum partes feci transmitti ; usque utrobique ergo quod debui exsolvi, qui et imperatori obedientiam prebui et pro Deo quod sensi minime tacui.' Multi sunt enim locutionum modi, multa et genera, quibus pro diversitate causarum et personarum non solum sanctorum sermones, sed et communes et vulgares dispensantur locutiones. Sancti enim, quia homines esse se meminerant, modo humano suas locutiones formabant. Solent enim homines ita loqui vel cognatis vel amicis vel certe extraneis : ' Implevi quod imperasti ' et : ' Quodcumque iusseris ut servus tuus implebo ' et : ' Nullus tuus proprius libentius obedit

voluntati tuæ.' . . . Secundum hunc igitur locutionis modum beatus Gregorius obedientiam se dicit debere et non ex alicuius debiti necessitate. . . . Cum igitur hæc ita esse certa comprehendantur ratione, certe tamen, si Gregorius aliqua temporis vel causarum dispensatoria ratione funestam legem ad omnium noticiam non distulit insinuare fecitque transmittere, certe, inquam, hoc facto sedem beato Petri divinitus concesso nequaquam privavit privilegio. At si sanctissimus ille, corpore quod corrumpitur animam aggravante, aliquid ut homo, quod cum gratia ipsius dicam, excessit, nullatenus in hoc aliquem suorum successorum ad sui imitationem constringit, quia nec Petrus princeps utique apostolorum in hoc se imitandum docuit, quod gentes iudaizare coegit, nec Cyprianus, quia Donatistas rebaptizandos censuit, rebaptizandi nobis necessitatem imposuit. Neque sanctorum excessus ad imitandum sunt conscripti, sed potius, ut caveantur, denotati sunt."

[1] Wenrici, Epistola, 6.

violates the agreement under which he was elected, and disturbs and confounds that which he was to set in order, the people is justly and reasonably absolved from its obedience, since he has broken that faith which bound him and them together. The people never binds itself by an oath to obey a ruler who is possessed by fury and madness.[1]

There are, Manegold points out, two cases which have to be considered, that of the man who takes a just and reasonable oath to the king, and that of him who takes an unjust and unreasonable oath, and he examines the two cases separately. He who takes a just and reasonable oath to the king swears that he will be his companion and helper in maintaining the government of the kingdom, in preserving justice and establishing peace, and this oath is binding so long as the king demands his help in doing those things which he has sworn to do. But if the king ceases to govern the kingdom, and begins to act as a tyrant, to destroy justice, to overthrow peace, and to break his faith, the man who has taken the oath is free from it, and the people is entitled to depose the king and to set up another, inasmuch as he has broken the principle upon which their mutual obligation depended. This, Manegold maintains, is what the German princes had done ; they had perhaps sworn allegiance rashly when Henry IV. was too young to understand the nature of an oath, but they had striven to keep their oath, until he threw aside his obedience to the apostolic see, and forced them to apostatise from the Christian religion. When for this crime the Synod of Rome had deposed him, and

---

[1] Manegold, ' Ad Gebehardum,' xlvii. : "In hoc namque natura humana ceteris prestat animantibus, quod capax rationis ad agenda queque non fortuitis casibus proruit, causas rerum iuditio rationis inquirit nec tantum, quid agatur, sed cur aliquid agatur intendit. Cum enim nullus se inperatorem vel regem creare possit, ad hoc unum aliquem super se populus exaltat, ut iusti ratione inperii se gubernet et regat, cuique sua distribuat, pios foveat, inpios perimat, omnibus videlicet iusticiam inpendat. At vero si quando pactum, quo eligitur, infringit, ad ea disturbanda et confundenda, que corrigere constitutus est, eruperit, iuste rationis consideratione populum subiectionis debito absolvit, quippe cum fidem prior ipse deseruerit, que alterutrum altero fidelitate colligavit. Huc accedit, quod populus nequaquam iuramento ad hoc se cuiquam obligat, ut ad quoscumque furentis animi inpetus obediat, aut, quo illum furor et insania precipitat, illum necessitudo subiectionis sequi compellat."

deprived him of the royal dignity, the Christian people no longer owed him any reverence. It was the proper function of the apostolic see to reassure the people, which was concerned and anxious about the obligation of the oath it had taken, and it is therefore clear that it justly loosed the oath which was certainly and manifestly null and void, and publicly annulled that which was inherently invalid.[1]

The discussion of the second case, that of the man who has sworn to do something in itself evil and unjust, does not demand any detailed consideration. Manegold urges, and supports his contention with a number of patristic quotations, that such oaths are obviously from the outset null and void.[2]

It should be observed that Manegold's treatment of the real nature of the authority which was exercised, when a man was absolved from the obligation of an oath, was not in any way peculiar or eccentric, but represents what was probably the

[1] Id., xlvii. : "Aut enim quisque juste et qua fieri debet ratione regibus et principibus iurat, aut iniuste et qua fieri non debet ratione. Sequamur utraque et, qua servanda sunt ratione, videamus.

xlviii. : Ut enim ab adversariis inducto utamur exemplo, si, ut Augustinus diffinit, per Deum est iurare Deo ius reddere, ille, qui iuste et qua fieri debet ratione regibus vel principibus iurat, hoc sacramento confirmat, ut ad regni gubernacula tuenda, iusticiam servandam, pacem stabiliendam individuus et inremotus comes et adiutor existat. Hoc namque sacramentum iurantem tam diu debiti necessitate obstringit, quam diu is cui iuratum est ad iurata facienda iurantem poposcit. At vero, si ille non regnum gubernare, sed regni occasione tyrannidem exercere, iusticiam destruere, pacem confundere, fidem deserere exarserit, adiuratus iuramenti necessitate absolutus existit, liberumque est populo illum deponere, alterum elevare, quem constat alterutre obligationis rationem prius deseruisse. Sic, inquam, sic principes nostri, quamvis vestro Hein-

rico minus caute, parum considerate iurassent, adhuc utpote parvulo ac necdum fidei sacramentis iniciato, tamen sacramenti consideratione omni reverentia studebant obedire, donec illos, apostolicam abiurando obedientiam, idolatriam cogebat exercere et a cristiana religione apostatare. 'Quasi,' inquid Samuel, 'peccatum ariolandi est repugnare et quasi scelus idolatrie nolle acquiescere.' Super quo igitur scelere postquam hunc Romana sinodus iusta, ut supra prolatum est, ratione deposuit, regia dignitate privavit, nulla regie potestatis reverentia a christiano populo fuit exhibenda. Pertinuit igitur ad apostolici officium populum de his securum reddere, quem de exhibitis sacramentis vidit sollicitum estuare. Constat ergo illum iuste sacramenta solvisse, que omnibus fidelibus et rationali intellectu nitentibus certum et manifestum est nulla existere. Implevit igitur officium suum, fecit quod erat apostolicum, dum ea quæ intus soluta cognovit foris discindere non distulit."

[2] Id., xlix.

normal conception of the canonists.[1] We are not here dealing
with the claim of the ecclesiastical or papal authority to have
the power of deposing kings ; with that we propose to deal
in the next volume, and we shall then have to consider the
treatment of this subject by Manegold. In the meanwhile we
must observe that his contention that the oath of allegiance
is not binding to the king who abuses his authority is really
independent of this. In his opinion the Pope merely declares
that obligation annulled which is already null and void.

We can now approach the consideration of that well-known
passage in which Manegold sets out his theory of the nature of
political authority and obligation in the sharpest and clearest
terms. We have already indeed cited the first words of the
passage, the words in which he expresses his judgment of the
greatness and dignity of the royal office, and of its high moral
function in maintaining justice.[2] The royal dignity excels all
earthly authority, and he who is to hold it, who is to have the
care and government of all, should be superior to all in virtue,
that he may exercise this power with the highest equity. So
far we have already followed Manegold's argument, but suddenly he turns to the other side of the principle. The people
does not exalt him in order that he should act as a tyrant
towards them, but in order that he should defend them from
the wickedness and tyranny of others. If he, who has been
elected to put down the wicked and to defend the good, turns
to wickedness, oppresses the good, and plays the part of a
tyrant over his subjects, it is clear that he justly falls from the
office which was conferred upon him, and that the people are
free from his dominion and from their subjection, inasmuch as
he has violated that agreement (pactum) in virtue of which he
was appointed. The people cannot in such a case be accused
of a breach of faith, for it is he who has first broken faith.

And then Manegold, with characteristic audacity, reinforces
this principle by a comparison from humble life. If a man has
given his swine for a suitable wage into the charge of a swine-
herd, who, in place of keeping them safe, steals, slays, or loses

[1] Cf. vol. ii. pp. 202, 203.   [2] Cf. p. 112 and p. 161.

them, he will refuse to pay the wage, and will dismiss him from his service.   If this is just in such humble matters, how much more is it clear and just that the man to whom the rule of men has been committed, and who uses his power not for the true government of men, but to lead them into error, should be deprived of all power and dignity.   This principle is surely right in Christian times, for even the Romans drove out Tarquin for the outrage which his son had committed against Lucretia. It is one thing to reign, it is another to act like a tyrant, and, while men should render faith and reverence to kings and emperors in order to maintain the true government of the kingdom, yet, if they play the tyrant, then they deserve neither faith nor reverence.[1]

---

[1] Manegold, 'Ad Gebehardum,' xxx. : " Regalis ergo dignitas et potentia sicut omnes mundanas excellit potestates, sic ad eam ministrandam non flagitiosissimus quisque vel turpissimus est constituendus, sed qui sicut loco et dignitate, ita nichilominus ceteros sapientia, iusticia superet et pietate. Necesse est ergo, qui omnium curam gerere, omnes debet gubernare, maiore gratia virtutum super ceteros debeat splendere, traditam sibi potestatem summo equitatis libramine studeat administrare. Neque enim populus ideo eum super se exaltat, ut liberam in se exercendæ tyrannidis facultatem concedat, sed ut a tyrannide ceterorum et improbitate defendat. At qui cum ille, qui pro coercendis pravis, probis defendendis eligitur, pravitatem in se fovere, bonos conterere, tyrannidem, quam debuit propulsare, in subiectos ceperit ipse crudelissime exercere, nonne clarum est, merito illum a concessa dignitate cadere, populum ab eius dominio et subiectione liberum existere, cum pactum, pro quo constitutus est, constet illum prius irrupisse ? Nec illos quisquam poterit iuste ac rationabiliter perfidiæ arguere, cum nichilominus constet illum fidem prius deseruisse.

Ut enim de rebus vilioribus exemplum trahamus, si quis alicui digna mercede porcos suos pascendos committeret, ipsumque postmodo eos non pascere, sed furari, mactare et perdere cognosceret, nonne, promissa mercede etiam sibi retenta, a porcis pascendis cum contumelia illum amoveret ? Si inquam, hoc in vilibus rebus custoditur, ut nec porcarius quidem habeatur, qui porcos non pascere, sed studet disperdere, tanto dignius iusta et probabili ratione omnis, qui non homines regere, sed in errorem mittere conatur, omni potentia et dignitate, quam in homines accepit, privatur, quanto conditio hominum a natura distat porcorum. Quid igitur mirum, si hæc disciplina sub Christiana religione custoditur, dum antiqui Romani, etate videlicet illustrium virorum Collatini et Bruti, Tarquinii regis superbiam non ferentes, pro stupro, non quod ipse, sed quod filius eius in Lucretia nobili matrona commiserat, cum filio pariter illum patria et regno depellerent, ac, ne quisquam imperii diuturnitate insolesceret, annua sibi imperia per binos exinde consules crearent ? Aliud est regnare, aliud in regno tyrannidem exercere. Ut enim imperatoribus et regibus ad tuenda

We have in this passage not only the summary of the political conceptions of Manegold himself, but the crystallisation of a movement of political thought and principle into a great phrase. For when Manegold represents the relation between the king and the people as embodied in an agreement or "pactum," a contract binding equally upon each party, he is not only giving the first definite expression to the conception which came in later times to be known as the theory of the "social contract," but he is summing up in one phrase the main principle of mediæval political society. This conception is the same as that which finds its classical expression in the phrase of the "Declaration of Rights" that James II. had broken the original contract between the king and the people, and it is also the expression of the mediæval principle of the relation of the king to the law and the administration of justice. It is, indeed, of the first importance to observe that Manegold's conception is not constructed upon some quasi-historical conception of the beginnings of political society, but rather represents in concrete form the constitutional principle of the mediæval state as embodied in the traditional methods of election or recognition, and of the reciprocal oaths of the coronation ceremonies. The people have indeed sworn obedience, but their oath is related to and conditioned by the oath which the king has at the same time taken to administer justice and to maintain the law. It is in virtue of this that he has been elected or recognised, and it is these reciprocal oaths which constitute the contract. The oath of the people is indeed "ipso facto" null and void if the king does not on his part faithfully observe the obligations which he has taken. Men do not undertake so great an obedience except for reasonable causes, and it is not reason to think that they are bound to obey one who refuses to recognise the principles and conditions in virtue of which they promised obedience.

regni gubernacula fides et reverentia est adhibenda, sic certe, sic firma ratione, si tyrannidem exercere eruperint, absque omni fidei lesione vel pietatis iactura nulla fidelitas est vel reverentia impendenda. 'In maximo enim imperio' ait hystoricus, 'minima est licentia.' "

Cf. id. xlvii., p. 164, note.

It is no doubt true that the phrases of Manegold are related to a period of great confusion and civil war, and if they stood alone they would represent at the best an interesting and important anticipation of later developments of political principle or theory. But they do not stand alone, there is indeed no other writer of the eleventh or twelfth centuries who expresses the principle in exactly the same phrases, but the principle expressed by his phrases is the normal principle of the political theory of these centuries.

CHAPTER VII.

THE CONCEPTION OF A UNIVERSAL EMPIRE.

WE have endeavoured to set out the main aspects of the theory of political authority in the eleventh and twelfth centuries, and we have so far made no distinction between the theory as it may have been related to the empire and the other Western states. We do not indeed find any reason to think there was any substantial distinction ; on the contrary, the principles of political organisation appear to us to have been substantially the same in all the European communities.

There is, however, one conception which has been thought to have been important in the theory of the structure of mediæval society with which we have not dealt, and this is the conception of the political unity of the world. It has been sometimes thought that as the Middle Ages present us with a unified ecclesiastical system under the headship of the Pope, so, at least in principle, they represent a unified political system under the headship of the emperor. There is, indeed, no doubt that at least in the fourteenth century, when abstract political theory was very highly developed, many writers, of whom Dante was the most illustrious, were much occupied with this conception, and it might well be supposed that this represents the natural survival of the impression of the great attempt of Charlemagne to gather together into one the divided members of the ancient Roman empire.

It is indeed clear that the conception of the one empire embracing and including all lesser states, and claiming some indeterminate superiority over them, was from the first frequently held among the people of the empire which the Ottos built up in the tenth century, and that they conceived of the position of the Roman emperor as being something different from that of a German king.   The expeditions to Italy represented the claim not merely to political authority in Italy, but to the succession of Charles the Great and of the ancient empire.

This is the conception which is represented in the Annals of Quedlinburg.   They speak of the consecration and coronation of Otto III. in 996 as being done with the acclamation not only of the Roman people, but of the people of almost all Europe.[1]   And they enlarge these phrases, and make them even more emphatic in describing the position of Conrad II. (the Salic).   They speak of the chief men of all Europe and the envoys of many peoples as hastening to his court,[2] and of the emperor as one to whom all parts of the world bow the neck.[3]

The author of the life of St Adalbert, writing probably about the end of the tenth century, uses a phrase which serves well to illustrate the conception of the emperor as supreme lord of the world.   He speaks of Rome as the head of the world, and says that Rome alone can transform kings into emperors.   It is Rome that keeps the body of the Prince of saints, and it is right therefore that the lord of the world should be appointed by Rome.[4]   Berno, the Abbot of Reichenau, in a letter to the Emperor Henry II., addresses him as his lord, the propagator of the Christian religion, Emperor and Augustus,

---

[1] 'Annales Quedlinburgenses, Continuatio,' 996 : "Hic ergo sede intronizatus apostolica, dominum Ottonem, huc usque vocatum regem, non solum Romano, sed et pene totius Europæ populo acclamante . . . imperatorem consecravit Augustum."

[2] Id. id., 1024 : "Emensa itaque imperator quam coeperat via, cunctis, ut ita dicam, Europæ primis ibidem confluentibus, diversarumque gentium missaticis ad imperiale eius obsequium undique properantibus, sacrosanctum dominicæ resurrectionis gaudium, toto iam corridente mundo, prout decuit

talem, eximia celebrant gloria."

[3] Id. id. : "Et quid de victoriosissimi imperatoris referam gratulatione ? Cui cuncta mundi climata colla subdendo inserviunt, quique eo magis super accumulata gloria merito gaudet, quo se, Deo donante, altiorem ceteris, præminentem laetatur universis."

[4] Vita S. Adalberti, 21 : "Roma autem cum caput mundi et urbium domina sit et vocetur, sola reges imperare facit ; cumque principis sanctorum corpus suo sinu refoveat, merito principem terrarum ipsa constituere debet."

the lord both of lands and sea, and gives thanks to God, who
has made his magnificence excel that of all kingdoms.[1]   And
Wippo, in his panegyric on Henry III., says : "Thou art the
head of the world, while thy head is the ruler of Olympus,
whose members thou dost rule with the just order of the law." [2]

Such are some of the phrases used by the earlier writers as
expressive of the conception that in some sense the emperor
was lord not merely of the German and Italian kingdoms, but
of Europe and of the world. And the tradition was not lost,
but continued throughout the Middle Ages. Thus St Peter
Damian, in the second half of the eleventh century, in his
treatise on the disputed election of Alexander II. and
Cadalous of Parma, adjures the royal counsellors and the
ministers of the Apostolic See to labour together that the
"summum sacerdotium" and the Roman empire may be united
in alliance with each other, and that the race of men which is
ruled by these two may not be divided.[3]   And in a letter
addressed by him to Henry III. he speaks of all the kingdoms

[1] Berno, Abbas Augiæ Divitis, Ep.
iii. : "Domino suo, Christianæ religionis propagatori orthodoxo, Heinrico
imperatori Augusto, nec non terrarum
marisque domino. . . . Iure immenso
cordis iubilo grates rerum omnium
persolvimus Domino, qui, in modum
excelsæ pyramidis, vestræ dignitatis
magnificentiam universis superex-
cellere fecit regnis."

[2] Wippo, ' Panegyricus Heinrici
Regis ' :—
"Tu caput es mundi, caput est tibi
    rector Olympi,
Cuius membra regis iusto modera-
    mine legis."

[3] St Peter Damian, ' Disceptatio
Synodalis,' ' Clausula dictionis ' :
"Amodo igitur, dilectissimi, illinc
regalis aulæ consiliarii, hinc sedis apostolicæ comministri, utraque pars in hoc
uno studio conspiremus elaborantes,
ut summum sacerdotium et Romanum simul confœderatur imperium,
quatinus humanum genus, quod per
hos duos apices in utraque substantia

regitur, nullis—quod absit !—partibus,
quod pro Kadaloum nuper factum est,
rescindatur ; sicque mundi vertices in
perpetuæ karitatis unionem concur-
rant, ut inferiora membra per eorum
discordiam non resiliant ; quatinus
sicut in uno mediatore Dei et hominum
hæc duo, regnum scilicet et sacerdotium, divino sunt conflata mysterio,
ita sublimes istæ duæ personæ tanta
sibimet invicem unanimitate iungantur,
ut quodam mutuæ caritatis glutino et
rex in Romano pontifice et Romanus
pontifex inveniatur in rege, salvo
scilicet suo privilegio papæ, quod nemo
præter eum usurpare permittitur.
Ceterum et ipse delinquentes, cum
causa dictaverit, forensi lege coher-
ceat, et rex cum suis episcopis super
animarum statu, prolata sacrorum
canonum auctoritate, decernat. Ille
tanquam parens paterno semper iure
premineat, iste velut unicus ac sin-
gularis filius in amoris illius amplexi-
bus requiescat."

of the world as being subject to his empire.[1] Again, we may notice how, in a treatise ascribed to Cardinal Beno, in the last years of the eleventh century, Hildebrand is vehemently censured for applying certain words of St Gregory the Great to the emperor, as though there were no difference between him and any " provincial " king.[2]

It is thus that when the empire reached its highest point under Frederick I. (Barbarossa), we find a frequent recurrence of phrases indicating the notion that the Empire was superior to all other States, and even in some sense supreme over them. Thus Frederick uses of himself a phrase which might seem to be a claim to universal authority. In the introduction to a document of 1157 he styles himself "Frederick, by the grace of God emperor and always Augustus," and says that he holds by the Divine providence "Urbis et Orbis gubernacula." [3] Again, in a document relating to the enfeoffment of the Count of Provence, he speaks of the dignity of the Roman empire as having a more excellent glory and greatness than all other kingdoms, authorities, or dignities, as it is adorned by the greater number and merit of its illustrious princes and wise men.[4]

It is, however, in one of the documents relating to the Council of Pavia (1159-1160) that the imperial claims are most forcibly expressed. On the death of Hadrian IV. there had been a double election to the papacy, and both Alexander III. and Victor

[1] St Peter Damian, Epist., Bk. vii. 1 : "Et cum omnia regna terrarum, quæ vestro subiicitur imperio, teste mundo, largissima vestræ pietatis abundantia repleat."

[2] M. G. H., 'Libelli de Lite,' vol. ii., 'Benonis aliorumque cardinalium Scripta,' iii. 9 : "Vel si iubentis sunt non recte divisisti, dum preceptum adversus provinciarum regem compositum cæsari oposuisti, quasi nulla sit differentia cæsaris et cuiuslibet provincialis regis."

[3] M. G. H., Legum, Sect. IV., Constitutiones, vol. i. 161.

[4] Id. id. id., vol. i. 216 (1162):

"Fridericus divina favente clementia Romanorum imperator augustus. Cum Romani imperii dignitas, sicut nulli mortalium in dubium venit, per se principaliter ac singulariter nullo nisi divino innixa podio, totius honestatis omniumque virtutum sit adornata fulgoribus, tanto comparacione solis, quam habet ad alia sydera, excellentiori gloria et magnitudine omnia regna et reliquas potestates vel dignitates videtur præcellere, quanto illustrium principum ac sapientum virorum, qui portant orbem, ampliori numero et merito decoratur."

claimed to have been duly elected. Frederick maintained that in such a circumstance the emperor had the responsibility of taking the proper steps to prevent a schism, and he therefore called together a council at Pavia to inquire into the matter and to decide which of the two claimants had a just title. It is in the letter of invitation to the German bishops that he uses the strongest phrases about the position and dignity of the empire. When Christ, he says, was content with the two swords, this pointed to the Roman Church and the Roman Empire, for it is by these two that the whole world is ordered in sacred and human things. For as there is one God, one pope, one emperor, there must be one Church. And thus it is the Roman emperor who must take measures to provide a remedy for this great mischief. He has therefore called together an assembly of the bishops of the empire, and of the other kingdoms, France, England, Spain, and Hungary, in order that they should in his presence decide which of the claimants should lawfully rule over the universal Church.[1]

We are not here concerned with the question of the relation between the secular and the ecclesiastical authorities which was raised by this attempt to deal with the disputed succession to the papacy, we deal with Frederick's letter here only as illustrating his assertion of a special and unique position of the

---

[1] M. G. H., Legum, Sect. IV., Constitutiones, vol. i. 182, ' Encyclica Invitatoria ad Episcopos Teutonicos ' : " Quod in passione sua Christus duobus gladiis contentus fuit, hoc in Romana æcclesia et in imperio Romano credimus mirabili providentia declarasse, cum per hæc duo rerum capita et principia totus mundus tam in divinis quam in humanis ordinetur. Cumque unus Deus, unus papa, unus imperator sufficiat, et una æcclesia Dei esse debeat, quod sine dolore cordis dicere non possumus, duos apostolicos in Romana æcclesia habere videmur.

. . . .

Ne itaque in tantæ discrimine discordiæ universalis æcclesia periclitari possit, Romanum imperium quod ad

remedium tam perniciosi mali divina clementia providit, universorum saluti debet sollicite providere et, ne tanta mala in æcclesia Dei premineant futuris casibus sollerter obviare. . . .

. . . .

curiam sollempnem et generalem conventum omnium æcclesiasticorum virorum in octava epiphaniæ Papiæ celebrandam indiximus, ad quam ambos qui se dicunt Romanos pontifices vocavimus omnesque episcopos imperii nostri et aliorum regnorum, Franciæ videlicet, Angliæ, Hispaniæ atque Ungariæ, ut eorum in presentia nostra iusto declaretur examine, quis illorum regimen universalis æcclesiæ de iure debeat obtinere."

empire. If we were to take the encyclical letter to the German bishops alone, we might well think that Frederick definitely claimed that the empire stood above all other political authorities. When, however, we take account of the other documents relating to the Council of Pavia, we observe that his tone is somewhat different. His letter to Henry II. of England has been preserved, and it is noticeable that in this the more pretentious phrases about the position of the empire are omitted, and that he confines himself to the invitation to send as many of his bishops and abbots as possible to the meeting at Pavia, that they may assist in restoring the peace of the Church.[1] And in another of these documents, a letter addressed to the Archbishop of Salzburg asking him to postpone his recognition of either of the claimants to the papacy, he tells him that he has entered into communication with the Kings of France and England, and asked them also not to accept either of the claimants unless he had been recognised by them all.[2]

There is, however, a passage in a letter of Henry II. to Frederick I. cited by Rahewin, which seems to recognise the superior authority of the emperor in a very large sense ; he speaks of the emperor as having the right to command, and assures him that he will not fail in obedience.[3] And Roger of Hoveden relates that Richard I. of England being a prisoner in Germany, and in order to procure his release from captivity, handed over his kingdom of England to the Emperor Henry VI.,

---

[1] M. G. H., Legum, Sect. IV., Constitutiones, vol. i. 183 : " Set quia hoc iam diu desiderabile votum nostrum necessarie cure prepediunt, dilectionem tuam modis quibus possumus exoratum esse cupimus, quatinus de venerabili collegio episcoporum regni tui et abbatum aliorumque orthodoxorum, quorum sapientia et religione Anglorum prefulget ecclesia, quotquot potes, nobis transmittas et prædicto sacro conventui interesse facias, ut eorum ceterorumque ecclesiasticorum virorum salubri dictante consilio unitas Romanæ æcclesiæ, eo mediante qui facit utraque unum, reformetur et status ecclesiarum nulla deinceps dissensionum turbine collisus,

nostris temporibus incolumis in summa tranquillitate possit permanere."

[2] Id. id. id., vol. i. 181 : " De cetero noster predictus legatus hoc verbum electionis de Romano pontifice in cordibus eorum ita firmabit, ut ipsi una nobiscum unum inde velint et sapiant, nec in aliquam personam favorem suum tam subito ponant, nisi quam nostrum trium unicus laudaverit assensus."

[3] Rahewin, ' Gesta Friderici, Imperatoris,' III. 7 : " Regnum nostrum vobis exponimus. . . . Vobis imperandi cedat auctoritas, nobis non deerit voluntas obsequendi." Cf. Bryce, ' Holy Roman Empire,' p. 186, note k.

"as to the Lord of all," and that the emperor then invested him with it on the terms of the payment of an annual tribute.[1] He adds that the emperor released him from this on his deathbed, but he also mentions that Richard was summoned in virtue of his oath and faith to be present at Cologne in 1197, as being a chief member of the empire, to take part in the election of Henry VI.'s successor, and that he sent envoys to represent him.[2]

It is difficult to say what credit is to be attached to this story ; if it is true, it has to be observed that Richard was acting under compulsion. But it is possible that there may be some confusion about it, as Richard was at the same time invested, according to Hoveden, with the nominal kingdom of Arles by Henry VI.[3] There may be some confusion, and it is possible that it was in this connection that he was summoned to the election.

Such are some of the most important illustrations of the survival in the eleventh and twelfth centuries of the conception of the emperor not only as holding a position and authority different from that of all other rulers, but as in some sense the supreme lord of a united world, as representing the conception of a political unity of the civilised world. It must be observed that with the exception of the last passages, all of these phrases represent the opinion or feelings of those who were emperors, or members of the empire. When we turn to the consideration of the question how far the sentiments of men in other western countries corresponded with them, we find ourselves in a somewhat different atmosphere.

---

[1] Roger of Hoveden, ' Chronicle,' ed. Bp. Stubbs, Rolls Series, vol. iii. p. 202, A.D. 1193 : " Ricardus rex Angliæ in captione Henrici Romanorum imperatoris detentus, ut captionem illam evaderet, consilio Alienor matris suæ, deposuit se de regno Angliæ et tradidit illud imperatori sicut universorum domino, et investivit eum inde per pilleum suum : sed imperator sicut prælocutum fuit, statim reddidit ei, in conspectu magnatum Alemanniæ et Angliæ, regnum Angliæ prædictum, tenendum de ipso pro quinque millibus librarum sterlingorum singulis annis de tributo solvendis, et investivit eum inde imperator per duplicem crucem de auro. Sed idem imperator in morte sua de omnibus his et aliis conventionibus quietum clamavit ipsum Ricardum regem Angliæ et hæredes suos."

[2] Id. id., vol. iv. p. 37.

[3] Id. id., vol. iii. p. 225.

There has survived a very significant letter written in 988 by Gerbert (afterwards Pope Sylvester II.), in the name of Hugh, King of France, to the Emperor of Byzantium, which indicates very clearly the attitude of the newly established kingdom of the Western Franks. It is possible, indeed, as M. Havet has suggested, that the letter was never actually sent, but it is hardly the less significant. It expresses the desire for close and friendly relations, and, in order that these may be secured, proposes a marriage between Robert, the son of the French king, and the daughter of one of the emperors, and assures them that the French king will resist any attempt on the part either of the "Gauls" or the "Germans" to attack the Roman Empire.[1] It is no doubt very probable that the project of a matrimonial alliance with Byzantium was suggested by the marriage of Otto II. with Theophano, and that the letter may represent nothing more than a project of Gerbert's for the glory of the French kingdom. But the recognition of the Easterns as rulers of the Roman Empire, and the undertaking to defend it against a possible attack on the part of the "Germans," are very significant of the attitude of the French kingdom.

In a curious poem by Adalbero, Bishop of Laon, there are some lines which seem to assert the dignity of the French kingdom and its independence.[2] In a letter of William, the Abbot of St Benignus, at Dijon, addressed as has been thought

[1] Gerbert, Epistolæ, 111 : " Basilio et C. imperatoribus orthodoxis, Hugo gratia Dei rex Francorum.

Cum nobilitas vestri generis, tum etiam gloria magnorum actuum ad amorem vestrum nos hortatur et cogit. Ii quippe esse videmimi, quorum amicitia nihil dignius in humanis rebus possit existimari. Hanc sanctissimam amicitiam iustissimamque societatem sic expetimus, ut nec regna, nec opes vestras in ea requiramus : sed haec conditio, quæ nostri iuris sunt, vestra efficit. Magnoque usui, si placet, hæc nostra coniunctio erit, magnosque fructus afferet. Etenim nobis obstantibus nec Gallus, nec Germanus fines lacesset Romani imperii. Ergo ut hæc

bona fiant perpetua, quoniam est nobis unicus filius, et ipse rex, nec ei parem in matrimonio aptare possumus propter affinitatem vicinorum regum, filiam sancti imperii præcipuo affectu quærimus."

[2] Adalbero, Bishop of Laon, ' Carmen,' 389 :—

" Regnum Francorum reges sub tempore patrum
Subjugat, et semper sublimi pollet honore,
Regum sceptra patrum nullius sceptra coercent
Quisque regit, gaudens virtutibus, imperat æque
Novimus imperium iam regibus esse fugatum."

to Pope John XIX. (1024-1033), he asserts that the Roman Empire, which once ruled over the whole world, is now broken up, and is ruled by many kings, and that the power of binding and loosing in heaven and earth belongs to the jurisdiction of St Peter.[1] We are not now concerned with the ecclesiastical question, but the emphatic assertion of the contrast between the unity of the ecclesiastical authority and the fragmentary and divided nature of political authority is very noteworthy. And again, while as we have seen St Peter Damian in some places speak as though the world was united under the rule of the one emperor and the one Pope, in another work he expresses himself very differently, and contrasts the one Pope who rules over the world with the many kings whose authority is limited to their particular territories, and explains that this is the reason why the death of the Pope is notified throughout the world, while there is no reason why the death of a king should be thus announced.[2]

There is then some evidence that the idea of the unity of the world continued to influence men's thoughts and expressions, that the tradition of the universal empire of Rome, and the great unity of the Carolingian empire was never wholly lost, and that from time to time it was asserted by emperors, or those who were under the imperial rule. On the other hand, we find occasional statements which seem to repudiate the conception of a unity of political control, and we can find no examples of any attempt seriously and practically to assert this. This does not mean that there was no conception of a unity of the Christian

[1] William of Dijon, Epistle (in Rodolphus Glaber, Hist., iv. 1): " Quoniam licet potestas Romani imperii, quæ olim in orbe terrarum monarches viguit, nunc per diversa terrarum loca innumeris regatur sceptris, ligandi solvendique in coelo et in terra potestas incumbit magisterio Petri."

[2] St Peter Damian, ' Opusculum,' xxiii. 1 : " Ad quod facile respondetur, quia cum unus omni mundo papa præsideat, reges autem plurimos in orbe terrarum sua cuiusque regni meta concludat, quia quilibet imperator ad papæ vestigia corruit, tanquam rex regum, et princeps imperatorum, cunctos in carne viventes honore ac dignitate præcellit. . . . Porro quia terreni principes regni sui quisque ut dictum est, limitibus includuntur, causa non est cur per alienas mundi provincias eorum obitus diffundatur ; papa vero, quia solus est omnium ecclesiarum universalis episcopus, cum luce privatur, mors eius per ampla terrarum regna diffunditur."

and civilised world. We shall have to consider this more carefully when in our next volume we endeavour to deal with the
question of the relation of the spiritual and temporal powers.

It is important to observe that, although there has been
preserved a great mass of political writing of the eleventh and
twelfth centuries, it is only in a few incidental phrases that we
find any trace of the conception of a political unity of the
world. It is not till the latter part of the thirteenth century,
or rather till the fourteenth century, that the conception of a
universal empire takes an important and conspicuous place in
political theory—that is, not until it had ceased to have any
relation to the actual political circumstances of Europe. What
may have been the conditions under which the idea of political
unity became important, just when the actual development of
the modern nationalities was rendering it practically impossible,
we cannot at present consider, though we hope that we may be
able to deal with this later.

The truth is that, if we are to be in a position to consider
this whole question seriously, we must begin by taking account
of the actual trend and movement of European civilisation
during the Middle Ages. As soon as we make the attempt to
do this we shall recognise that the most important aspect of the
living growth of the centuries, from the tenth to the sixteenth,
was the development of the great nationalities of Europe out of
the chaotic welter of incoherent tribes. For a moment these
had been united by Charles the Great under the Frankish
lordship, but the unity was merely artificial and apparent.
Once his great mind and strong hand was removed Europe fell
back into confusion, and it was only slowly out of the complex
of oppositions and sympathies that there arose the various
European nationalities. The movement was thus both towards
unity and towards division, unity within certain areas, and the
political separation of these great areas from each other.

No doubt the position of the emperors and their relation to
Rome gave them a place which was formally different from that
of other European rulers, and it is probably true to say that
few men would have doubted that this gave them a certain
priority or precedence. But the position of the new monarchies

was in the main that of independent states, recognising no authority over them but that of God. We are therefore driven to the conclusion that while the tradition of a universal empire was not dead in these centuries, and while in those parts of Europe which were closely connected with the Empire the conception was always more or less present to men's minds, it is yet impossible to recognise that during the eleventh and twelfth centuries the conception had any living part in determining either men's ideals, or the principles and theory of the structure of society.[1]

[1] For a further discussion of this question, see vol. v. Part I. chap. 10.

CHAPTER VIII.

SUMMARY.

THERE are three great conceptions expressed in the political literature of the Middle Ages, so far as we have yet examined it. The first is the principle that the purpose or function of the political organisation of society is ethical or moral, that is, the maintenance of justice and righteousness. We have seen in an earlier volume that this was continually and emphatically maintained in the political literature of the ninth century, and our examination of the general literature of the eleventh and twelfth centuries, and of the feudal law books to the thirteenth, has been sufficient to show that no one ever seriously questioned it. If there has been any doubt among modern scholars it has arisen from a misunderstanding as to the influence of St Augustine on the mediæval theory of the state, and from a hasty interpretation of some phrases of Hildebrand.

No doubt there lay behind St Augustine's treatment of the state a real difficulty which had its origin in the fact that, as we can see in the later philosophical systems of the ancient world and in the Christian theory of life, men had become more clearly aware of the existence of characteristics of human nature and personality which cannot be adequately expressed in the terms of the political organisation of society. It is this new apprehension of the nature of human life which is struggling for expression in St Augustine's 'De Civitate Dei.' His apprehension is often profound, but the expression of it is sometimes crude and ill-considered. As we have seen in the first volume, St Augustine at times seems to deny to the

State as such the character of justice, though at other times he speaks in different terms.[1] But the difficulty is not to be measured by these hasty phrases of St Augustine. The difficulty lay in the fact that men had begun to apprehend that there are aspects of the moral and spiritual life which the coercive machinery of the state cannot adequately represent. This is no doubt the principle which lay behind the development of the conception of the independence of the spiritual power. It was conceived of as the embodiment of moral and spiritual ideals which could not be adequately represented by the temporal power. When the distinction was crudely conceived, the former was spoken of as being concerned with " divine " things and the latter with " secular." We cannot here discuss these questions adequately, we shall have to return to them when in our next volume we deal with the relations of the ecclesiastical and political powers in the Middle Ages. We can, however, recognise at once that behind the formal aspects of this question there lay great and profound difficulties, difficulties for which we have not yet found any complete solution.

It is necessary to recognise the existence of real perplexities for the mediæval political thinkers. But, having done this, we must also recognise that the broad common-sense of these men refused to allow itself to be entangled in these perplexities to such an extent as to admit any doubt whether the State had a moral character and purpose. It is clear that no mediæval thinker seriously doubted the moral function of the State, and that this moral function was the securing and maintaining of justice. Even when Hildebrand urged that the State had its origin in sin, he did not mean that the State was sinful. It may have been sin which made it necessary, but also it was the remedy for sin, the divinely appointed remedy for the confusion which sin produced, the means of curbing and restraining the sinful passions and actions of men.

This is the real meaning of the doctrine of the New Testament, and the Fathers, and of the Middle Ages, that the authority of the king is a divine authority. He is God's minister for

[1] Cf. vol. i. pp. 164-170.

the punishment of the wicked and the reward of the good. It is true that here again a certain confusion had crept in, owing mainly to some rash phrases of St Gregory the Great, and, as we have seen, there were some even in the Middle Ages who were carried away by this tradition into the impossible theory that the authority of the king was in such a sense divine, that he was responsible only to God, and that it was always unlawful to resist him even when his conduct was unjust and illegal. But again the robust good sense of the mediæval political thinkers and the force of circumstances counteracted this influence. They believed firmly in the divine nature of the state, they looked upon the ruler as God's representative and servant, but only so far as he really and in fact carried out the divine purpose of righteousness and justice.

This, then, was the first principle of the political theory which we have been considering. And the second is closely related to the first, for it is the principle of the supremacy of law as the concrete embodiment of justice. Mediæval thinkers upon politics were not disturbed by some of our modern perplexities, they were satisfied to regard the law of any society as the expression of the principle of justice for that society. It is very difficult for us to put ourselves back into the mood and temper of these times ; we look upon all legal regulations as being at the best reasonable applications of general principles which make for the wellbeing of human life, we look upon laws as the expression of the judgment of the legislative authority, representing more or less adequately the judgment of the community, and normally we recognise the laws as reasonable, though not necessarily the best possible ; we take them to be rules laid down by men yesterday or to-day, and perhaps to be changed to-morrow. Our difficulty is to make it clear that there ought to be, and to feel certain that there is, a real moral sanction behind them, and that they justly interpret the actual needs of society. To the men of the Middle Ages the law was a part of the local or national life ; it had not been made, but had grown with the life of the community, and when men began to reflect or theorise on the nature of law, they assumed that these customary regulations represented the principles of justice.

To the mediæval political theorist then the supremacy of justice meant the supremacy of law, and though the expression of this conception by John of Salisbury is stronger and more systematic than that of most writers of the period which we have been considering, yet it does not really go beyond their principles. To them the conception of an arbitrary authority was simply unthinkable, the distinction between the king who governs according to law and the tyrant who violates it, was not a rhetorical phrase, but the natural and normal expression of their whole mode of thought.

And if we now compare the conceptions which are embodied in the general political literature with those of the feudal lawyers, we find that they are substantially identical. Indeed Bracton and the authors of the Assizes of the Court of Burgesses of Jerusalem speak as sharply and definitely as John of Salisbury. "There is no king where will rules and not law," "The king is under God and the law," "La dame ne le sire n'en est seignor se non dou dreit," these phrases are as unequivocal as those of John of Salisbury, and their doctrine is the doctrine of all feudal lawyers.

The third great principle of mediæval political theory is again related to the others, and it is the principle that the relation between the king and the people is founded and depends upon the mutual obligation and agreement to maintain justice and law. We have considered the clear and somewhat harsh terms in which this is expressed by Manegold of Lautenbach. It may be urged that he represents an extreme position which was not generally approved,[1] but we must not allow ourselves to be misled into the judgment that the principles which he expressed were strange or unfamiliar. On the contrary, it is clear that he was only putting into definite if hard form a principle which was generally assumed as that which determined the relations between subject and ruler. This is, we think, the conclusion

---

[1] Cf. Gerhoh of Reichersberg, 'Epistola ad Innocentium Papam.' M. G. H., 'Libelli de Lite,' vol. iii. pp. 232, 233.

which must be drawn from the literature which we have just been examining, and our judgment is only confirmed when we turn to the strictly feudal literature. The feudal obligation may have once been conceived of as one of unconditional personal loyalty, but, as we find it in the feudal law books of the twelfth and thirteenth centuries, it is clear that this loyalty was limited and conditioned by the principle of the necessary fidelity of lord as well as of vassal to the mutual and legal obligations which each had undertaken.

Manegold may express the principle in one way, John of Salisbury in another, and the authors of the Assizes of Jerusalem in a third, but their meaning is the same. Manegold speaks of deposing the ruler who has broken his contract, John of Salisbury of the lawfulness of slaying the tyrant, the authors of the Assizes of refusing to discharge any of their feudal obligations to the lord who refuses to do justice to his vassal according to the law and the judgment of the court ; the forms of expression are different but the principle is the same. The mediæval conception of contract is not a speculation of a pseudo-historical kind, related to some original agreement upon which political society was founded, but rather a natural and legitimate conclusion from the principle of the election or recognition of the ruler by the community, and the mutual oaths of the ceremony of coronation ; it is an agreement to observe the law and to administer and maintain justice.

INDEX.

Abbo of Fleury—
    Function of the king is to maintain
        justice, 108.
    The king cannot conduct affairs
        of kingdom without advice of
        bishops and chief men, 149.
    Elective character of kingship, 149.
Adalbero, Bishop of Laon : Seems to
    assert complete independence of
    French kingdom, 177.
Adalbert, St, Vita : Emperor is lord of
    the world, 171.
Administrative system : Lack of this
    in Middle Ages, 31.
Alcuin, 107 (note 3).
Alexander II., Pope : Disputed elec-
    tion, 172.
Alexander III., Pope : Disputed elec-
    tion, 173.
Alfred the Great : His victory over the
    Danes, 15.
Allegiance (ligece, ligancia)—
    William the Conqueror requires all
        landowners in England to take
        oath of fidelity to himself, 76.
    All sub-vassals in kingdom of
        Jerusalem, and inhabitants of
        cities and castles, take oath of
        allegiance to chief lord, 77.
    Form of oath of allegiance in king-
        dom of Jerusalem, 77, 78.
    Made only, according to Glanvill,
        to lord from whom vassal holds
        his " capitale tenementum," 79.
    All men in Normandy bound by
        fidelity and allegiance to Duke
        alone, 82.
Amauri I., King of Jerusalem—
    His Assize, 56, 57.
    Dispute between him and Girard
        of Seeste, 77.
Ambrose, St : Differs from St Gregory
    the Great on nature of political
    authority, 116.
Ambrosiaster : His phrase that king

has the image of God, bishop that
    of Christ, cited by Hugh of Fleury,
    111.
Aquinas, St Thomas : Recovery of
    Aristotle's Politics, 3, 5.
Ardizone, James of—
    Lombard civilian of thirteenth
        century, 80.
    Vassal not to follow his lord against
        overlord or prince, 80.
    Ambiguous phrase about this
        matter, 80, 81.
Aristotle, Politics—
    Their recovery in thirteenth cen-
        tury, 3, 5, 10.
    His theory of the naturally servile
        man, 4.
    Contrast between him and Stoics
        about personality, 7.
    Modern political thought Aristo-
        telian, but with a difference, 8.
    Distinction between King and
        Tyrant in St Isidore and Mediæ-
        val writers probably derived from
        Cicero, not directly from Aris-
        totle, 126.
Arles, kingdom of : Richard I. of Eng-
    land invested with this by Emperor
    Henry VI., 176.
Assizes of the Court of Burgesses—
    Illustrate principle that authority is
        founded on law and justice, 32, 33.
    Influenced by Roman law, 34, 44.
    Definition of justice, 34.
    Origin and date, 44, 45.
Assizes of Jerusalem, 22.
    Story of origin of Assizes, 43.
    Primarily customs of various West-
        ern countries, 43, 44.
    Court for Syrian population, ad-
        ministering their customs, 45.
    Mutual obligations of lord and
        vassal, 52-59.
    Enforcement of these by Court, 53-
        59.

Nature of the feudal Court, 54-56, 65.

Mode of enforcing its decisions, 56-59, 74.

Agreement in principles of political authority with John of Salisbury and Manegold, 185.

Atto, Bishop of Vercelli—

Asserts divine authority of secular ruler whether Christian or Pagan, 100.

Maintains unlawfulness of resistance to king, even when unjust, 117.

Augustine, St—

His theory of temporal power, 9, 10.

Mistaken interpretation of his phrase about "contract," 12.

Question of his influence on mediæval theory of source and nature of political authority, 93, 94.

Denies that justice is necessary quality of the State, 106.

No trace of this conception in eleventh and twelfth centuries, 106.

Cited as affirming duty of obedience by Christian men even to unbelieving emperors like Julian, 122.

His omission of justice from the theory of State has no real influence in Middle Ages, 181, 182.

Augustus, Emperor : Forbade men to call him lord, 145.

Authority, Political—

Vulgar impression that it was looked upon as irresponsible and arbitrary in Middle Ages, 30, 31.

Its relation to law and justice in feudal theory, 30-40.

Its divine origin and nature, 92-105.

Question of the influence of St Augustine on mediæval theory about this, 93, 94, 106, 114.

Phrases of Gregory VII. which seem to deny its divine nature, 94, 96, 97.

Phrases of Gregory VII. which represent another view, 94-96.

Condemnation of Gregory VII.'s phrases by Hugh of Fleury, 98.

Writings which seem to support Gregory VII.'s phrase — 'De Ordinando Pontifice,' 98 ; Bernald, 99 ; Deusdedit, 99.

Normal mediæval view that it is divine in origin and nature, 100-105.

Illustrations of this form—Atto of Vercelli, 100 ; Wippo, 100 ; Peter Damian, 100 ; Gerhoh of Reichersberg, 102 ; John of Salisbury, 102 ; Manegold, 103 ; Honorius of Augsburg, 103, 104.

Its moral function, 106-114.

Its purpose to secure justice, 106.

Its relation to beginning of organised society, 106, 107.

Illustration of its moral function—Abbo of Fleury, 108 ; Ratherius of Verona, 108, 109 ; Wippo, 109 ; 'De Unitate Ecclesiæ Conservanda,' 109, 110 ; Hugh of Fleury, 111 ; Manegold, 111, 112 ; Berthold of Constance, 112, 113 ; Lambert of Hersfeld, 113, 114 ; John of Salisbury, 113.

Theory of the "Divine Right," 115-124.

Theory of relation of political authority to justice and law, 125-146.

Distinction between king and tyrant, 126, 127.

Illustrated from John of Salisbury, 126, 127.

No king without justice, Ratherius of Verona, 127.

Relation of king to law, Wippo, 127, 128.

Justice and law necessary for political authority, illustrated from Lambert of Hersfeld, 130, 132 ; Bruno, 131 ; Berthold of Constance, 132 ; Herrand, 133 ; Hugh of Fleury, 134 ; 'Tractatus Eboracenses,' 135 ; Manegold, 136 ; John of Salisbury, 137-146.

Constitutional theory of political authority, and theory of contract, 147-169.

Three fundamental conceptions of mediæval political theory, 181-185.

Beaumanoir, 22.

All pleas determined according to custom, 42.

Great feudatories and King of France bound to maintain customs, 42.

Tests of legally valid custom, 42.

Ambiguity in his view of legislative power, 48, 49-51.

Maintains original freedom of all men, 49, 90.

Account of creation of kingship, 49.

His use of the word "souverain," 50, 84.

King can make "establissemens " for the whole kingdom, 50.

Legislation must be for the common good, and "par tres grant conseil," 50, 51.

Mutual obligations of vassal and lord, 63, 64.

Violation of these involves loss of fief or homage, 64.

Feudal court is composed of vassals, 64, 65.

Court is judge in all cases between an individual vassal and the lord, 64, 65.

Cases between whole body of vassals and their lord go to lord's council and to king as overlord, 64.

Cases cannot go to overlord till they have been considered in court of lord, 65.

Lord can take no part in court when it considers a case which he brings against his vassal, 65.

In Beauvoisis lord is in no case judge in his court, 65.

Vassal can renounce his fief and challenge his lord, 65, 66, 185.

Lord can renounce homage and challenge vassal, 66.

Obligation to follow lord in battle does not hold against overlord or king, 80.

King is supreme over all jurisdictions and persons, 84.

Any one can be summoned before king's court "pour defaute de droit ou pour faus jugement," 84.

Origin of slavery in violence, &c., 90.

All men in the beginning free, 90.

Emancipation a good thing, 90.

Beneficium, its place in development of feudalism, 23, 24.

Beowulf, 23.

Bernald—
His treatise 'De solutione iuramentorum,' 99.

If Pope has authority to depose patriarchs, he has the same authority over secular princes, 99.

Dignity of secular prince, of human rather than divine origin, 99.

Berno, Abbot of Reichenau : Addresses Emperor Henry II. as lord of lands and sea, 171, 172.

Berthold, Duke of Carinthia : Admits justice of complaints against Henry IV., but urges that they should be submitted to meeting of all the princes, 156.

Berthold of Constance—
Restates St Isidore's distinction between king and tyrant, 112, 132.

Reports that some clergy maintained that neither Pope nor any other authority could judge kings however unjust, 119, 132.

Maintains that this opinion was absurd, and urges difference between king and tyrant, 132.

Reports that at council of Forchheim princes at first assumed that Gregory VII. had finally deposed Henry IV., but papal legates deny this, 158.

Deposition of Henry IV. and election of Rudolph of Suabia by princes at Forchheim, 158.

Bracton—
Reverence due from vassal to lord, 27.

Relation of authority of king to justice and law, 34-37.

King is vicar of God, 34, 35, 67, 68, 69, 73, 85.

King has no equal or superior in his kingdom, 35, 38.

King is bound by the law, 35.

Influence of Roman law on Bracton, 36, 37, 67, 70 (note 2).

King is under God and the law, 38, 39, 67, 68, 70, 72, 73.

Discussion of coronation oath, 34, 40.

King is God's servant when he does right, but the servant of the devil when he does wrong, 35, 73.

There is no king where will rules and not law, 38, 67.

English law is custom, 41, 42, 48.

Legislation the act of king, great men, and the whole commonwealth, 48.

Laws approved "consensu utentium," 48.

Laws can only be changed or abolished with consent of those by whose counsel and consent they were made, 48.

They may be improved without this, 48.

Mutual obligations of lord and vassal, 27, 66.

Disputes about these decided in the court of the lord, with appeal to county court, and, by permission of king, to his court, 66.

No man can dispute the king's charters, 70.

King is compared to the least in receiving justice, 71, 73.

Assize of "Novel Disseisin" cannot be demanded against him, 71.

"Universitas regni " and " Baronagium " may correct the king's action, 71, 73.

Probably interpolated passage which says that the court is the king's superior, 72-74.

Cites phrases drawn from St Isidore of Seville about king as tyrant, 73.

King has "ordinary " jurisdiction over all men, 84.

No difference between men before God, but only before men, 90 (note 1).

Bruno, St, Bishop of Würzburg—
Quotes phrase from Cassidorus's Commentary on Psalms that king transgresses only against God, 118.

No man can judge him, 118.

Bruno, ' De Bello Saxonico '—
Report of speech of Otto to the Saxons, 131.
Otto urges them to revolt in name of liberty and justice, 131.
No allegiance due to king who had broken his faith, 131, 132.
Burke, Edmund : Overthrew theory of conventional nature of government, 3.

Cadalous of Parma : Disputed election to Papacy, 172.
Cæsar, Julius : Treatment of his murder by John of Salisbury, 145.
Caligula : Slain as tyrant, 145.
Cambrai, ' Gesta Pontificum Cameracensium ' : Order and justice among men began with cities, 107.
Canon law—
Its influence on political theory of Middle Ages, 1.
Restates Pauline and Stoic conceptions of slavery, 5.
Treatment of relation of spiritual and temporal authorities, 7.
Possible influence on development of conception of legislation, 45, 48.
Capitale Tenementum : " Ligancia," according to Glanvill, only made to lord from whom a man holds this, 79.
Cardinals : Collection of epistles, &c., of the cardinals opposed to Gregory VII. and Urban II., 122.
Cassiodorus : King transgresses against God only, for no man can judge him, 118.
Cathulfus : His phrase that king has image of God, bishop that of Christ, cited by Hugh of Fleury, 111.
Charlemagne—
Breaking up of his empire, 15, 75.
Consequences of this, 15, 16.
His attempt to unite the divided members of ancient empire, 170.
Unity of his empire artificial, 179.
Chrysippus : His definition of law cited by John of Salisbury, 141.
Chrysostom, St : Saying that while people elect the king, once he is elected they cannot depose him, attributed to him : but this really comes from " Privilegium " of Pope Leo VIII., 117, 122.
Church. See Spiritual Power.
Cicero—
His repudiation of inequality in human nature, 4.
Origin of cities and states, 107 (note 3).
His treatment of law as embodiment of justice, and of function of the state to maintain law, quoted from ' De Civitate Dei ' in treatise ' De unitate ecclesiæ conservanda,' 110.
St Isidore's conception of difference between king and tyrant probably derived from him, 126.
Civilians—
Restate Stoic and Pauline theories of human nature and slavery, 5.
Treatment of relation of spiritual and temporal authorities, 7.
Law requires consent of those concerned, 48.
Their definition of equity cited by John of Salisbury, 141.
Comitatus : Its place in development of feudalism, 23, 24.
Commendatio : Its place in development of feudalism, 23, 24.
Consuetudines Feudorum—
Feudal law book of Lombardy, 59.
If vassal fails to discharge his obligation to his lord he loses his fief, 59, 60.
Vassal can only be deprived of his fief for definite and proved offence, 60.
Decision in such cases belongs to court of his peers or to court of emperor, 60.
Court can compel lord to make restitution to his vassal, 60.
Lord can only proceed against his vassal in court, 60.
Relation of these principles to " Edictum de beneficiis regni Italici " of Conrad II., 60 (note 3).
Conrad II., Emperor—
His " Edictum de beneficiis regni Italici," 60 (note 3).
Annals of Quedlinburg speak of chief men of Europe hastening to his court and of envoys of all nations hastening " ad imperiale eius obsequium," 171.
Constitutional theory—
And social contract, 147-169.
Political authority dependent upon election or recognition of great men or community, 147.
Is exercised normally with consent and counsel of great men of the community, 147, 148, 154, 160.
Illustrations of this principle in early Middle Ages in Gerbert (Sylvester II.), 148 ; Abbo of Fleury, 148, 149 ; in formulas of legislation of Empire, 149, 150 ; in the eleventh and twelfth centuries, in Hermann of Reichenau, 151 ; Bruno, 151 ; circular letter of archbishops and princes on death of Henry V., 151, 152 ; Frederick I. (Barbarossa), 152 ; Sachsenspiegel, 153 ; formulas of legislation in Empire, 153, 154 ; in France, 154 (note 4).
Claim by princes of authority to judge and depose emperor, 156-159.

Claim by princes of authority to control government of Empire, 159, 160.

Political theory of Manegold with regard to the conditions and limitations of royal authority, 160-169.

The "Pactum," in virtue of which the king is appointed, 163-167.

Relation of this conception to "Social Contract" of the seventeenth and eighteenth centuries, 168, 169.

Theory of mutual agreement to maintain law and justice by people and ruler a fundamental part of political theory in the Middle Ages, 184, 185.

Coronation oath : King swears to maintain justice and law, 33, 34-37, 39, 40.

Coulanges, Fustel de, 11.

Court, Decisions of—
Test of valid custom, according to Beaumanoir, 42.
Accepted as law in kingdom of Jerusalem, failing Assizes, 44.

Court, Feudal—
Is judge in all cases of dispute about mutual obligations of lord and vassal, 52-74.
Composition of it, 54-56, 60-65, 72.
Means of enforcing the decisions of court upon lord, 56-66, 71-74.
Cannot judge, according to Beaumanoir, in cases of dispute between whole body of vassals and lord, 64.
Relations of the court to the king, in Bracton, 71-74.

"Couronnement de Louis" : Function of authority is to maintain justice, 32.

Custom—
Primary source of law, 41-45, 47.
English laws are customs, according to Glanvill and Bracton, 41, 48.
All pleas, according to Beaumanoir, are determined according to custom, 42.
Customs must be maintained, according to Beaumanoir, by feudatories and kings of France, 42.
Tests of legal custom, 42.
Assizes of Jerusalem based on customs of various countries, 43.
Cases in kingdom of Jerusalem to be decided by custom, failing Assizes, 44.
Court for Syrians administering justice based on their customs, 45.

Dante : His conception of political unity of the world, 170.

'De Civitate Dei '—
Question of the influence of its conception of political authority, 93, 94.
Passages which deny that justice is

a necessary quality of the state never cited in eleventh and twelfth centuries, 106.
Passages in it from Cicero describing function of the state as maintenance of law and justice, quoted in treatise 'De unitate ecclesiæ conservanda,' 110.

Declaration of Rights : Original contract between king and people, 168.

'De Duodecim Abusivis Sæculi '—
Function of king to maintain justice, 108.
Cited by Abbo of Fleury, 108.
Probably of Irish origin, 108 (note 1).

Demosthenes : His definition of law cited by John of Salisbury, 141.

Deusdedit, Cardinal—
Royal authority founded on human institution, with permission of God, but not by His will, 99.
Refers to creation of monarchy in 1 Samuel, 99.

Divine origin and nature of political authority, 92-105, 115-124.

"Divine Right," 10, 115-124.
Conception that resistance to king is always unlawful, derived from some Fathers, and especially St Gregory the Great, 116-124.
Conception set out by Atto of Vercelli, 117 ; by St Bruno of Würzburg, 118.
Question raised in acute form by Saxon revolt of 1073, 118.
Henry IV.'s reply to bull of deposition by Gregory VII., 119.
Maintained by some German clergy, 119 ; by Wenrich of Trier, 119 ; by author of 'De unitate ecclesiæ conservanda,' 120 ; by supporters of Henry IV., 121 ; by Sigebert of Gembloux, 122 ; by Gregory of Catino, 122.

Domitian, Emperor : His murder, 145.

Eglon, King of Moab : His murder, 145.

Ekkehard Uraugiensis : Reports Henry IV.'s appeal to German bishops and princes against his son, 159.

Election of King or Emperor—
Abbo of Fleury, 149.
Authority of ruler normally depends upon election or recognition, 150.
This is true even in England or France, 150, 151.
Elective principle finally established in Empire during Henry IV.'s reign, and at death of Henry V., 151.
Election of Henry IV. subject to condition that he should prove a just ruler, 151.
Principle laid down by council of Forchheim, 1077, 151.

Circular letter of German archbishops and princes on death of Henry V., 151.

Letter of Frederick I. to Pope Eugenius III., 152.

Elective principle laid down in Sachsenspiegel for all authority, 153.

Emperor. See under King.

Empire—
Conflict with Papacy, 7.
Conception of a universal empire, 170-180.

England—
English law is custom, 41, 42, 48.
William the Conqueror requires oath of fidelity from all landowners in England, 76.
Fidelity to king always reserved in doing homage, 79.
Election or recognition necessary for succession to throne, 150, 151.

Equality in human nature—
In Stoics and Fathers, 3, 4.
Treatment of the subject by Beaumanoir, 49, 90.
Ratherius of Verona, 88.
Sachsenspiegel, 89.
Schwabenspiegel, 89 (note 3).
Bracton, 90 (note 1).

Eugenius III., Pope, 152.

Ezekiel : Conception of individual responsibility, 8.

Fathers, Christian—
Their influence on mediæval political theory, 3-10.
Political institutions conventional not natural, 4.
Freedom and equality of human nature always real, 4.
Slavery a punishment for vice, 4.
Private property conventional not natural, 5.
Property the result of greed, and a remedy for it, 5.
Property the creation of the State, 5.
Almsgiving an act of justice not of charity, 5.
Divine nature of political authority, 9, 93.
Political institutions, results of and remedies for sin, 97.
Theory of " Divine Right " derived from some of them, 10, 116.
Others draw sharp distinction between king and tyrant, 116.

Feudalism—
Its influence on political theory of Middle Ages, 1, 19-86.
Takes shape in ninth and tenth centuries, 15, 16.
Two principles, loyalty and contract, 21.
Contrast between literary and legal conceptions of it, 21-23.

Comitatus, Commendatio, Beneficium, elements in it, 23, 24.
Personal loyalty of vassal to lord, 24-29.
Illustrated in ' Raoul of Cambrai,' 24, 25, 28, 29.
In Fulbert of Chartres, 25, 26 ; in Jean d'Ibelin, 26, 27 ; in Glanvill, 27 ; in Bracton, 27.
Conception of law and justice in feudal law books, 30-40.
Conception of source of law, 41-51.
Conception of method of maintaining law, 52-74.
Feudal system in its essence contractual, 74.
The antithesis of absolutism, 74.
Its anarchical and disintegrating tendency, 75, 76, 86.
Its origin in period when central government had broken down, 75, 76.
Gradual victory of national principle over the disintegrating forces, 76-86.
Fidelity to king reserved in homage, 77-81.
King recognised by all feudal jurists as having full jurisdiction over all persons, 81-85.

Fidelity. See Loyalty.

Flach : " Le Compagnonnage dans les Chansons de Geste," 25 (note 2).

Flanders, Count of : Case between him and city of Ghent, 65.

Forchheim, Council of—
Determines that German kingdom shall be elective, 151.
Deposition of Henry IV., 158.
Election of Rudolph of Suabia, 158.

France—
Kings of France and feudatories must maintain the customs of the kingdom, 42.
Question whether legislative practice of France was different from others, 49.
Reservation of fidelity to king in homage, 79, 80.
Election or recognition necessary for succession to throne, 151.
Formulæ of legislation, with advice and consent of great men, 154 (note 4).

Frederick I. (Barbarossa), Emperor—
Recognises his election and promises justice, 152.
Feudal constitution of Roncaglia made with counsel of great men, 154.
Admits that in grave matters he cannot act without consulting princes, 154.
Phrases which claim universal authority, 173-175.
Letter of Henry II. of England to

him which seems to recognise this, 175.

Frederick II., Emperor : Case of his representative and the lord of Beyrout, 57.

Fulbert, Bishop of Chartres : His definition of feudal obligations, 25, 26.

Gelasius I., Pope—
Statement of relation of spiritual and temporal authorities, 6.
Cited by Hugh of Fleury, 111.

Gerbert. See Sylvester II.

Gerhoh of Reichersberg—
Divine origin and authority of secular power, 102.
Condemns Manegold's phrases, 184.

Gerstengen : Meeting there between Saxon princes and those of the imperial party, 157.

Ghent : Case between the city and the Count of Flanders, 65.

Girard of Seeste : War between him and King Amauri I., 77.

Glanvill—
Reverence of vassal for lord, 27.
English law is custom, 41, 42.
Laws of England though unwritten may properly be called laws, 46.
Cites " Quod principi placet, legis habet vigorem," 46.
Laws are promulgated by prince with counsel of great men, 46.
Vassal perhaps entitled to defend himself against his lord, 61 (note 1), 79 (note 4).
Fidelity to king always reserved in England, in doing homage, 79.
" Ligancia " only made to lord of whom a man holds his " capitale tenementum," 79.

Government—
A conventional institution according to Fathers, 3 ; and Stoics, 5.
A result of sin, 5.
Conception of it as natural by St Thomas Aquinas, 5.
This had little influence till end of thirteenth century, 5, 6.

Gratian : His dictum that no law is valid unless it is accepted by the custom of those concerned, 47, 48.

Gregory, St, the Great—
Probable reference to his statement of a heavenly hierarchy, by Hugh of Fleury, 98 (note 1).
Source of the theory of the "Divine Right," 10.
To his influence it can generally be traced in Middle Ages, 116 ; i.e., Atto of Vercelli, 117 ; Wenrich of Trier, 119 ; ' De unitate ecclesiæ conservanda,' 120.

Gregory II., Pope : His action in restraining Italians from revolt against Leo the Iconoclast, cited by Gregory of Catino, 123.

Gregory VII., Pope—
His phrases about sinful origin and character of secular authority, 94.
Other phrases seem to recognise its divine origin and purpose, 94-96.
Discussion of this apparent contradiction, 96-98.
Excommunication of Henry IV. in 1076, 157.
Revolters wish to refer charges against Henry IV. to him, 157.

Gregory of Catino—
' Orthodoxa defensio imperialis,' written in name of monks of Farfa, 122.
Condemns all revolt against royal authority, 122.
No saint of Old or New Testament had ventured to condemn or depose king or emperor, even though a heretic, 122, 123.
Pope Gregory II. restrained Italians from revolt against Leo the Iconoclast, 123.
God only gives or takes away kingdoms and empires, 123.

Hadrian IV., Pope : Disputed succession on his death, 173.

Harold, King of Denmark : Letter of Gregory VII., 95.

Henry II., Emperor—
Constitution of 1022 issued by him along with great men, 150.
Berno of Reichenau addresses him as lord of lands and sea, 171, 172.

Henry II., of England—
Frederick I. invites him to send bishops and abbots to Council of Pavia, 175.
His letter recognising Frederick I.'s supremacy, 175.

Henry III., Emperor—
His conduct about Papacy attacked by a French Churchman, 98.
Procures election of his infant son as king, subject to condition that he should prove a just ruler, 151.
Wippo speaks of him as head of the world, 172.
Peter Damian speaks of all kingdoms of the world as subject to him, 172, 173.

Henry IV., Emperor—
Demands of Saxon and Thuringian revolters, 113, 130, 155.
Maintains in his reply to Gregory VII.'s bull of deposition that kings could only be judged by God, and only deposed for heresy, 119.
Civil wars of his reign check development of hereditary succession to throne in Germany, 151.
Development of constitutional conceptions in course of revolts against him, 155-159.

Excommunicated by Gregory VII., 157.

Deposition by princes at Forchheim, 158.

His appeal to bishops and princes against his son, 159.

Henry V., Emperor—
Hereditary succession to German kingdom finally destroyed on his death, 151.

Circular letter of Archbishops of Cologne and Mainz and other princes, arranging for election of successor to him, 152.

Henry VI., Emperor : Roger of Hoveden's account of submission of Richard I. of England to him as vassal, 175.

Hermann, Bishop of Metz : Letters of Gregory VII. to him, 94-98.

Herrand, Bishop of Halberstadt—
His answer to Waltram of Naumburg, written in name of Louis, Count of Thuringia, 133.

Corrects misinterpretations of St Paul's words about obedience to ruler, 133.

Quotes Hosea as speaking of princes who reigned, but not as of God, 133.

Obedience due to an ordered power, but government of Henry IV. could not be called ordered, 133.

No order where there is not justice and law, 133.

Hildebrand. See Gregory VII.

Holofernes, tyrant, 145.

Honorius Augustodunensis—
His treatise ' Summa Gloria,' 103.

Temporal authority not primitive, but established by God, 104.

Temporal authority must be obeyed by clergy as well as laity, 104.

Hoveden, Roger of—
His story of Richard I. making himself vassal of the Emperor Henry VI., 175, 176.

Richard I. summoned as Elector of German Kingdom, 176.

Hugh, King of France—
Letter written in his name by Gerbert, assuring Archbishop of Sens that he proposed to govern with advice and judgment of his "fideles," 148.

Letter written in his name by Gerbert to Emperor of Byzantium recognising him as Roman emperor, 177.

Hugh, Abbot of Flavigny : Urges difference between king and tyrant, probably from St Isidore, 133.

Hugh, Monk of Fleury—
Repudiates indignantly the assertion (probably Gregory VII.'s) that royal authority is not of divine origin, 98.

Statement of heavenly hierarchy, probably derived from Gregory the Great, 98 (note 1).

Cites both St Paul and Gelasius, 111.

Reproduces saying of Ambrosiaster and Cathulfus, that king has image of God, bishops have that of Christ, 111, 134.

Function of king is to maintain justice, &c., 111.

King has authority over all bishops in his kingdom, as Christ is subject, not in nature but order, to the Father, 111.

Even heathen rulers must receive due honour, 134.

Warns rulers that those who do not keep commandments of God are wont to lose their power, 135.

People often revolt against such kings, 135.

d'Ibelin, Jean—
Special obligations of vassal to lord, 26, 27.

Coronation oath of King of Jerusalem ; king swears to maintain law and justice, and men of kingdom swear to maintain good usages and customs of kingdom, 39.

Account of origin of Assizes of Jerusalem, 43, 44.

Failing Assizes, Court determines according to custom and the previous decisions of Court, 44.

Mentions Court for Syrians, 45.

Mutual obligations of lord and vassal, 53-59.

These are enforced by Court, 53-59.

Breach of these involves loss of fief or service, 53.

Discusses composition of feudal court, and especially the place of the lord in it, 54-56.

Method of enforcing decisions of Court upon the lord, 56-59.

Sub-vassals and inhabitants of cities and castles take oath to chief lord, 77.

"Ligece" in kingdom of Jerusalem only due to chief lord, 77.

Form of "Ligece," 77, 78.

Sub-vassals must support chief lord against their immediate lord, unless he refuses to do justice in his Court, 78, 79.

Sub-vassals must prevent their lord doing wrong to the chief lord, 78, 79.

Chief lord must protect sub-vassals against unlawful action of immediate lord, 79.

Icelandic Sagas, 23.

Innocent I., Pope : Exercise of justice upon criminals founded upon authority of God, 103.

Institutio Traiani—
Reference to it by John of Salisbury, 141, 142.
Its origin, 142 (note 1).

Isidore, St, of Seville—
Distinction between king and tyrant, 116, 126, 132.
Probably derived from Cicero, 126.

James II., of England : Said by Declaration of Rights to have violated the original contract between king and people, 168.

John of Salisbury—
Authority of prince comes from God, 102.
Function of the prince is to maintain justice and law, 113.
Prince said to be "legis nexibus absolutus" only because it is his character to do justice, 113.
Distinction between prince and tyrant, 127, 137, 138.
Influence on him of Roman law, 140.
Interpretation of its phrases about relation of prince to law, 140.
Nature and origin of law, its relation to equity, 141.
Definition of the commonwealth derived from 'Institutio Traiani,' 141, 142.
Relations of people to ruler, his theory in part affected by St Augustine and St Gregory the Great, 142, 143.
Maintains that tyrants have no rights against people and may justly be slain, 143-145.
Examples of the fate of tyrants from Roman and Jewish history, 145.
Influence of classical literature and history on him, 146.
Agreement of his principles with those of Assizes of Jerusalem and Manegold, 185.

'Jostice et Plet '—
Prince is under the law, from which he derives his privileges, 38 (note 1).
Vassal must be judged in King's Court by his peers, 63.
Fidelity to King always reserved in homage, 80, 83.
King has plenary jurisdiction everywhere and always, 83.
King holds of no one, 83.

Julian, Emperor—
Henry IV. urges that Fathers had not judged or deposed him, though an apostate, 119.

St Augustine cited by Imperialists as affirming duty of obedience even to an unbelieving emperor like him, 122.

Justice—
Its treatment in feudal law books, 30-40.
The principle which lies behind all authority, 32-37.
Its relation to law in feudal law books, 37-40.
Is end of political authority, 106-114.
Justice and law necessary to political authority, 125-146.
To govern justly is to govern according to law, 125, 126.
Without justice there is no king but only a tyrant, 126.
Maintenance of justice the first principle of mediæval political theory, 181, 182.
Supremacy of law as embodiment of justice, 183, 184.

King—
Theory of Divine Right of, 10.
Contrast between Roman and Teutonic conceptions, 11.
Contempt of king or overlord in feudal poetry, 28, 29.
King is only "seigneur dou dreit," 32.
Swears to maintain law and justice, 33 40.
He is Vicar of God, Bracton, 34, 35, 68, 69, 85 ; the Vicar of Christ, Wippo, 100, 109 ; title used in ninth century, 115.
He is the servant of God when he does right, of the devil when he does wrong, 35, 68, 73.
He is bound by the law, 35.
He is under God and the law, 38, 67.
There is no king where will rules and not law, 38, 67.
Account of creation of monarchy by Beaumanoir, 49.
People to restrain the king if refuses to do justice, 52.
Vassals to restrain the King of Jerusalem if he does wrong, 52-59.
Emperor liable to be judged by Count Palatine, 61.
Vassal has right to make war on King of France if he refuses to do him justice in his Court, 63, 72
Bracton corrects misrepresentations of phrase "Quod principi placet, &c.," 69.
King has no equal or superior in his kingdom, 70.
King is like the least when he seeks justice, 71.

Some maintain, according to Bracton, that "Universitas regni et baronagium" may and should correct his wrong actions, 71, 72.

Court is king's superior, probably a passage interpolated in Bracton, 72-74.

Evil king a tyrant, Bracton, 73.

Relation between king, as representing the nation, and feudalism, 78-86.

William the Conqueror requires all landowners to swear fidelity to him, 76.

Sub-vassals of kingdom of Jerusalem must do "ligece" to king only, 77, 78.

Fidelity to king always reserved in England, France, and Lombardy in doing homage, 79-81.

He has full jurisdiction over all persons and in all causes in the judgment of all feudal jurists, 81-85.

Qualities of a true king, according to Ratherius, 108, 127 ; Wippo, 109, 128 ; Hugh of Fleury, 111.

King has image of God, bishop that of Christ, Hugh of Fleury, 111, 134.

Greatness and dignity of his office, Manegold, 111, 112.

Divine right of king, 115-124.

Distinction between king and tyrant, Manegold, 112, 136 ; Berthold of Constance, 112, 132 ; John of Salisbury, 127, 137-146 : Tract. Ebor., 135.

This distinction probably derived through St Isidore from Cicero, 126.

The king governs according to law, John of Salisbury, 127, 128.

Revolters against Henry IV. willing to obey him if he governed according to law and custom, 130-133.

No kingdom where there is not rightful order, 133.

King represents the divine nature, priest the human nature of Christ, Tract. Ebor., 135.

Lambert of Hersfeld—
Oath of allegiance only binding to king who maintains justice and law, 113, 130, 131.

Demands of the Saxons and Thuringians, 130-132, 155-157.

Distinction between king and tyrant, 132.

Council of princes have right to determine justice of charge against Henry IV., 157.

Latin literature : Influence of its revived study in eleventh and twelfth centuries, 146.

Law—
Contrast between Roman and Teutonic conception of its origin, 11.

In Middle Ages, usually the custom of the country, 12.

Conception of it in feudal law books, 30-86.

Relation of law to justice, 30-40.

Reverence for it in Middle Ages, 31, 32.

King is bound by the law and under it, Bracton, 35, 38 ; 'Jostice et Plet,' 38 (note 1).

No king where will rules and not law, Bracton, 38, 67.

Source of law, according to feudal law books, 41-51.

Law primarily custom, Bracton, 41, 42, 48 ; Beaumanoir, 42 ; Jean d'Ibelin, 43-45 ; Philip of Novara, 45 ; Glanvill, 42, 46.

Summa de legibus, 46.

Beginning of conception of legislation, 41-45.

Legislation the action of prince, great men, and people, 46-51.

Illustrated in Glanvill, 46 ; Summa de legibus, 46, 47 ; Bracton, 48.

Position of Beaumanoir with regard to this, 48-51.

Decision of courts to be taken as law in kingdom of Jerusalem failing the Assizes, 44.

Importance of conception of laws as "a populo conservati," 47.

And of the customs of those concerned, 47, 48.

Method of maintenance of law in feudal law books, 33, 52-71.

Place of feudal court in this, 52-74.

Maintenance of law and justice the end of the state, 110, 113.

Prince said to be "legis nexibus absolutus" only because it is his essential character to do justice, John of Salisbury, 113.

Distinction between king and tyrant lies in relation to law, John of Salisbury, 127, 137-140.

Laws made by king, great men, and people in Empire, 149, 150, 153, 154 ; in France, 154 (note 4).

Supremacy of law as embodiment of justice, the second great principle of mediæval political theory, 183, 184.

Leo VIII., Pope : People elect king but cannot depose him, 117.

Leo the Iconoclast, Emperor : Gregory of Catino cites the action of Gregory II. in restraining Italians from revolt against him, 123.

'Liber Canonum contra Henricum quartum,' represents supporters of Henry IV. as bringing forward

authority of St Augustine and St
Chrysostom to prove wrongfulness
of his excommunication, 121, 122.

Liberty—
Natural condition of human nature,
3.
All men in the beginning free,
Sachsenspiegel, 89 ; Beaumanoir,
49, 90.
Contrary to God's will and Scrip-
ture that one man should belong
to another, Sachsenspiegel and
Schwabenspiegel, 89.

Liège—
Letter in name of clergy of Liège,
by Sigebert of Gembloux, 122.
Wickedness of resisting the emperor, 122.

Ligece. See under Allegiance.

Lothair III., Emperor : Constitution
" de Feudorum distractione," made
with consent of great men, 154.

Louis the Pious, Emperor : His deposition, 162.

Louis, St, Etablissements de—
Mutual obligations of lord and
vassal, 62.
Violation of vassal's obligations
entails loss of fief, 62.
Refusal of lord to submit case between him and his vassal to the
court involves forfeiture of service, 62.
Certain offences against vassal do
the same, 62.
Dispute between king and vassal
about questions concerning his
fief must be decided by court,
including the vassal's peers, 63.
If king refuses to do justice to
his vassal in court, vassal can
make war against king, and his
sub-vassals must follow him,
63.

Lord—
Conception of personal loyalty to
him, 19-29.
" Lady " or " Lord " only " seigneur dou dreit," 32, 37.
Mutual obligations of lord and
vassal, 26, 53, 59-66.
Question how far he was a member
of the feudal court, 54-56, 65.
Means of enforcing decision of
court against him, 56-66, 71-74.

Loyalty, personal—
An element of feudalism, and a new
conception in political theory,
21, 27, 30.
Treatment in mediæval literature,
24-29.
Relation to tribal loyalty, 28.
Difficult to reconcile with nationa
idea, 28, 29.

Lucretia : Expulsion of Tarquin from
Rome on account of the outrage done
her, 167.

Magyars—
Their invasions, 15, 75.
Their defeat by Otto the Great, 15.

Manegold of Lautenbach—
Office of king is sacred, 103, 161.
Exercise of criminal justice founded
upon authority of God, 103.
Temporal power, of divine origin,
111, 161.
Derived immediately from the
community, 111, 112, 163, 164,
166.
Function of royal authority is to
maintain justice, 112, 162.
Distinction between king and
tyrant, 136, 164.
People under no obligation of
obedience to tyrant, 136, 164.
Examination of his political theory,
160-169.
Question of obligation of oath of
allegiance, 163-166.
Nature of papal authority in de-
claring it void, 163-166.
The contract (" pactum ") on
which royal authority is founded,
136, 166-169.
Agreement of his principles with
those of Assizes of Jerusalem
and John of Salisbury, 185.

Marcus Aurelius : His justice and
felicity, 145.

Nation : Relation between national
government and feudal system, 75-86.

Nature—
Institutions of society conventional
not natural, according to Fathers
and Stoics, 3, 4.
By nature all men are free
and equal, Stoics and Fathers,
3 ; Ratherius, Sachsenspiegel,
Schwabenspiegel, and Beaumanoir, 88-91.

Nero, Emperor : The most monstrous
and wicked of men, 145.

Nerva, Emperor : His just and happy
rule, 145.

Normandy—
Supreme jurisdiction of Duke over
all causes and persons, 82.
All men bound by fidelity and allegiance to prince alone in Normandy, 82.

Norsemen : Their invasions, 15, 75.

Novara, Philip of—
Origin of Assizes of Jerusalem, 43.
Method of enforcing decision of
court against lord, 56-59.
Discusses relations of chief lord
and sub-vassals in same terms
as Jean d'Ibelin, 79.

Oath—
Wenrich of Trier attacks Gregory
VII. for absolving the subjects
of Henry IV. from it, 163.

Manegold discusses the question of binding nature of an oath, 163-166.

Olaf, King of Norway : Letter to him by Gregory VII., 95.

'De Ordinando Pontifice '—
Its author a French Churchman, 98.
Criticises severely Henry III.'s action about Papacy, 98.
Denies that emperors hold the place of Christ, 98, 99.
Maintains that they hold the place of the devil when they shed blood, 99.

Othloh of St Emmeran : Peace impossible unless men are subject to each other, 107.

Otto I., Emperor—
Victory over Magyars at the Lechfeld, 15.
His Capitula issued at Verona, along with princes and people, 149.

Otto III., Emperor : Annals of Quedlinburg speaks of his coronation as acclaimed by all Europe, 171.

Overlord—
Contempt for him expressed in some feudal literature, 28, 29.
Relation between him and sub-vassals, 75-86.

Papacy—
Conflict with Empire, 7, 16, 129.
Falls under tyranny of Roman nobles in tenth century, 16.
Rescued from them by the Ottos and Henry III., 16.

Papinian—
Possible influence of his definition of law on feudal jurists, 47, 69 (note 3).
His definition of law cited by John of Salisbury, 141.

Paul, St—
Slavery an external condition, 4.
His doctrine that all authority is from God, 100, 101, 104, 111, 117, 123 (note 1), 135.

Pavia, Council of, 1159 and 1160 A.D.—
Documents relating to disputed election to Papacy, 173-175.
Some of them seem to set out the supremacy of the Empire over the world, 173, 174.
Others make no such claim, 175.

Peter, St : His command to obey the king, 102, 103, 104, 161.

Peter, Damian—
Temporal as well as spiritual authority (" Regnum ac sacerdotium ") is derived from God, 100, 101.
Function of temporal authority is to maintain justice, 101.
Race of men ruled by Papacy and Empire, 172.

Speaks of all kingdoms of the world as subject to Henry III., 172, 173.
In another place he speaks of secular authority as limited to particular territories, 178.

Pierre de Fontaines, Conseil—
Professes to record the customs of the Vermandois, 61.
Consists largely of citations from Code and Digest, 61.
Court is judge between lord and vassal in cases concerning the fief, but not in other questions, 61, 62.

Plato : Conception of social contract, 12.

Plutarch : Author of ' Institutio Traiani,' according to John of Salisbury, 141, 142.

Property, private—
Conventional and not natural, according to Stoics and Fathers, 5.
Result of greed, 5.
Created by the State, 5.
Almsgiving, an act of justice, not charity, 5.

Quedlinburg, Annals of : Phrases about relation of Empire to Europe, 171.

" Quod principi placet legis habet vigorem "—
Cited by Glanvill, 46.
Bracton warns against wrong interpretations of this, 68, 69.

' Raoul de Cambrai '—
Illustrates conception of feudal loyalty, 24, 25.
Illustrates contempt for overlord or king, 28, 29.

Ratherius, Bishop of Verona—
His conception of human equality, 88, 89.
No kingship without justice, 108, 109, 127.
A peasant who is prudent, just, brave, &c., may well be called a king, 127.

Rau de Tabarie : Dispute between him antl King Amauri, 57 (note 1).

Recognition of king. See under Election.

Richard I., King of England—
Story of his submission as vassal to the Emperor Henry VI., 175, 176.
Said to have been invested with kingdom of Arles by Henry VI., 176.

Roger of Hoveden—
Relates that Richard I. of England accepted position of vassal of Emperor Henry VI., 175, 176.
Relates that Henry VI. invested Richard I. with kingdom of Arles, 176.

Roman Law (Civil Law)—
Its influence on political theory of Middle Ages, 1.
Contrast between its conception of political authority and Teutonic, 11.
Special influence on Assizes of Court of Burgesses, 44, 45.
Influence on conception of legislation, 45.
Possible influence of revived study of it on Beaumanoir, 49, 51.
" Conseil " of Pierre of Vermandois consists largely of citations from it, 61.
Its influence on Glanvill, 46.
Its influence on Bracton, 35-37, 67-69.
Its influence on John of Salisbury, 140, 141.
Romances, Arthurian, 23.
Rome, its relation to mediæval Empire, 171.
Rousseau : Overthrow theory of conventional nature of government, 3, 6.
Rudolph of Suabia—
Letter to him of Gregory VII., 94.
Refuses in 1073 to be elected King of Germany until question of deposition of Henry IV. had been considered by all the princes, 157.
Election as King at Forchheim, 1077, 158.

' Sachsenspiegel '—
King when elected must swear to maintain law, 40.
Vassal may wound or slay his lord in self-defence, 61.
Emperor liable to judgment of Count Palatine, 61.
King is " gemene richtere " over all men, 81.
When king is present all other jurisdictions are superseded, 81.
Original freedom of all men, 89.
No slaves when Germans first settled in their country, 89.
It is not in accordance with the truth that one man should belong to another, 89.
King to be elected by the Germans, 153.
All judicial authority founded upon election, 153.
Saxons—
Their demands in revolt against Henry IV., 113, 129-132, 155, 156.
Their revolt raised question how far resistance to royal authority was consistent with divine nature of grant, 118, 119.
Active political speculation and controversy begins with their revolt, 129.

' Schwabenspiegel '—
According to scripture no man should be a slave (eigen sin), 89 (note 3).
Slavery arose from force, and is now according to law, 89 (note 3).
Emperor liable to judgment of Count Palatine, 61.
All judicial authority founded upon election, 153.
Seebohm : Roman influence on Teutonic institutions, 11.
Seneca—
Repudiates inequality of human nature, 4, 89.
Men's bodies may be enslaved, the mind is free, 4.
Government the result of vice, 5.
His conception of personality, 7.
Sigebert of Gembloux—
Letter written in name of clergy of Liège against Pope Paschal II., 122.
Even if emperor was wicked, subjects must obey, 122.
Slavery—
A conventional institution according to Fathers, 3.
A punishment and remedy for human vice, according to Fathers, 4.
Aristotelian conception of it, 4.
Its relation to natural law, 87-91.
Treatment of subject in Fathers and Stoics, 89 ; in Sachsenspiegel, 89 ; in Schwabenspiegel, 89 (note 3) ; in Beaumanoir, 90 ; in Bracton, 90 (note 1).
Social contract—
A mediæval conception, 12, 13.
Anticipated in Plato's Laws, 12.
Feudalism in essence a system of contractual relations, 74.
Constitutional theory and social contract, 147-169.
Treatment of subject by Manegold, 160-169.
The agreement or " pactum," 164, 166-169.
Relation of this to " Original Contract " of the " Declaration of Rights," 168.
Relation to " social contract " theories of seventeenth and eighteenth centuries, 168, 185.
Sovereignty—
Common conception of this has no place in Middle Ages, 41, 46.
Beginning of conception in relation to legislation, 45.
Limited in mediæval theory by justice, natural law, and law of God, 46.
Beaumanoir's use of the word " souverain," 50, 84.

Spencer, Herbert : The police theory of the State, 6.

Spiritual life : Source of conception of its independence, 6-9.

Spiritual Power—
Authority of, source of the conception, 6-9.
Expression of this by Pope Gelasius I., 6.
Treatment of the principle by Civilians and Canonists, 7.
Conflict with Temporal power, 9, 16.

State. See Authority, Political.

' Statuta et Consuetudines Normaniæ ' : Duke of Normandy swears to maintain justice and law, 40.

Stoics—
Their influence on mediæval political theory, 4, 89, 97.
Their conception of personality, 7.

Stubbs, Bishop—
Relation of ancient to Teutonic institutions, 10, 11.
Cites account of William the Conqueror's action in making all landowners in England take the oath to him, 76 (note 1).

' Summa de Legibus '—
Law created to maintain order and justice, 37.
" Consuetudines " are customs observed from ancient time by prince and people, 47.
" Leges et a populo in provincia conservate " made by prince, 47.
Fidelity to Duke always reserved in doing homage to a lord in Normandy, 79 (note 4).
In last resort vassal who thinks himself wronged can renounce his fief and challenge his lord, 66 (note 1).
Lord in same case can renounce homage and challenge his vassal, 66 (note 1).

Sutri, Council of : Deposition of Popes, 98, 99.

Sweyn, King of Denmark : Letter of Gregory VII. to him, 95.

Swords, Two : Interpreted as pointing to Papacy and Empire by Frederick I., 174.

Sylvester II., Pope—
Authority of man over man arose from transgression, to restrain his unlawful desires, 106.
Royal authority in France exercised with advice and judgment of " fideles," 148.
His letter recognising Emperor of Byzantium as Roman emperor, 177.
Seems to repudiate claim of Germans to Roman empire, 177.

Syrians : Court for them, in Jerusalem, administering their own customs, 45.

Tarquin : His expulsion from Rome for the outrage on Lucretia, 167.

Temporal Power—
Its relation to Spiritual, 6-9.
Divine nature and origin, 9, 10, 92-105.
Its function to maintain justice and law, 106-114.
Theory of the " Divine Right," 10, 115-124.

Teutonic principles of government : Relation to Roman, 10-12.

Theodoric, Bishop of Verdun : Letter written in his name by Wenrich of Trier, 119, 120.

Thuringians. See under Saxons.

' Tractatus Eboracenses '—
Cites Gregory the Great's letter to Emperor Maurice, promising obedience to his command, though he thought it wrong, 120 (note 2).
Sets Temporal power higher perhaps than any other writer in the Middle Ages, 135.
Priests represent the human nature of Christ, kings the divine nature, 135.
Distinguishes king and tyrant, 135.
Distinction between the authority, which is good, and the ruler, who may be evil, 135, 136.

Tribur, Council of : Election in 1053 of infant son of Henry III. on condition that he should prove a good ruler, 151.

Tyrant. See under King.

' De unitate ecclesiæ conservanda '—
Author possibly Waltram, Bishop of Naumburg, 109, 110.
Written against Hildebrandine tradition, 109.
Quotes from ' De Civitate Dei,' Cicero's description of law and state as existing to maintain justice, 110.
Contrasts conduct of Gregory VII. with that of Gregory the Great, 120.
Cites Gregory the Great's phrases about duty of submission to kings, 121.
Looks upon deaths of Rudolph of Suabia and Henry of Luxemburg as examples of God's judgment upon rebels, 121.

Unity of the world—
Question of importance of the idea in Middle Ages, 2.
Conception of a universal empire, 170-180.
Conception of unity under Pope, 170, 178.

Vacarius : John of Salisbury's reference to him, 140.

Vassal—
  Personal loyalty to lord, 19-29.
  Mutual obligations of lord and vassal, 26, 27, 53, 62, 64, 66.
  Failure to discharge his obligations to his lord is treason, 53.
  Involves forfeiture of fief, 53.
  Failure of lord to discharge obligations to vassal involves loss of service, 53.
  Judge of disputes between lord and vassal is the court, 53-74.
  Court is composed of the vassals, 54, 60, 63, 65, 71, 72.
  Obligation of vassals to support each other in maintaining their legal rights, and the decisions of the courts, 56-59.
Vicar of Christ—
  King "gerit vices" of Christ on earth, Bracton, 68 (note 2).
  King is vicar of Christ, Wippo, 100, 109.
Vicar of God—
  King is God's vicar, Bracton, 34, 35, 67, 68, 69, 73, 85.
  The title frequently used in ninth century, 115.
Victor: Disputed election to Papacy, 173.
Vitellius, Emperor: His murder, 145.

Waitz, 10.
Waltram, Bishop of Naumburg—
  Possibly the author of the treatise 'De unitate ecclesiæ conservanda,' 110.
  His letter to Count Louis of Thuringia, 133.
Wenrich—
  Head of the school at Trier, 119.
  Afterwards Bishop of Vercelli, 119.
  Protests against deposition of Henry IV. by Gregory VII., and his encouragement of German princes to revolt, as being contrary to law of God, 120.
  Cites Gregory the Great's letter to the Emperor Maurice, 120, 162.
  Urges that Ebbo, Archbishop of Rheims, was deprived for taking part in deposition of Louis the Pious, 161.
  Attacks Gregory VII. for absolving the subjects of Henry IV. from their oath of allegiance, 163.
William, Abbot of St Benignus: Asserts that Roman Empire is now broken up, 177, 178.
William the Conqueror—
  Requires all landowners in England to take the oath of fidelity to him, 76.
  Letter of Gregory VII. to him, 96.
Wippo—
  Life of Conrad the Salic, 100.
  God is the source of all human dignity, 100.
  King is the vicar of Christ, 100, 109.
  Function of the king is to do justice, 109.
  King must hearken to the law, for to keep the law is to reign, 128.
  Speaks of Emperor Henry III. as "caput mundi," 172.
Worms: 'Privilegium Imperatoris,' in which Henry V. agreed to resign right of investiture of bishops with ring and staff, 153.
Würzburg—
  Council of princes held there in 1121, 159.
  Declaration that princes intend to settle the investiture question, &c., 159.

THE END.

Printed in Great Britain by
WILLIAM BLACKWOOD & SONS LTD.

THE END.